·Tidings of the King·

Tidings of the KING

A Translation and Ethnohistorical Analysis of the *Rāyavācakamu*

PHILLIP B. WAGONER

UNIVERSITY OF HAWAII PRESS
HONOLULU

Printed in the United States of America
93 94 95 96 97 98 5 4 3 2 1

Library of Congress Cataloging-in-Publication Data
Rāyavācakamu. English.
Tidings of the king : a translation and ethnohistorical analysis of the Rāyavācakamu / Phillip B. Wagoner.
p. cm.
Includes bibliographical references and index.
ISBN 0–8248–1495–9
1. Krishnadeva Raya, King of Vijayanagar, d. 1529 or 30.
2. Vijayanagar (Empire)—Kings and rulers—Biography. I. Wagoner. Phillip B., 1955– . II. Title.
DS460.K714R3913 1993
954.02'52—dc20 93–18879
CIP

Designed by Paula Newcomb

University of Hawaii Press books are printed on acid-free paper and meet the guidelines for permanence and durability of the Council on Library Resources

C·O·N·T·E·N·T·S

APPENDIXES · 163

NOTES TO PART ONE · 171

NOTES TO PART TWO · 181

WORKS CITED · 221

INDEX · 231

I·L·L·U·S·T·R·A·T·I·O·N·S

MAPS

FIGURES

All maps and illustrations by the author unless otherwise noted.

P·R·E·F·A·C·E

The inception of the present book can be traced back to a warm moonlit night in February 1984, when I was a guest of John M. Fritz and George Michell, co-directors of the Vijayanagara Research Project, at their archaeological camp in the midst of the ruins of Vijayanagara. They were then in their fifth season of fieldwork devoted to documenting and interpreting the form of this ruined city that was once the capital of South India's greatest empire, and in the course of the evening our discussion turned to the question of Telugu literary sources relevant to the study of the city. I mentioned the *Rāyavācakamu*, a work with which I had only a slight acquaintance at the time, and told them that I believed it contained an account of the founding of the city as well as many details of the reign of Krishnadevaraya, Vijayanagara's greatest ruler. Their curiosity led to a commission for a translation of several passages that promised to shed light on the nature of the city; subsequently, my own curiosity to come to a better understanding of this unusual text eventually led to the complete translation and interpretation offered here. In recognition of their original commission, and in token of their continuing encouragement and friendship, this work is dedicated to John Fritz and George Michell.

My initial work on the text was supported by the Vijayanagara Research Project (VRP) with funds provided by a grant from the National Endowment for the Humanities. Subsequently, my continued work was assisted by a grant from the Joint Committee on South Asia of the Social Science Research Council and the American Council of Learned Societies with funds provided by the Ford Foundation and the National Endowment for the Humanities. Support from the Smithsonian excess foreign currency program made possible my participation in the VRP's 1987 field season at Vijayanagara, part of which was devoted to working out some of the ideas presented in the fourth section of the introduction, "The 'City of Victory' as Talisman of Authority." My work at the site was greatly facilitated by the hospitality of the Directorate of Archaeology and Museums (Government of Karnataka), who graciously permitted me to enjoy the amenities of their archaeological camp. I am also grateful to the director of the manuscripts library of the Oriental Research Institute at the University of Mysore for enabling me to obtain a microfilm copy of the Sanskrit *Vidyāraṇya-kṛti* manuscript in their collection (translated in Appendix B) and to the Archaeological Survey of India and the American Committee for South Asian Art Color Slide Project for granting permission to reproduce photographs from their archives.

I have benefited greatly from criticism and suggestions kindly offered by a number of colleagues. Richard Davis, Richard M. Eaton, Allan Shapiro, David Shulman, James H. Stone, and Cynthia Talbot all generously gave of their time to read and comment on an earlier draft of the work; their criticism and suggestions have been invaluable and deeply appreciated. It also pleases me to acknowledge my debt and gratitude to R. Sarat Babu, who first introduced me to Old Telugu and Telugu historiographic literature, and to Malathi Rao, who offered guidance in several passages of the *Rāyavācakamu*. Special thanks are due to Burton Stein, but for whose trenchant criticism some of the central ethnohistorical questions would have remained unaddressed, and to my guru Velcheru Narayana Rao, for a series of enlightening conversations on the *Rāyavācakamu*, for his invaluable assistance with a number of difficult readings and textual problems, and, most important, for his generous friendship over many years. I would also like to thank Sharon F. Yamamoto of the University of Hawaii Press for her kindness and wisdom in seeing the book through all stages of editing and production and Joseph H. Brown for his meticulous copyediting. Finally, to my wife Rieko and son Gene, whose help and understanding have been inexhaustible throughout the course of my obsession with the *Rāyavācakamu*, I hope this book may stand as a small token of my gratitude.

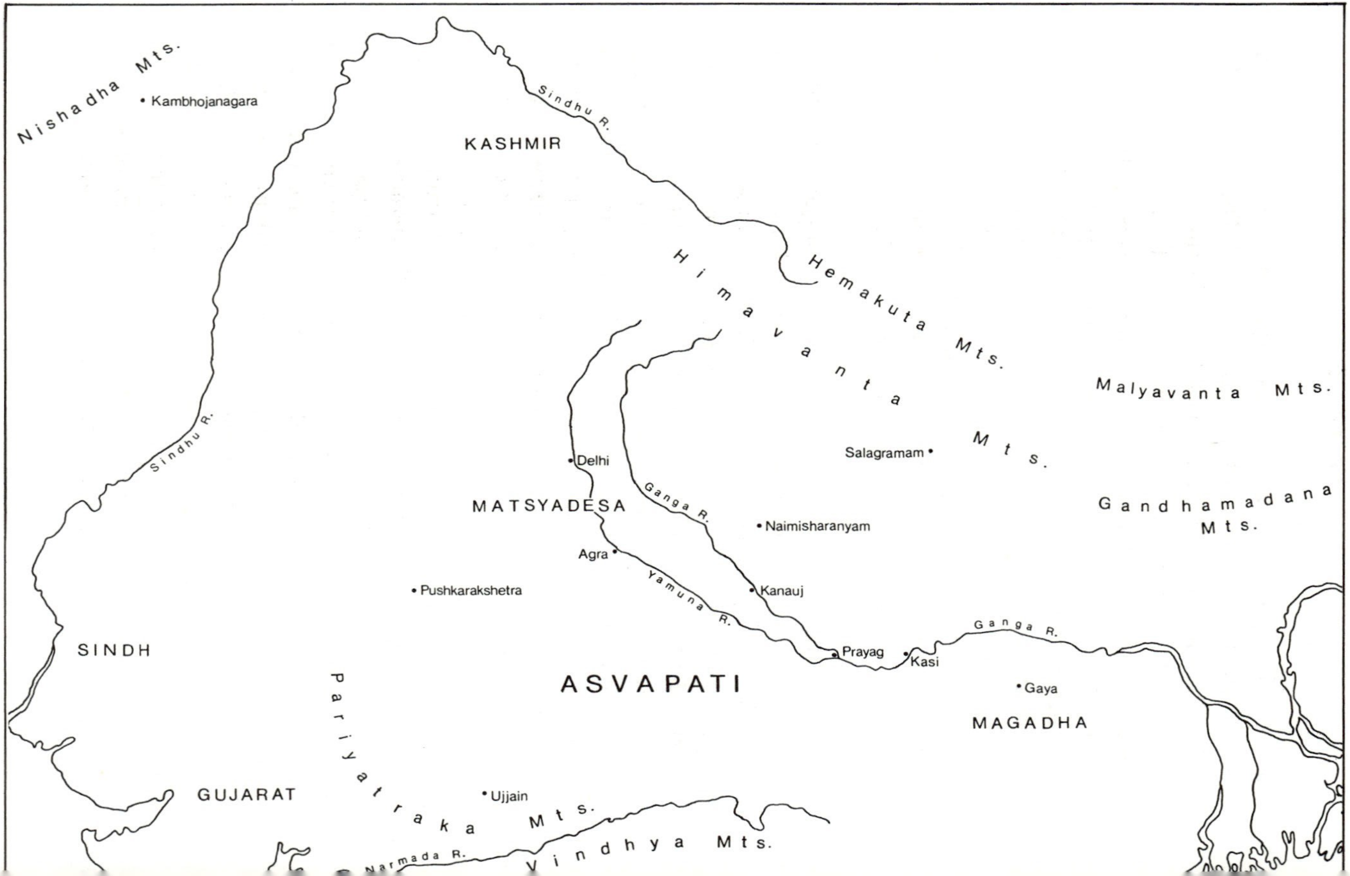
Nishadha Mts.
Kambhojanagara
KASHMIR
Sindhu R.
Hemakuta Mts.
Himavanta Mts.
Malyavanta Mts.
Salagramam
Gandhamadana Mts.
Delhi
MATSYADESA
Ganga R.
Naimisharanyam
Agra
Yamuna R.
Kanauj
Pushkarakshetra
Sindhu R.
SINDH
Prayag
Kasi
Ganga R.
Gaya
ASVAPATI
MAGADHA
Pariyatraka Mts.
GUJARAT
Ujjain
Narmada R.
Vindhya Mts.

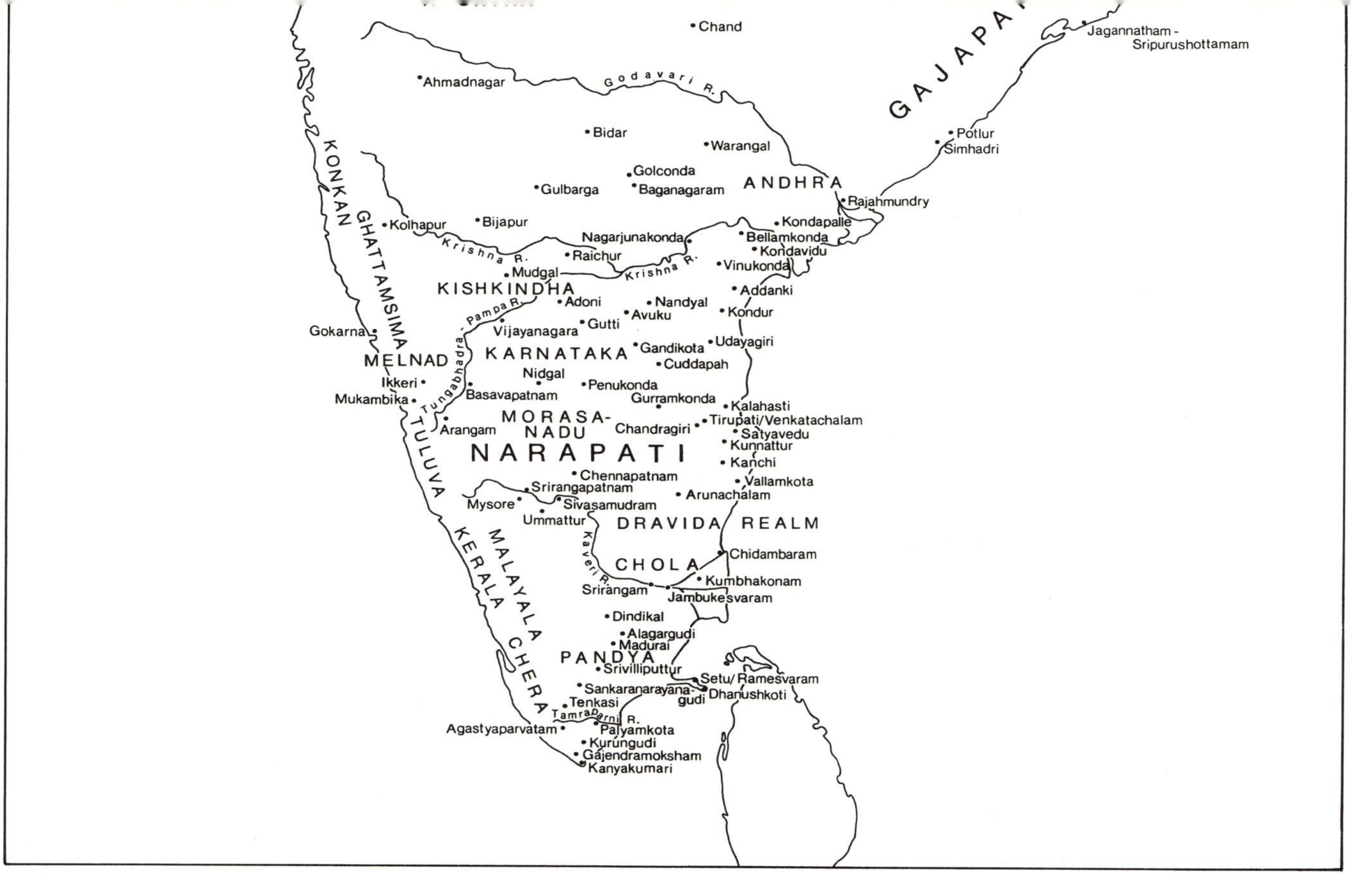

Map 1. Sixteenth-century India according to the *Rāyavācakamu*.

Part One

An Ethnohistorical Perspective

THE *RĀYAVĀCAKAMU*: A SOURCE OF VIJAYANAGARA HISTORY?

The work translated here as *Tidings of the King* is a unique specimen of Telugu historical prose dating from the sixteenth century. While there is a substantial body of historical literature preserved in Old Telugu, with a majority of the texts dating from the period of the sixteenth and seventeenth centuries, the present work defies classification in terms of any of the usual historiographic genres.[1] As is suggested by the very title of the work—*Rāyavācakamu,* literally, "report" or "tidings" *(vācakamu)* of "the king" *(rāya)*—the author of the text rejects the established conventions of historiographic narrative and instead casts his account in the form of a diplomatic report outlining events from early in the reign of the most famous king of Vijayanagara, Krishnadevaraya (r. 1509–1529; see fig. 1). For nearly three centuries, Vijayanagara dominated the history of medieval South India, and it was during Krishnadevaraya's reign that the empire was at its apogee, holding sway over almost all of peninsular India south of the Tungabhadra and Krishna rivers, and meeting significant opposition only from the Gajapati kingdom of Orissa to its northeast and the Muslim kingdoms of the Deccan to its north (see map 1). The period was a time of cultural florescence, marked by important new formulations in the realms of architecture, literature, and music; not only did Krishnadevaraya extend lavish patronage to the arts, but he was himself a major poet in Telugu and Sanskrit. It is hardly surprising that he is remembered today as the paradigm of royal virtue and is referred to simply and affectionately as "the king," *rāya* or *rāyalu.*[2]

The *Rāyavācakamu* first attracted the attention of modern scholars in the opening decades of this century, when two manuscripts were discovered at Pudukkottai in the Tamil country.[3] In 1914, the manuscripts were edited and published by Jayanti Ramayyapantulu in the Telugu literary journal *Āndhra Sāhitya Pariṣat Patrikā,* and the text was immediately seen as a potential source for the history of Vijayanagara. In part, this assessment was due to an important reorientation then under way in Indian historical scholarship, based on the premise that contemporary literary sources were as relevant to the

Fig. 1. Life-size portrait sculptures of Krishnadevaraya and his queens Tirumaladevi and Chinnadevi, ca. 1514–1518, Tirupati, Venkateshvara Temple. (Photo courtesy Archaeological Survey of India.) These are the sculptures described on p. 157 of the text: "And then he had a copper image made of himself, with his hands folded in respect and flanked by his queens Tirumaladevi and Chinnadevi, so that he could always remain standing there in the eastern doorway to attend on his lord . . . Venkateshvara."

study of medieval South Indian history as the more familiar sources provided by epigraphy and archaeology.[4] Innovative scholars such as S. Krishnaswami Ayyangar and N. Venkataramanayya had begun to expand the horizons of historical research by examining the dedicatory verses and colophons of Sanskrit and vernacular works of *kāvya* poetry and by carefully sifting the wealth of local records *(kaifiyat)* and family histories *(vamśāvaḷi)*, inevitably in the regional vernaculars, that had been collected by British administrators a century earlier.

It was within this context that historians first began to study the *Rāyavācakamu*, mining it for whatever veins of historical data it might contain embedded among more legendary and fanciful strata. The text was approached simultaneously along two fronts. On the one side, the more "historical" and factual sections were extracted from the text and published with synopses and commentary in sourcebooks together with extracts from other comparable works. Thus, in 1919, a twelve-page excerpt dealing with Krishnadevaraya's Deccan and Kalinga campaigns was reprinted together with an English synopsis in Krishnaswami Ayyangar's widely circulated *Sources of Vijayanagara History,* and, in 1946, all remaining portions of the text that were deemed to have historical value were included with translations or synopses in a three-volume sequel, Nilakanta Sastri and Venkataramanayya's *Further Sources of Vijayanagara History.*[5] Along the second front, scholars began subjecting these historical sections of the text to careful analysis and critical exegesis, and their findings were incorporated in the articles and monographs they produced on the history of Vijayanagara. Two works by N. Venkataramanayya, *Studies in the Third Dynasty of Vijayanagara* (1935) and *Kṛṣṇadēvarāyalu* (1972), stand out as particularly fine examples of this trend. Both monographs include discussions not only of political history but also of social and economic institutions that are informed by careful analysis of passages from literary sources of the period, including the *Rāyavācakamu*.

Paradoxically, however, even while this work served to advance scholarly understanding of Vijayanagara's history, at the same time it had the deleterious effect of dismembering and obscuring the text itself. The result was that, by mid-century, the *Rāyavācakamu* as an integral totality had been lost—sacrificed, in effect, on the altar of history. Soon after publication, both Ramayyapantulu's 1914 edition of the text and its 1933 reprint in book form had become rare collector's items, and all that remained accessible of the text were the dismembered fragments in *Sources* and *Further Sources* and the equally fragmented exegetical scraps that surfaced here and there in monographs and articles. The text itself had never been made available in a complete English translation for scholars—Indian as well as foreign—with no knowledge of medieval Telugu; nor even had any comprehensive discussion of the nature, date, and purpose of the text ever been presented. And, while recent years have in fact seen important advances in scholarship on the *Rāyavācakamu* and similar historiographic works, the significant studies have all been published in Telugu and thus remain inaccessible to the majority of specialists in the history of medieval South India. The average scholar still has no choice but to rely on the English synopses and discussions in *Sources* and *Further Sources* to approach the *Rāyavācakamu,* and it is for this reason that the text is so poorly known and misconceptions about it so abundant.

Indeed, with only the fragmentary evidence of translated excerpts to go on, it is impossible to gain even the most basic understanding of the nature and functions of the *Rāyavācakamu* as a textual whole. It is thus not in the least surprising that the text has recently been conceived of by non-Telugu specialists of Vijayanagara variously as "a poem," "a courtly poem," and "the diary of Krishnadevaraya," none of which is an accurate characterization of the work.[6] But it is clearly not the historians who are at fault here; the onus must fall instead on the specialist scholars of Telugu literature and historiography for failing to make available translations of either the text itself or its most current scholarly studies. Given the impossibility of any one person's attaining full mastery in more than a few of the more than ten languages offering primary source material for medieval South India,[7] there is a clear and urgent need for translations and studies of significant sources in each language. Works such as the *Rāyavācakamu* must be made available to the broader scholarly community, not in the form of abridgements and excerpts that inevitably obscure the overall structure and real purposes of such texts, but in their entirety so that these crucial dimensions can stand clearly revealed.[8]

What, then, is the value of a work such as the *Rāyavācakamu?* Earlier scholars readily concluded that the text's primary value was as a source for the history of Vijayanagara and, in particular, for the period of Krishnadevaraya's reign. This seemingly unexceptionable conclusion was based not merely on the fact that the work is *about* Krishnadevaraya but, more important, on the explicit suggestion of the text itself that it was written, in A. Rangaswami Sarasvati's words, "to the governor of a province under Krishna Deva Rāya, by name Viśvanātha Nāyanayya, by an agent *(sthānāpati)* of his at the imperial headquarters" (Krishnaswami Ayyangar 1919, pp. 110–111). Indeed, the text opens (after four introductory verses) with an explicit declaration to the effect that it is a report to Vishvanatha Nayanayya by his *sthānāpati* and concludes with the *sthānāpati* promising to send news of further events as they develop (see the discussion below). Taking these framing passages at face value, and identifying the "governor" in question as Vishvanatha Nayaka, the famous younger contemporary of Krishnadevaraya and founder of the Nayaka kingdom of Madurai, scholars concluded that the text was not just a description of events in Krishnadevaraya's reign but, far better, a direct, contemporary eyewitness account dating to the period that it describes. Thus, confident of the text's status as a primary historical document for Vijayanagara, the scholars were free to turn their attention to the contents of the text and identify those passages that could stand as reliable historical testimony for the Krishnadevaraya period.

It was not until the 1940s that the dating of the text began to be called into question. In his introduction to *Further Sources,* N. Venkataramanayya first suggested that the text must have been composed "either at the end of the 16th century or at the commencement of the 17th" (Nilakanta Sastri and Venkataramanayya 1946, 1:187), although he did not at this time explain his reasoning for this conclusion. Later, in a 1954 article published in the Telugu journal *Bhārati,* Venkataramanayya supported his later dating by calling attention to the fact that the text mentions a number of historical individuals who did not rise to prominence until the end of the sixteenth century, long after Krishnadevaraya's reign and the period of Vishvanatha Nayaka's rule in Madurai (1529–1564). More recently, and again on the basis of internal evidence, C. V. Ramachandra Rao (1982, pp. ii–iii) has argued compellingly that the text must date from the period 1595–1602 and that the Vishvanatha Nayaka mentioned as the recipient of its report was not Kotikam Vishvanatha Nayaka but rather this figure's great-grandson and namesake,[9] who, along with his brother Krishnappa II, was co-ruler of Madurai from 1595 to 1602. The text must thus be removed from the events that it describes by a period of some eighty or ninety years, and, accordingly, the veristic assumption that the work is an actual eyewitness report by a Nayaka's ambassador becomes patently untenable. The unavoidable conclusion is that the *Rāyavācakamu* cannot possibly be a contemporaneous report of events in Krishnadevaraya's reign, that it is instead a later historiographic representation of those events, anachronistically cast—for reasons to be explored presently—in the form of a diplomatic report of the period.

Obviously, this conclusion seriously calls into question the text's status as a primary source for events in Krishnadevaraya's reign. The *Rāyavācakamu* is no longer a direct record of events in that period; rather, it has become an indirect account mediated through the experience and sensibilities of a later time—the world of early Nayaka Madurai at the opening of the seventeenth century. But even as this change of status potentially devalues the text as a source for the Krishnadevaraya period, it simultaneously invests it with a new and unquestionable relevance as a document of Nayaka-period Madurai. To be sure, the text contains no direct account of events in Madurai at the opening of the seventeenth century (as it appeared to do for early sixteenth-century Vijayanagara), yet, to the extent that any text is a direct expression of the intellectual world in which it is produced, the *Rāyavācakamu* has a high value as a primary ideological document. Most important, it offers clear testimony to the nature of an indigenous historiographic discourse in early Nayaka Madurai, demonstrating the forms through which the past could be represented and suggesting the ideological uses to which this knowledge could be applied. Clearly, then, the text's primary value is not as a historical document of the Vijayanagara period but as an ethnohistorical document of the Nayaka period, and, as such, it must be read, in Bernard Cohn's words, not "to establish chronologies, or to sift historical fact from mythic fancy, but to try to grasp the meanings of [its] forms and contents in [its] own cultural terms" (Cohn 1981, p. 247).

Nicholas Dirks has aptly characterized the goal of ethnohistory as "the reconstruction of an indigenous discourse about the past" and has suggested that the chief value of the method lies in the fact that "it frees us to examine any given text (or tradition) in its own terms before we ask (or simply classify) in what sense it is or is not 'historical' " (1987, pp. 58, 57). Indeed, to sift "historical fact" from "mythic fancy" is to interpret on the basis of exogenously conceived criteria, and, while such a strategy may admittedly yield information about the past represented in such a text that we might deem "useful" or "of interest," it tells very little about how and to what purposes that representation was produced in the first place—at least little beyond the dubious conclusions typically drawn from such an approach concerning the "disregard for historical facts" and the "penchant for myth and exaggeration" among peoples who do not share our own historiographic methods and assumptions. Certainly, in the case of the *Rāyavācakamu,* there is nothing to suggest that the culture that produced the text thought in terms of the dichotomy implied by such an evaluation.[10] In approaching the *Rāyavācakamu,* I prefer to take the position of Dirks, who argues that the various "fanciful" or mythical episodes occurring in such a text are by no means superfluous embellishments that detract from the text's historical value; rather, they provide the very coordinates of the text's narrative structure and as such are "as integral to the text as any of the other episodes" (1982, p. 680). Thus, when the editors of *Sources* and *Further Sources* rejected the less clearly "historical" sections of our text, what they were discarding was not just so much mythical chaff but the very passages that would have provided the keys to understanding the *Rāyavācakamu*'s unique vision of the past—sections such as the legend of Vidyaranya's founding of the city and the story of the Sixteen Patras' brave defense of their ambushed Gajapati king.

The reading of the *Rāyavācakamu* that I will offer in the following pages is guided by my belief that the text is best understood as an organically coherent literary whole and that it is only through examination of the "coordinates" that structure the narrative and generate this coherence that one may begin to understand how the past is being used in the text. Stated in the most general terms, my reading suggests that knowledge of the Vijayanagara past was constructed and deployed in the *Rāyavācakamu* as part of an ideological argument for the political legitimacy of the Madurai Nayaka regime. The precise details of how and why this was done form the subject matter of the remaining sections of this essay.

Because of my belief that it is more profitable to view the *Rāyavācakamu* primarily as a document of Nayaka Madurai rather than simply as a source of Vijayanagara history, I have devoted the next section, "Text and Context," to a discussion of those factors that have led me to conclude that Nayaka Madurai was indeed the historical context in which the work was produced. While the late sixteenth-century dating of the *Rāyavācakamu* has by now been convincingly established by the arguments of Venkataramanayya and Ramachandra Rao, attempts to solve the problems of the text's authorship and patronage—and, by extension, its geographic situation—have not met with equal success. In my belief, this is in part due to the fact that most authors have failed to come to terms with the unusual report *(vācakamu)* format in which the *Rāyavācakamu* is cast. Accordingly, my own consideration of these problems begins with a discussion of the *vācakamu* format and of the institution of the written *sthānāpati*'s report on which it is based.

With the third section of the introduction, "The *Rāyavācakamu* and the Use of the Past," we begin to address the question of what the relevance was, for early Nayaka Madurai, of historical knowledge of the Vijayanagara past. It is now widely recognized that, despite their real power and de facto independence, the early rulers of Madurai and the other Nayaka kingdoms never assumed the titles and positions of "great kings or universal overlords" (Dirks 1987, p. 45) but instead remained content to follow the political mode of dependent kingship, professing subordination to the Vijayanagara throne and thereby strengthening their own authority through a reflected glory. What has not been recognized—and what is one of the most important points suggested by the present text—is that, by the closing years of the sixteenth century, the then-reigning Vijayanagara king Venkatapati II (r. 1586–1614) was seen by some in Madurai as no longer possessing the ritual authority sought after by dependent kings to augment their own power. As I shall argue below, the *Rāyavācakamu* may on one level be understood as an intellectual exercise devoted to the resolution of this dilemma. Exploring Vijayanagara's past in search of an alternate source for the legitimacy that had been lost under Venkatapati, and finding it in the reign of Krishnadevaraya, our author sets about to produce a freely creative construction of the recent past. By emphasizing certain events and ignoring or suppressing others, he is able to argue that the throne of Madurai derives its legitimacy and power, not from the faded, contemporary Vijayanagara of Venkatapati, but directly from the glorious Vijayanagara of Krishnadevaraya, some ninety years earlier.

Why Venkatapati's Aravidu house should have been perceived as bankrupt of ritual authority is considered in the fourth section, "The 'City of Victory' as Talisman of Authority." Here too, the implications of the text are clear and unmistakable: if the Aravidus are lacking in authority, it is because one of the most important sources of that ritual authority—the very city of Vijayanagara itself—had ceased to exist in 1565 and the rulers of this fourth and final dynasty had never been able to find an adequate replacement for the lost city as a source of that power. Our text accords a deep importance to the "City of Victory" (the literal meaning of *Vijayanagara*), devoting an entire chapter to the story of its founding, even though this occurred some three hundred years[11] before the reign of Krishnadevaraya, on which the work primarily focuses. We learn from this narrative that, because of a supernatural power derived from its physical siting, the City of Victory is a powerful talisman bestowing an invincible authority on its possessor. In this and other passages, the text is unequivocal in its insistence that the greatness of the Vijayanagara king—even in the case of an ideal ruler like Krishnadevaraya—is not the concomitant of an innate personal or even dynastic authority but is to the contrary totally dependent on his continued physical possession of the capital. The natural corollary of such a view is that the destruction of the capital implies the destruction of legitimate dynastic authority and, thus, that the Aravidus cannot be seen as anything other than vain pretenders to the throne.

Clearly, the destruction of Vijayanagara precipitated a number of linked problems within the realm of early Nayaka political culture, eliminating the principal source of ritual authority for the "great king" at the apex of the Vijayanagara state, and thereby eroding the legitimacy and local power of the subordinate kings, such as the Nayakas of Madurai, who occupied the next tier of the system. Given the far-reaching consequences of this situation,[12] it is not surprising to find that our text offers, among other things, an extended reflection on the persons who happened to be the agents of this change: the Muslim kings of the northern Deccan. It is not that the connection between these Muslim rulers and the destruction of the old order is ever explicitly articulated, but the sustained cultural polemic that our author builds against these rulers and the alien forms of their Islamic civilization is difficult to view in any other light: it is as though an attempt is being made, through historiography, to contain the forces of these enemies who had already dealt such a blow to the traditional cultural order. The final section of this introduction, "Demons of the Kali Age," examines the textual strategies adopted in the *Rāyavācakamu* to effect this end. By fitting these dangerous aliens and their abhorrent social practices into the template afforded by a well-known cultural paradigm—that of the demons or *rākṣasas,* whose endless fight with the gods provides the central theme of Hindu mythology—our author attempts to domesticate these menacing foreigners, reducing their threat by bringing them more fully within the realm of the familiar.

Text and Context

The Vācakamu *Format*

We have already noted that, unlike the majority of sixteenth- and seventeenth-century Telugu historiographic writings, the *Rāyavācakamu* is cast in the form of a diplomatic report. Apart from being implied in the work's very title, which means literally "report" or "tidings" *(vācakamu)*[13] of "the king" *(rāya),* the unusual format of the text becomes immediately and vividly manifest in the first prose passage that opens the work (following four introductory verses). Through this brief passage, the narrator establishes his persona as a *sthānāpati* or ambassador, residing at the Vijayanagara court and submitting a report to his lord Kashi Vishvanatha Nayanayya, who is, by implication, one of the *nāyakas* or feudatories of the Vijayanagara throne: "This is the report of his lordship's devoted *sthānāpati,* submitted with true humility, fear, and devotion, to the divine lotus feet of the prosperous king of great kings Shri Kashi Vishvanatha Nayanayya, the prosperous great ruler, respected by kings, who is endowed with boundless good qualities, who is as steadfast as great Mount Meru, who is resplendent with imperishable riches. . . ." At the end of the text, the *sthānāpati* closes with a promise to continue sending news of further events as they transpire: "And so, my lord, I have recorded for you everything that has happened up to this point, and I will be sending you news of whatever continues to happen in the future. I remain in devoted attention at my lord's lotus feet, deserving of your protection. . . ." Through the device of these two framing passages, every intervening word of the text is established as part of the *sthānāpati*'s report. As will gradually become clear in the course of the following discussion, the text cannot be construed as an actual, real report; even so, it is obvious that the author had the mimetic intention of making it *appear* as if it were such. Thus, in order to understand this aspect of the text better, we may begin by considering the nature of the *sthānāpati* institution and of the reports that *sthānāpatis* were expected to file.

The office of *sthānāpati* is not, to my knowledge, attested epigraphically,[14] nor, apparently, are there any actual specimens of *sthānāpati*'s reports known to survive from the Vijayanagara or Nayaka periods. Nonetheless, the nature of the institution may be inferred clearly enough from circumstantial evidence afforded both by the present text and by other sixteenth-century literary sources. We may start with the observation that the primary purpose of *sthānāpatis* does not appear to have been actual diplomatic representation (as might be suggested by my choice of *ambassador* to translate the term). To the contrary, the *sthānāpatis* represented in the *Rāyavacakamu* are almost entirely concerned with the gathering and reporting of political intelligence. They differ from spies *(cārulu, vēgarlu)*—who also play an important part in the text—only by virtue of their more open manner of action and the fact that they send written reports while the latter invariably return in person from their missions and report orally to the king. Indeed, the fact that Vijayanagara's *sthānāpati* Kamalanabhayya sends his report back to Krishnadevaraya's camp through the agency of a spy is suggestive of the close connections that actual *sthānāpatis* would likely have maintained with their more covert counterparts.

The *Rāyavācakamu* is absolutely clear in its implication that the reports filed by *sthānāpatis* were written rather than oral. Whenever a *sthānāpati* has witnessed anything of importance, he writes out *(vrāyu)* a report or letter on paper or palm leaves (the materials can be inferred from the fact that the reports are designated variously as *kākitamulu*, "papers," or *kamma-kākitamulu*, "palm leaves and papers") and sends it immediately to his lord. Thus, for example, when the aforementioned Kamalanabhayya learns of the Gajapati's firm resolve to repel Krishnadevaraya's attacking force, he immediately sets about the task of writing a report *(kākitamu vrāyiṃci)* to inform Krishnaraya of the enemy's strategy. He affixes his seal *(mudra-baḍi-jēsi)* and entrusts the report to a spy, instructing him, " 'Go with the greatest possible secrecy . . . and put this [report] directly into the hands of Rayalu himself [*āyana cētanē kākitamulu yimmani*] when he is alone in his innermost quarters.' "

Among the numerous *sthānāpatis* who would have been in residence at any given court, there would have been not only those who represented the kingdom's allies and enemies but also those who served the kingdom's own feudatories. Thus, according to the *Rāyavācakamu*, in addition to the *sthānāpatis* at the Vijayanagara court who represent the kingdoms of the Turks (referred to by the Persian term *muqim*) and the Gajapati kingdom (the *sthānāpati* Subuddhi), there are also those who represent Vijayanagara's own subordinate Nayakas. Examples of the latter class are the unnamed *sthānāpatis* in the service of Vithalappa Nayadu and the *sthānāpati* Virabhadrayya, who is identified simply as "one of the *sthānāpatis* of the Amaranayakas." Clearly, then, it is to this latter category that the *sthānāpati* who narrates the text itself would belong. A passage in the sixteenth-century Portuguese chronicle of Nuniz further corroborates the testimony of the *Rāyavācakamu* and sheds additional light on the functioning of these *sthānāpatis* who served the feudatories of the court (referring to them as "secretaries"): "The captains and lords of this kingdom of Bisnaga [i.e., Vijayanagara], as well those who are at Court as those who are away from it, have each one his secretary who goes to the palace in order to write to him and let him know what the King is doing; and they manage so that nothing takes place of which they do not soon know, and day and night they are always in the palace" (Sewell 1962, p. 355).

This, then, is the contextual situation implied by the narrative conventions adopted by our author. As a *sthānāpati* stationed "day and night" at the Vijayanagara court, the narrator enjoys a powerful position of centrality that affords him the opportunity to witness and report any and every event of importance. Paradoxically, however, this same position of ideal centrality would appear to create a potential textual dilemma by restricting the narrator's range of observation to those events that transpire within the immediate spatial locus of the court. But, by rigorously carrying the convention to its logical conclusion, the author is able to transcend any such limitations: just as the narrator's lord maintains his *sthānāpati* at the Vijayanagara capital, so too does Krishnadevaraya maintain his own *sthānāpatis* and spies to inform him of events at the courts of the Muslim kings and the Gajapati. While the narrator as *sthānāpati* could not possibly be a personal witness to events transpiring in these distant places, he would just as certainly have the opportunity to witness other *sthānāpatis* or spies reporting to Krishnadevaraya about such events and then transmit this information in his own report. Through frequent recourse to such internal narration, the author is able to maintain the basic narrative convention of the *vācakamu*, even while transcending the restrictions that would otherwise be imposed on the narrator through his limiting identity as a *sthānāpati*.

The text's internal narratives are typically framed between an introduction describing the arrival of the spies or a written message and a conclusion in which the king rewards the spies or the messenger. Within the framework thus established, the narration proceeds in the direct words of the spy or *sthānāpati*. A representative example is the report of the Gajapati kingdom:

> A little while later the king was talking with Appaji and his other trusted friends when the spies Vayuvegi Hanumantayya and Manovegi Purushamrigayya were ushered in. They had just returned from the city of Shripurushottamam in the Gajapati kingdom. They stood before the king and submitted their report. Here are the full details of what they told Rayalu:
>
> "Hurrying on our way from Vidyanagara, we went to the Gajapati kingdom to survey its various districts. We inspected Rajahmundry, Cuttack, and some other places; finally, since Mukunda Bahubalendra Gajapati was staying in the presence of Lord Jagannatha, we went to Shripurushottamam."

The spies continue their report with a detailed description of "everything they had seen and heard and all the discussions they had overheard as well," accounting for a substantial portion of this translation. Once they have finished speaking, the *sthānāpati* narrator closes the internal narrative as follows:

> When the spies had finished reporting . . ., Appaji spoke up. "Yes," he said to Rayalu, "the Gajapati king is a great man. . . ."
>
> Marveling at the Gajapati's excellence of character, Rayalu gave thousands of bundles of areca nuts and betel leaves to the spies. He told them to continue traveling from land to land, bringing back reports of whatever further incidents they might learn. And thus he dismissed Vayuvegi Hanumantayya and Manovegi Purushamrigayya.

Thus, the secondary level of internal narration created by such passages fulfills an important function within the *Rāyavācakamu*, and it is in fact largely from the author's systematic reliance on this "narration within narration" that the work derives its unique stylistic quality. The continuously repeating shifts from one narrative level to the next produce an unusually rich and complex narrative texture that contrasts sharply with the more even fabric generated by the omniscient narrator of other Telugu historical genres.

Authorship and Date of the Rāyavācakamu

This more complex narrative texture is not the only factor that differentiates the *Rāyavācakamu* from other works of Telugu historiographic literature. With regard to what the text reveals of its authorship and context of production, the *Rāyavācakamu* again represents a departure from the norm. Many medieval historiographic works unambiguously record the names of their authors, and some go even further to follow the conventions of courtly *prabandham* poetry in giving further information regarding the circumstances of their production. Works of this latter class are thus typically divided into cantos *(āśvāsamu)*, each of which concludes in a colophon *(āśvāsāntamu)* giving detailed information about the author's identity, including his name, details of his ancestry, and, if he is a brahman, other pertinent information about his lineage such as the clan *(gōtra)* and school of Vedic recitation *(śākha)* to which he belongs. In many cases, the introductory canto *(avatārika* or *pīṭhika)* will even contain further biographical information about the author and the circumstances of his patron's commissioning the work, provided in the context of the formal dedication.[15] The *Rāyavācakamu*, however, offers none of this information. The text has no colophons (for that matter, it is not even divided into cantos or chapters); it likewise lacks a formal dedication. Nowhere does the author even offer his name—let alone any other explicit biographical details—and, accordingly, it is impossible to say anything definite about his identity as a specific individual.[16]

Given the ethnohistorical commitment to the historiographic text, not as a source of knowledge about the society that is taken as the subject of its representation, but rather as a means of understanding the society that has constructed this representation,[17] successful ethnohistorical analysis of any text depends initially on a proper understanding of the historical context of the work's production. In the case of the *Rāyavācakamu*, even though nothing is known of the author's actual identity, circumstantial evidence contained in the text yet makes it possible to infer three general points, which together serve to situate the text in the specific historical and social context of early Nayaka Madurai. This evidence suggests, first, that the author wrote at some time during the closing years of the sixteenth century or the opening years of the seventeenth; second, that the geographic locus of the author's activity was indeed the Madurai country; and, third, that the social context of the text's production can have been only a royal court.

Addressing the problem of the text's dating, C. V. Ramachandra Rao (1982, pp. ii–xiii) has demonstrated unequivocally that the text must have been composed at some point between 1591 (the foundation date of Baganagaram—present-day Hyderabad—a site that is mentioned in the text) and at the latest circa 1675 (the date of composition of Kumara Dhurjati's *Kṛṣṇarāyavijayamu,* a verse composition based on the present text), but with the bulk of the evidence further suggesting a date nearer the turn of the seventeenth century. Ramachandra Rao's evidence falls into two general categories: quotations from other datable literary works and references to historical personages and events of known date. Although only two of the Telugu and Sanskrit literary works from which the text quotes date from after the period of Krishnadevaraya,[18] the evidence provided by the text's numerous references to historical events and personages is more conclusive. First, the work contains an oblique reference to the destruction of the city of Vijayanagara in 1565. Thus, the date given in the text for the city's foundation (Ś. [Śaka] 1127 or A.D. 1205), when taken together with the prophecy that the city will last for 360 years (i.e., until Ś. 1487 or A.D. 1565), provides clear evidence that the author knew the date of the city's destruction and in fact used this date as a means of "determining" the date of its foundation. Another piece of evidence that pushes the date of composition at least into the second half of the sixteenth century is the name given for the Gajapati king with whom Krishnadevaraya fights: instead of his actual contemporary, Prataparudra Gajapati (r. 1497–1538), the text names Bahubalendra Mukunda Gajapati, a later king who revived the Gajapati dynasty and ruled from 1557 to 1568. The inclusion of Mysore, Chennapatnam (the modern Channapatna, Bangalore District), and Baganagaram (the modern Hyderabad) among the list of places to which Krishnadevaraya sends spies pushes the date of composition still later into the sixteenth century, for Mysore was not founded until after 1571, Chennapatnam until 1580, and Baganagaram until 1591.

Finally, the *terminus ante quem* for the text's composition is brought all the way to the closing years of the sixteenth century by the fact that, among a listing of Krishnadevaraya's military commanders, the text includes the names of several major political figures from the time of the Aravidu king Venkatapatiraya II (r. 1586–1614): Rana Jagadeva, Matla Anantaraju, Saluva Makaraju, and Velugoti Yacamanayadu. Although Rana Jagadeva is known to have been active since at least 1580, Velugoti Yacamanayadu and Saluva Makaraju do not seem to have risen to importance until the closing years of the sixteenth century and remained active until at least as late as 1617. On the other side, an approximate *terminus ad quem* is provided by external evidence: at the latest, the *Rāyavācakamu* must have been composed by circa 1675, when Kumara Dhurjati composed his *Kṛṣṇarāyavijayamu,* a verse reworking of our text in Telugu *prabandham* style. But, given the number of personages from Venkatapati's reign who are mentioned in the text, it would appear likely that the text was composed during this period, when they were still active and well known.

As for the question of where the *Rāyavācakamu* was composed, we may notice that the text places an unusual emphasis on religious centers within the territory of the Madurai Nayaka kingdom. Not only does this suggest a close familiarity with this region's geography on the part of the author, but, more important, it implies a personal interest in these sites, such as might be expected from an inhabitant of the region. Thus, we find that, after successfully concluding his military campaign along the Kalinga coast, Krishnadevaraya does not march directly back to Vijayanagara, but instead turns south and takes a long detour through the Madurai country, where he repeatedly stops at local pilgrimage centers *(tīrthas)* to worship and make donations to the gods in their temples. While en route from Kalinga to the Madurai country, he stops only twice, to pay his respects at the major *tīrthas* of Tirupati and Kalahasti in southernmost Andhra, and again, while returning up the west coast from Madurai to his capital, he breaks his journey only to visit the gods at Gokarna and

Shrirangapatnam. But, during his passage through the Madurai country itself, he visits a total of eighteen separate sacred centers spread around the region,[19] from Alagargudi (i.e., Alagarkoil) just outside Madurai to Setu or Rameshvaram, the site of Rama's bridge to Lanka (see map 2). The fact that the text has Krishnadevaraya manifest such an extraordinary interest in the pilgrimage sites of the Madurai country—a number of which were most likely only of limited, regional importance—suggests Madurai in the clearest possible terms as the locus of the author's activity. By having Krishnadevaraya visit so many local centers in the Madurai country, even at the expense of more important sites elsewhere, the author is able to demonstrate the spiritual superiority of his home region, much as a *kṣetra-māhātmya* does by localizing the mythical activities of pan-Indian deities at the religious site *(kṣetra)* whose greatness *(māhātmya)* it proclaims. Moreover, by establishing direct contact with the person of the Vijayanagara emperor, the author invests Madurai with a superior political legitimacy.[20]

Finally, we may turn to the social context of the text's production. Although we have succeeded in situating the text in the Madurai country at some point near the end of the sixteenth century or the beginning of the seventeenth, the evidence examined thus far implies nothing about the particular social context in which the author worked. How are we to determine whether our author was working under the patronage of a royal court, as a servant of a god in a temple, as a member of a folk tradition located within a brahman village, or in yet some other distinct social situation? Here we must recognize certain aspects of content and style that clearly imply a courtly setting for the production of our text. One of the striking qualities of the *Rāyavācakamu* is its unusually high degree of historical specificity. Thus, the text names a great number of individuals whose historicity is confirmed by other sixteenth-century sources,[21] mentions numerous places that can be positively identified and mapped, even in regions far removed from Madurai,[22] and describes a number of political events and practices at the Vijayanagara court that agree closely in detail with the contemporary accounts of inscriptions and foreign visitors.[23] This attentive concern for specific detail and the high degree of historical accuracy manifest in the text

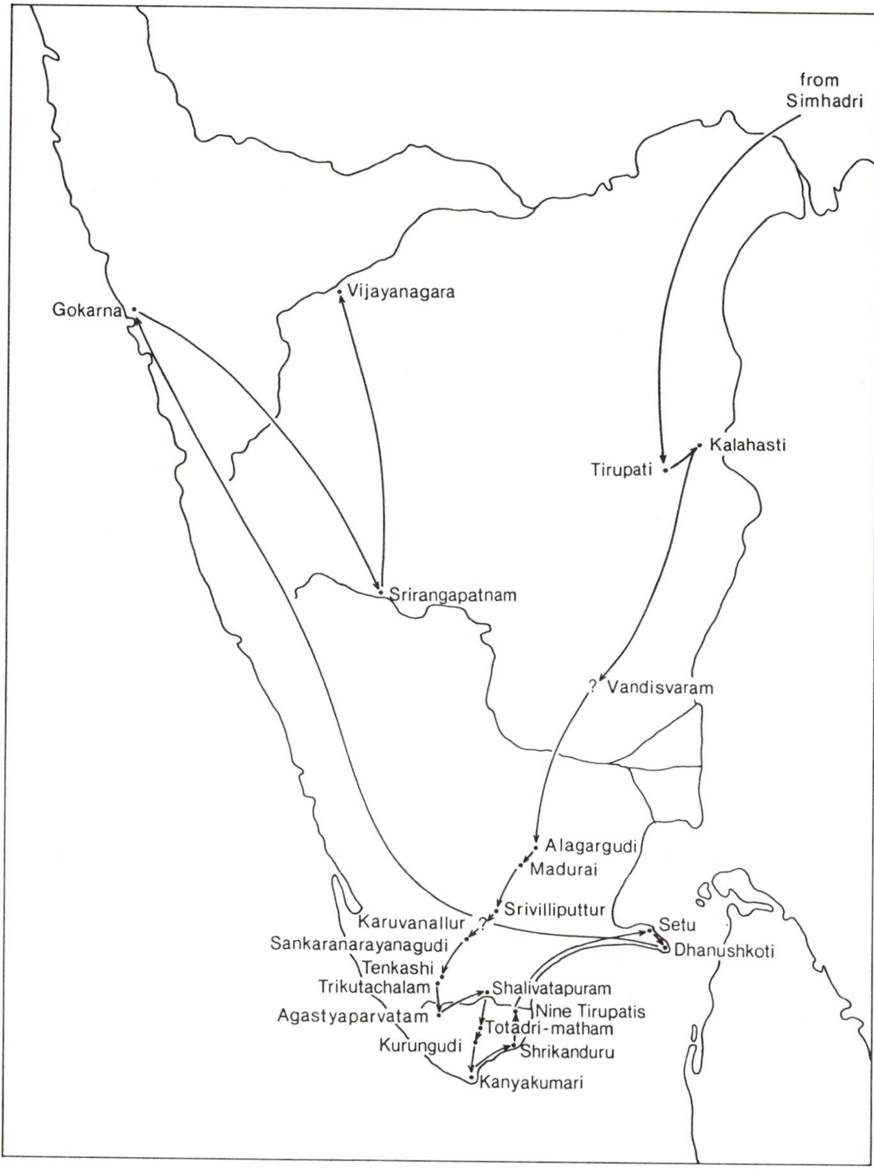

Map 2. Krishnadevaraya's pilgrimage to the Madurai country as narrated in the *Rāyavācakamu*.

would be inexplicable had the author been situated anywhere else but in a courtly, urban setting. These qualities reveal that the author had ready access to an abundance of accurate, detailed information, both about the Vijayanagara past and about contemporary political situations in other parts of the subcontinent. In medieval India, however, such information simply would not have been available outside the network of royal courts,[24] where storerooms or archives were customarily maintained to preserve the originals of royal documents *(rāja-śāsana)* such as edicts and land-grant charters (Sircar 1965, p. 99). Presumably, written diplomatic reports such as the *kamma-kākitamulu* discussed in the previous section would also have been kept in such archives, providing a written record of foreign relations. If the author of the *Rāyavācakamu* had been a servant of the court at Madurai with access to such an archive, this would account for the text's high degree of historic specificity. Older *kamma-kākitamulu* preserved from the Krishnadevaraya period filed by Madurai's *sthānāpatis* at Vijayanagara would have provided the author with a source of information on such topics as Krishnadevaraya's military reforms[25] and battle campaigns, while contemporary reports sent by *sthānāpatis* at the other courts of the subcontinent would have provided information on the current political climate in other regions of the subcontinent at the time of the text's composition.[26]

Taking these three factors together, then, we may conclude that the text was produced by an author who was a resident at the court of Madurai around the turn of the seventeenth century and that this author was most likely not a poet but rather a court functionary such as a clerk *(rāyasam)*, who would have had both a familiarity with the tradition of Telugu courtly literature (since a number of literary works are alluded to or quoted) and access to an archive containing *kamma-kākitamulu*. In light of these conclusions, the structure of the opening prose passage (quoted above) takes on an added significance. Although the work lacks a formal dedication in any strict sense, it is yet possible to view this passage as functionally analogous to such a dedication. Viewing the passage from within the logic of the text itself, the *sthānāpati* narrator is simply offering praise to the lord to whom he is about to submit his fictive report. If, however, one considers the passage extratextually, one cannot help but wonder whether the name of the report's fictive recipient, *Kashi Vishvanatha Nayanayya,* might not also reflect the actual name of the author's royal patron and whether thus, by extension, the author is not simultaneously praising his patron as a means of dedicating the work to him. There are indeed two rulers of the Nayaka house in Madurai who share the name *Vishvanatha* with the fictive recipient of the *Rāyavācakamu*'s report. (Remember that *Kashi* is an optional prefix that is sometimes added to the name *Vishvanatha* and that rulers in traditional India often used their name in several variant forms.) The first is (Kotikam) Vishvanatha Nayaka (r. 1529–1564), the younger contemporary of Krishnadevaraya who is celebrated as the founder of the Nayaka kingdom of Madurai, but he belongs to a period more than thirty years before the earliest possible date for the text's composition. The reign of the second Vishvanatha, however, coincides exactly with the likely date of the text's composition. This Vishvanatha was a great-grandson of Vishvanatha Nayaka and is generally known by the name *Vissappa,* a simplified form of *Vishvanatha;* he appears to have been co-regent of Madurai with his brother Krishnappa II and thus would have reigned from circa 1595 to 1602. Assuming that the text's Kashi Vishvanatha Nayanayya is indeed a representation of the author's patron, he must clearly be identified with this later Vissappa.

THE *RĀYAVĀCAKAMU* AND THE USE OF THE PAST

Early Nayaka Madurai and the Empire of Vijayanagara

We are now in a position to consider the significance of the anachronism implicit in the *Rāyavācakamu*'s report format. We have seen that the narrator is a *sthānāpati* serving his master Kashi Vishvanatha Nayanayya—identified as a textual representation of the author's patron Vissappa—but serving him by residing anachronistically in the bygone Vijayanagara of Krishnadevaraya and reporting back to his lord in present-day Madurai. With one foot anchored in the Vijayanagara past and the other firmly planted in the Nayaka present, the *sthānāpati* narrator effectively denies the existence of historical time. Not only does the stance of the narrator bridge any gulf that history threatens to open between past and present, but the substance of his representation itself effects this same end: thus, famous figures of the Nayaka present, like Matla Anantaraju and Velugoti Yacamanayadu, stand side by side and interact with Krishnadevaraya in this otherwise past world. This anachronistic fusion serves as a particularly poignant testament to the importance of the Vijayanagara past for those who lived in early Nayaka Madurai; in this text, at least, the past literally lives and is something with which one can enter into active communion. But why should the period of Krishnadevaraya have held such importance in late sixteenth-century Madurai that it should be singled out from all other pasts for representation in this text? An answer to this question is suggested by a brief consideration of the political history of South India between the fall of Vijayanagara and the rise of the Nayaka kingdoms and, in particular, of the special nature of the relation between these Nayaka houses and Vijayanagara.

The phase of South Indian history after the dissolution of the Vijayanagara empire is referred to as the Nayaka period, after the generic name of the kingdoms that dominated the southern peninsula until the late seventeenth and early eighteenth centuries. At the height of this period, most of the former Vijayanagara territory was divided up between five great Nayaka kingdoms: the Nayakas of Ikkeri and Mysore ruled over kingdoms located, respectively, in northern and southern Karnataka, while the Tamil country was dominated by the Nayaka houses of Gingee, Tanjore, and Madurai, situated, respectively, in the old Tondai, Cola, and Pandya Mandalams.[27] Although the various Nayaka dynasties were unrelated genealogically, they were united by their common political origins: all shared in a single ancestry of service to the Vijayanagara throne. Beginning as "feudatories" or subordinate kings toward the end of Krishnadevaraya's reign, they gradually moved toward a new status as independent sovereigns during the period of political confusion that reigned between the destruction of the Vijayanagara capital in 1565 and the civil wars that finally undermined the last remnants of Vijayanagara authority in the early seventeenth century.[28]

A major debate among historians of the Nayaka period has revolved around the question of when precisely these various "successor states" may be said to have emerged as independent kingdoms. Some have argued that this moment may have come as early as circa 1530, immediately after the reign of Krishnadevaraya, while others have attempted to push this moment as far forward as possible, in order to portray the Nayakas as loyal "governors" or "feudatories" right up until the fall of Vijayanagara's final dynasty (Stein 1989, pp. 121, 132). Although they arrive at very different conclusions, the arguments of both camps in fact rest on similar premises, including an implicit assumption that the political modes of dependence and independence are categorically opposed and, consequently, that any change from one to the other must be both decisive and datable. As Dirks has recently argued, however, this premise is thoroughly inadequate for sixteenth-century South India. It certainly does not explain the apparently anomalous references in Nayaka records to the greatness and superiority of Vijayanagara long after these kings had ceased paying tribute and when in many cases they were even actively engaged in warfare against their Vijayanagara "overlords." What Dirks suggests instead is that in this case it is more productive to analyze political relations "in terms of a logic in which there is a continuum between such poles as dependence and independence, inclusion and separation. . . . Neither pole is ever realized exclusively. Not only do the two poles define each other relationally but they cannot exist in total independence or separation from each other" (1987, p. 47).

The analysis of Nayaka political relations that Dirks subsequently offers begins with the recognition that Nayaka rulers derived their power from their strategic location as intermediaries between higher and lower tiers of the political order. The authority that a Nayaka would exercise over local chiefs and landholders can be constituted only through a relationship of service to a *dharmic* king at a higher level; Nayaka legitimacy is thus dependent on the status of subordination to the Vijayanagara emperor. Viewed historically, the relationship typically begins with an act of service to the superior king and is formalized when the superior rewards the servant with gifts of "limited sovereignty," including "titles, emblems and honors, rights to enjoy the usufruct of particular lands, and/or the privilege to rule on behalf of the superior over a particular area." Even though the sovereignty of the subordinate Nayaka is gifted, and thus dependent on that of the superior king, the fact that what is given is authority itself means that the relationship is at the same time not only binding but also potentially divisive: "The more gifts of honors and rights the overlord makes to his subordinate, and—in what is a logical and political consequence of this—the more the subordinate participates in the sovereignty of his overlord, the more the subordinate is represented as sovereign in his own right." But as long as the system remains intact, the source of sovereignty is not forgotten and thus, "[even] at the moments of greatest separation, or independence, the continued maintenance of certain forms of connection is not a contradiction" (Dirks 1987, pp. 47, 48).

In the case of the Nayaka kingdom of Madurai, Dirks' model provides a highly productive framework within which to comprehend the general course of this kingdom's relations with Vijayanagara. Indigenous historiographic texts trace the origins of Nayaka rule in Madurai to a dramatic episode in the reign of Krishnadevaraya or his successor Acyutaraya, in which Kotikam Vishvanatha Nayaka demonstrates his exemplary conduct as a loyal servant of the Vijayanagara throne.[29] Considering service to his king more important than filial obedience, Vishvanatha Nayaka leads an army to suppress his treacherous father Nagama Nayaka, who has revolted against the king and annexed the territories of Madurai and Tanjore as his own. The king rewards Vishvanatha for this unparalleled act of service by installing him on the throne of Madurai.

Once Vishvanatha and his Nayaka successors have been established in Madurai, however, their relationship with Vijayanagara develops along a course that oscillates between increasingly frequent demonstrations of Madurai's independence and continuing and repeated affirmations by Madurai's rulers of their status as subordinate Nayakas. Dirks traces a shift in the rhetoric of Nayaka donative inscriptions beginning in the 1560s; prior to this time, the early Nayaka rulers had characterized themselves as loyal "agents" (the Tamil word used is generally some form of *kāriyam* or *kāriyakārar*) acting on behalf of their Vijayanagara sovereigns. But, beginning with an inscription from the reign of Krishnappa Nayaka, the rhetoric is expressive of a new mode of relationship, one in which the Nayaka is not a mere agent but a petitioner *(vijñāptṛ)* who actively petitions the ruler to make a donation at his behest. Moreover, whereas the earlier inscriptions were issued locally by the Nayaka rulers, these new inscriptions differ in being issued by the Vijayanagara overlords in their own core territories while yet recognizing the power of the Nayaka petitioners. Dirks observes that, "on the one hand, these grants suggest a renewed solidarity in the relations between subordinate kings and their overlords; . . . [but] on the other hand . . . these imperial inscriptions . . . now had to incorporate the praiseworthy nature of these lesser kings . . . [who] have moved from being passive reflections of the great and undisputed overlordship of the Vijayanagara kings to acting in more innovative ways" (1987, p. 46).

If the Vijayanagara overlords had to begin recognizing the "praiseworthy nature" of their more innovative dependents, they also had to acknowledge the growing capacity of these Nayakas to express their very real sovereign power in ways that did not always accord with Vijayanagara's own imperial interests. Especially from the 1580s, the Madurai Nayakas challenged the authority of their Vijayanagara overlords with increasing frequency. Whether the challenge was in the form of a refusal to pay tribute or in the form of support lent to the "wrong side" in a succession dispute, the outcome was generally the same, culminating in open military conflict with Vijayanagara. The available evidence suggests that wars were fought between Madurai and Vijayanagara in 1583 (Heras 1927, pp. 285–286), 1595 (Heras 1927, pp. 342–343; *SVH,* no. 92), and 1599 (Heras 1927, pp. 348–349; *SVH,* no. 81), each time over the failure of Madurai to pay the tribute due the imperial throne. Then, in 1601, Madurai joined forces with a number of other Nayaka houses in a war against Venkatapati's loyal governor Yacama Nayadu, this time to demonstrate their solidarity with the Nayaka ruler of Vellore, whose *amaram* estate had been transferred to Yacama by the Vijayanagara king (*FSVH,* 1:321–324; *FSVH,* vols. 2 and 3, nos. 218, 219a, 219b, 222). In 1610, there was yet another war over tribute (Heras 1927, pp. 359–361), and then, from 1614 until 1629, Madurai fought on the side of those who opposed the legitimate successor to the Vijayanagara throne in the "civil war" that eventually led to the final collapse of Aravidu power (*FSVH,* 1:326–336; *FSVH,* vols. 2 and 3, nos. 230–233).

The increasing tension that marks Madurai-Vijayanagara relations starting in the 1580s may be viewed in part as a natural and inevitable concomitant of the gifting of sovereignty, but at the same time it is clear that the strains were further intensified by specific historical developments.[30] The problems had begun in 1565, when the Muslim kingdoms of the northern Deccan joined forces for a devastating campaign against Vijayanagara. After a pitched battle at Rakshasa-Tangadi, some distance north of the capital, the Muslim confederacy defeated the Vijayanagara army, slaying the de facto ruler Aliya Rama Raya and forcing his younger brother and successor Tirumala to take the captive puppet emperor Sadashivaraya and flee southward (see fig. 2). The invading army occupied and looted the city, and, according to the Italian Cesar Federici, who passed through the city several months later, "they remained [there] for six months, searching everywhere for money and valuable effects that had been hidden." After the retreat of the conquerors, Tirumala returned in an attempt to reoccupy and revive the city, but by 1567 he was forced to abandon the city "in consideration of the injury done to Bijanagur [Vijayanagara] by the four Mahometan kings" (Kerr 1824, pp. 157, 159). He took the puppet emperor and moved the capital southeast to Penugonda, where he attempted to reconsolidate the kingdom and inaugurate his own new dynasty, the Aravidu.

The period of six years between the fall of the capital and Tirumala's assumption of the throne in 1571 is described in local *kaifiyats* as a period of great confusion. "Anarchy prevailed in the country," we read in one such text, "and the people were considerably harrassed by thieves and the uncertainty caused by unsettled government" (*FSVH,* no. 190[f]). Much of the confusion apparently stemmed from a succession dispute between Tirumala and his nephew Peda Tirumala, son of the slain Rama Raya, who contested his uncle's right to the throne. But, even after the dispute was finally resolved in favor of Tirumala, disturbances continued in the form of fresh invasions by the Muslim kingdoms of Bijapur (1576) and Golconda (1579 and 1589–1590), during the course of which many strategic forts and a considerable amount of territory were lost to these rulers. Witnessing the apparent helplessness of the Aravidus in the face of these encroachments, many Vijayanagara chiefs and generals took the opportunity to rebel against their overlords.

Fig. 2. The battle of Rakshasa-Tangadi showing the slaying of Aliya Rama Raya, illustration from *Tārikh-i Husain Shahi* (Ahmadnagar, 1565.) Bharata Itihasa Samshodhaka Mandala, Poona. (Photo courtesy American Committee for South Asian Art Color Slide Project.)

Given the ideological basis for Nayaka legitimacy, the political situation in the latter half of the sixteenth century clearly must have generated a deeply problematic contradiction for the Nayakas of Madurai. Nayaka power in Madurai was real, but ideologically dependent, while Vijayanagara's power, even though remaining ideologically absolute, had all but vanished in any real sense. With the legitimacy of their legitimizing overlord itself now in question, Madurai's rulers were confronted with a serious dilemma that could be resolved only by means of a thorough transformation of the ideological system on which all political relations were based.

The Rāyavācakamu *and the Problem of Nayaka Legitimacy*

Eventually, the dilemma would be resolved by a simple but drastic solution: with the final collapse of Vijayanagara authority, the rulers of Madurai would themselves rise to assume the role of great kings, no longer "looking upward" for legitimation of their power, but now beginning to constitute their authority by "looking downward" to their own subordinates, the chiefly Palaiyakkarars, who would themselves be elevated to the new status of little kings (Dirks 1987, pp. 49, 104–105).[31] But this upward shift of positions within the legitimizing system did not come about immediately. To the contrary, the evidence suggests a long transitional period, during which attempts were made to modify the original structure so as to escape the dilemma posed by Vijayanagara senescence, without, however, offering any real challenge to the fundamental ideology of Nayaka dependence.

The creative vision of the Vijayanagara past constructed in the *Rāyavācakamu* represents one such attempt at modifying this ideology. Seen from this perspective, a primary accomplishment of the text is that it historicizes the relationship of dependence, so that it is no longer necessary for Nayaka authority to be constructed through a continuing relationship of present service and subordination to the Vijayanagara throne. The *Rāyavācakamu* is not unique in its reliance on this strategy; in fact, the primary importance of the story of Vishvanatha Nayaka's service to Vijayanagara within the various Nayaka chronicles stems from a similar concern for historicizing the relationship of Nayaka dependence. Once Vishvanatha proves his personal worthiness as a subordinate of the king, the gift of authority he receives legitimizes not only his own rule but also the position of his successors who inherit this empowerment. With Nayaka authority represented as deriving from Vishvanatha's original relationship with Vijayanagara, the continued existence of the imperial throne becomes irrelevant. Thus, in the chronicle discussed by Dirks, after the episodes recounting Vishvanatha's establishment of his kingdom, there is no further mention of Vijayanagara (Dirks 1987, p. 104).

While the *Rāyavācakamu* nowhere relates the story of Vishvanatha, certain aspects of the text's historiographic construction can be viewed as both implying and further refining this ideological myth. Kotikam Vishvanatha Nayaka is mentioned only once in the text, and then only in passing, as one among a group of military commanders summoned by Krishnadevaraya in preparation for war against the Muslim kingdoms. To a reader in Madurai at the close of the sixteenth century, it is quite possible that the mere mention of the name *Vishvanatha Nayaka* would have been sufficient to summon up recollections of the story of Madurai's founding, particularly if the context further implies—as it does here—his status as a loyal servant of the king. Far more important, however, is the way in which the text develops the attitude of indifference to Vijayanagara seen manifested in the Madurai chronicles subsequent to the episode of Vishvanatha Nayaka's empowerment. The *Rāyavācakamu* goes further than these texts in that it rejects later Vijayanagara history, not by a mere passive silence, but by an active historiographic construction that explicitly *denies* the existence of any kings after Krishnadevaraya. Thus, in the story of the founding of the Vijayanagara capital told to Krishnadevaraya's predecessor Viranrisimharaya (see chap. 1), the brahman soothsayer who narrates the story explains that, before Vijayanagara was built, the sage Vyasa had pronounced that the city would serve as the capital of a line of thirty kings who would rule for a total of 360 years. At the end of the story, the brahman proceeds to tell Viranrisimharaya that he is the twenty-ninth king and that there are only sixty years left for the city and dynasty to stand; at this point, Viranrisimharaya abdicates in favor of Krishnadevaraya, who is thus the last king and seal of the dynasty.

This dynastic paradigm is nowhere contradicted in the remainder of the text; Acyutaraya (who in actuality reigned as Krishnadevaraya's successor, from 1529 to 1542) and a "Chandramauli" (identity uncertain, but possibly Krishnadevaraya's nephew Sadashivaraya, who nominally ruled from 1542 until the Aravidu takeover) are each mentioned once in passing, but only as Krishnadevaraya's brothers, not as kings.

Even more striking is the obliteration of the entire Aravidu line by this historiographic construction. The only Aravidu who is mentioned at all is Araviti Bukka, whose name is included among a list of those present at Krishnadevaraya's coronation; although presented in later Aravidu records as the progenitor of the dynasty, he never ruled and was himself no more than a prominent military commander under Saluva Narasimha, founder of Vijayanagara's second dynasty, the Saluva. The names of all reigning Aravidu kings are conspicuously absent, from the famous Aliya Rama Raya all the way down to Venkatapati II, who continued to sit on the Vijayanagara throne at the very time that the text was composed. Thus, even though the text does not explicitly take part in the specific historicizing argument that Nayaka legitimacy derives from Vishvanatha's relationship with Krishnadevaraya, it does contribute an important ideological corollary, by closing the history of Vijayanagara after the reign that saw the Nayaka regime established, thus denying the right of any "successors" to exercise authority over Madurai's rulers.

One may wonder why, if the issue of Nayaka legitimacy was really such an important underlying concern, the text stops short of including some version of the narrative of Vishvanatha Nayaka and the founding of the Nayaka throne. If present Nayaka legitimacy was indeed conceived as an inheritance of the authority originally conferred by Krishnadevaraya, why should a text like the *Rāyavācakamu* not make at the very least some sort of affirmation of the importance of this original relationship? Here we may return once more to the unusual *vācakamu* format of the text. Whatever the text fails to do in narrative terms, it accomplishes just as effectively through the relationships implied in its basic discursive structure. Through the creative device of the *sthānāpati* narrator, fictively and anachronistically "reporting" to his Nayaka lord in present-day Madurai from

Krishnadevaraya's court at Vijayanagara eighty years in the past, the author is able to suggest an immediate and continuing relationship of dependence between the Nayakas and the Vijayanagara king who originally legitimated their rule. Through this playful but potent symbolism, the Nayakas are reaffirmed in their role as loyal subordinates—although their loyalty is no longer to any Vijayanagara sovereign of the corrupt present but to an ideal Vijayanagara in the inviolable past.

The "City of Victory" as Talisman of Authority

In the previous section, the destruction of the city of Vijayanagara was considered as one of the incidents that served to exacerbate the tensions already implicit in Madurai's relations with Vijayanagara. From the perspective of the analysis offered there, the destruction of the "City of Victory" was but one of several historical developments that could be viewed as symptomatic of the general decline in the power and authority of the imperial throne. From the perspective implicit in the *Rāyavācakamu*, however, the event is no mere symptom but rather the *cause* of the collapse of Vijayanagara authority. According to the text's own interpretation, it was the City of Victory itself that served as the fundamental source of its kings' power and authority; consequently, when the city was destroyed, its rulers were left with no source of power to uphold them, and thus the dynasty came to an end. The singular importance of the city and the nature of its symbolic power in fact emerge as key themes in the *Rāyavācakamu*, and we accordingly turn now to a consideration of the image of the City of Victory as it is represented in our text.

So important is the theme of the city as the basis of its rulers' authority that nearly an entire chapter at the beginning of the text is devoted to a narration of the circumstances of Vijayanagara's founding, thus explaining the source and nature of its power. According to the text's own chronology, the founding occurred three hundred years prior to the time of Krishnadevaraya; accordingly, the story is accommodated into the report through one of the text's many instances of internal narration. Thus, just before Krishnadevaraya's coronation, during the last days of his predecessor Viranrisimharaya,

Fig. 3. Vidyaranya in his palanquin, ca. seventeenth century, painting from *mahā-raṅga-maṇḍapa* ceiling, Virupaksha Temple, Hampi. (Photo Dee Foster, Vijayanagara Research Project.)

the then-reigning king suddenly interrupts the proceedings of his court to question his soothsayers about the city's origins. One of the soothsayers, Mullandradindima Pumbhava Sarasvati, comes forth and satisfies the king's curiosity by recounting the entire story. His long and complicated narrative provides one of the text's most fascinating and important episodes.

According to this account, the city was built not by its earliest rulers but by the sage Vidyaranya (see fig. 3) "as a favor" to those kings. The sage founded the city in his own name, thus giving rise to the appelation *Vidyanagara* (the City of Vidya[ranya]) that occurs in both this and other texts as an alternative designation for the city. Certain folk traditions current today in the Hampi region also recognize Vidyaranya as the "founder" of the city in that he is said to have provided financial backing by causing a rain of gold to fall on the site, but the *Rāyavācakamu* portrays the sage and his disciples as actually planning the city and directing the building activities themselves.

Building cities is hardly the ordinary business of sages, but then neither is it as a matter of his own choice that Vidyaranya comes to build the City of Victory. To the contrary, the narrative clearly establishes that it is his *fate* to build a city and that his realization of this fate is due entirely to the successive revelations of three other sagely personages. The first to guide Vidyaranya toward the realization of his fate is none other than his own earthly guru, Jnanendra Sarasvati. Jnanendra recognizes his disciple's unusual qualities when the latter comes home from his begging rounds bringing rice pudding instead of the usual alms fare. Concluding that this uncommon luck must be the unavoidable fruit of merit sown in his disciple's previous lives, Jnanendra orders Vidyaranya to leave the hermitage and go to Kashi, and, although he says nothing specific about building a city, his interpretation of the rice pudding as food that is "fit for a king" and thus inappropriate for "mendicants like us" is perhaps a veiled hint at what is to come.

Without questioning his preceptor, Vidyaranya sets out on a "circumambulation of the earth" (see map 3). As Vidyaranya proceeds through Central India on his way to Kashi, he encounters his second guide in the person of the forest ascetic Shingiri Bhatlu. Addressing

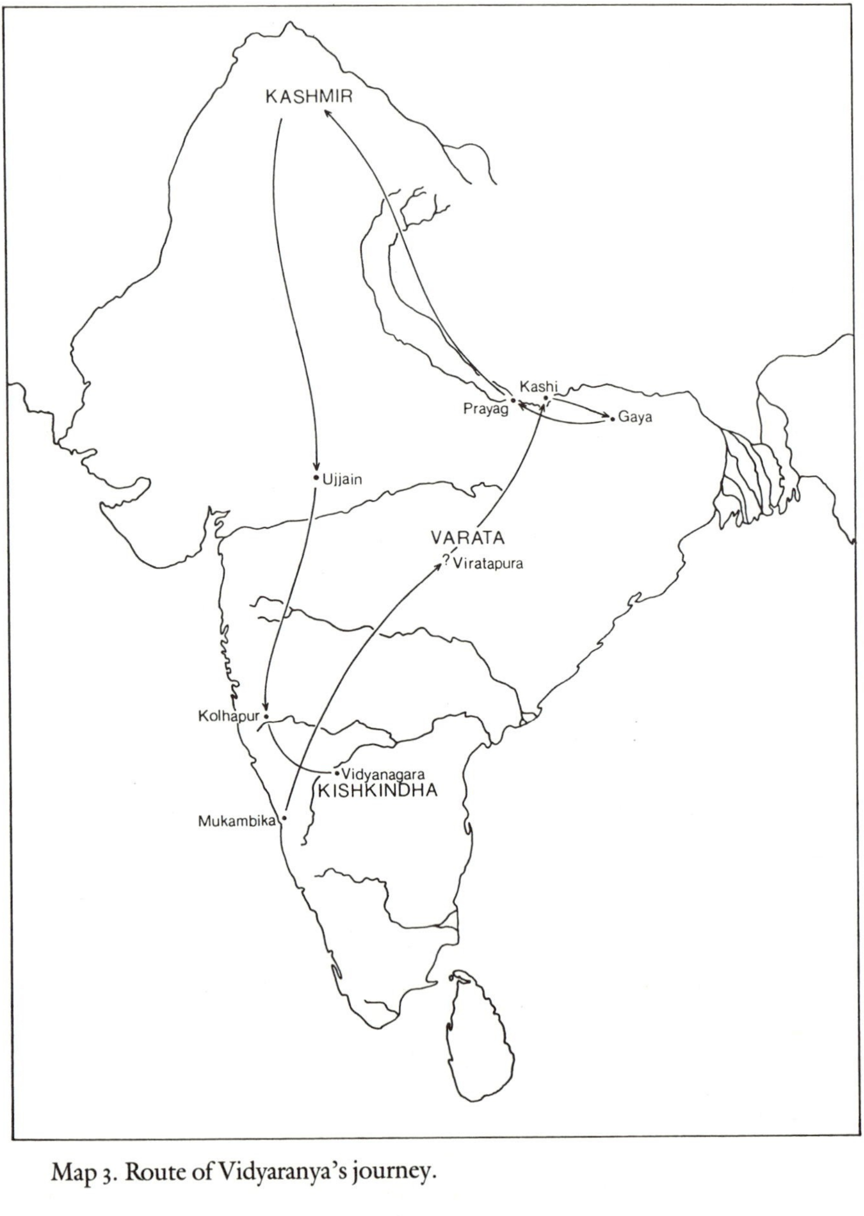

Map 3. Route of Vidyaranya's journey.

the wary Vidyaranya, Shingiri Bhatlu explains that he had once served as a sacrificial priest for none other than Rama himself, the semidivine king who had reigned in the Treta age many thousands of years before. Through his power of omniscience, the ancient and mysterious Shingiri Bhatlu openly proclaims Vidyaranya's fate: through the grace of the divine beings that he is to meet in Kashi, he will found a city on the banks of the Tungabhadra, and, after installing a king named Harihara[32] on its throne, he will enjoy prosperity and wealth forever after. Most important, Shingiri Bhatlu directs Vidyaranya to meet Vyasa—the archetypal, primordial sage who resides in Kashi—and gives Vidyaranya the instructions necessary to ensure that the great sage will appear before him.

Vidyaranya finally arrives in Kashi, where, thanks to Shingiri Bhatlu's instructions, he succeeds in recognizing Vyasa despite his appearance in the "vile form" of a pariah. In addition to reiterating several of the details that had already been revealed by Shingiri Bhatlu, Vyasa completes the revelation of Vidyaranya's fate by informing him of the life span and political functions of the city he will found. Vyasa explains that, through the power of the goddess of fortune, Vidyaranya's city will stand in prosperity for 360 years and that, during this time, it will serve as the capital for a line of thirty kings. Vidyaranya will be the preceptor of these kings, and he will instruct them to offer daily feedings for one thousand brahmans, "in order to make Shingiri Bhatlu happy." Now that he has come to the full realization of his fate and gained the blessings of Vyasa and the divinities of Kashi, Vidyaranya returns to Karnataka to build his city.

The city that he goes on to found is no ordinary city but has two special qualities as a result of the workings of divine power. In the first place—as Vyasa had revealed—the city is to exist and prosper for 360 years; this is thanks to the goddess Lakshmi, who agrees to dwell there in fulfillment of a boon she has granted to Vidyaranya. Second, the city is to be unconquerable throughout the entire term of its existence, through the power of an ancient curse that the sage Matanga has placed on Vali, the monkey king who had ruled over the region during the time of Rama. The circumstances and precise terms of the curse will be examined shortly; for the moment, we will simply note that the curse was originally placed on Vali, preventing him on pain of death from setting foot on Matanga's mountain hermitage. With the passage of time, however, the specific curse has transformed itself into a general protective power enveloping the mountain and insulating it from any attacker, "whether animal or man," as the local elders explain to Vidyaranya, who watches in amazement as a hare turns on an attacking dog to chase it from the spot. Vidyaranya decides to take advantage of the spot's great power and build here so that his city too will be protected from attackers by the curse of Matanga (fig. 4).

The story of Vidyaranya and his pivotal role in Vijayanagara's early history is not unique to the *Rāyavācakamu;* it occurs as well in a number of other texts dating from the sixteenth and seventeenth centuries. The narrative of our text is closely related to these other versions, yet there are important differences of detail that set the version of our text apart from the general body of Vidyaranya tradition. Clearly, in redacting his own version of the tale, our author has emphasized or suppressed certain themes and details—in some cases even adding totally new material—in order to produce an interpretation that is more fully consonant with his larger textual purpose. For this reason, comparison of the *Rāyavācakamu*'s account with that of another, more standard text will be useful as a means of identifying what is unique in our version and thereby bringing into sharper focus the concerns that guided the author in his redaction of the popular tale. We may take as our point of comparison a standard version of the tale as it occurs in the late sixteenth-century Sanskrit work *Vidyāraṇya-kṛti* of the *Vidyāraṇyakālajñāna* series[33] (a complete translation of this version is given in app. B).

While the primary focus of the *Vidyāraṇya-kṛti*'s narrative is on the scholarly activities of Vidyaranya and his role as *purohita* or priestly adviser to Harihara and Bukka's nascent dynasty, the real focus of the *Rāyavācakamu* redaction is on the founding of the city itself and Vidyaranya's role in that event. This point emerges most clearly from the differences between the two texts in their treatments of two points: the character and motivations of Vidyaranya and the circumstances of the city's founding. The *Vidyāraṇya-kṛti* depicts Vidyaranya as an active, purposive individual, devoted to the pursuit of scholarly, intellectual activities, while the *Rāyavācakamu* presents

Fig. 4. Mount Matanga, Vijayanagara: site of Vidyaranya's foundation of the City of Victory.

him as little more than a passive instrument of fate. Thus, in the *Vidyāraṇya-kṛti,* the story begins with Vidyaranya himself deciding to go to Kashi—in order to resolve some doubts he has about the commentaries on the four Vedas—while, in the *Rāyavācakamu,* it is his guru who orders him to go there for reasons that he himself does not yet understand. Once he has arrived at the holy city and met with the sage Vyasa, it is scholarly activity that dominates the *Vidyāraṇya-kṛti's* account of his stay, with Vyasa teaching him an ambitious curriculum, including "*śrutis, smṛtis, purāṇas,* and *itihāsas;* innumerable *artha-śāstras* and *kāma-śāstras;* and the works on the principles of religion, such as the sixty-four *saṃhitās.*" In the *Rāyavācakamu,* however, the emphasis is instead on Vyasa's revelation of his fate and favoring him with his grace.[34] Finally, when Vidyaranya has returned to Karnataka, the *Vidyāraṇya-kṛti* has him meeting Sayana and Mayana, accepting them as disciples, and helping them compose their scholarly studies *Sāyaṇīya* and *Māyaṇīya,* while in the *Rāyavācakamu* he is not represented as teaching or pursuing scholarship, and his disciples are introduced only as assistants who help in his efforts to build the city.

Likewise, in the circumstances of the city's founding, there are sharp differences between the two versions that are suggestive of the far greater importance accorded this event by the *Rāyavācakamu.* In the *Rāyavācakamu's* account, Vidyaranya builds the city on virgin land as a new foundation *(pratiṣṭha),* but, in the *Vidyāraṇya-kṛti,* the originality of the achievement is rudely deflated by the god Virupaksha's revelation that there had once before been a city named Vijayanagara standing on the site, with the result that Vidyaranya's action becomes in effect nothing more than a refoundation *(punar-pratiṣṭha).* With regard to the motive for building, the *Rāyavācakamu* explicitly states that it is Vidyaranya's fate to do so and that his city will ultimately be used for the benefit of a line of kings; the *Vidyāraṇya-kṛti* again trivializes the event by having Vidyaranya build the city primarily as a means of appeasing the appetite of Shringin, the hungry forest ascetic who is identical with the *Rāyavācakamu's* Shingiri Bhatlu. Finally, it is in the matter of the city's special qualities that the difference between the two texts is perhaps most clearly apparent. In the *Rāyavācakamu,* Vidyaranya finds the appropriate spot on which to build through the omen of the hare chasing the dog and then learns from the local elders of the curse of Matanga and the area's protective powers. Although the *Vidyāraṇya-kṛti* also relates the omen of the hare and the dogs—witnessed here not by Vidyaranya but by the hunting party of the kings-to-be Harihara and Bukka—and has Vidyaranya advising the kings of the spot's suitability on the basis of this sign, there is no mention of either Matanga's curse or any specific protective powers possessed by the site.

To summarize the differences between the *Vidyāraṇya-kṛti*'s earlier, more standard version and that of the *Rāyavācakamu,* in the redaction of the latter text, the traditional emphasis on Vidyaranya as a paradigm of the scholarly *purohita*—who incidentally happens to build a city—is eclipsed by a new emphasis on the "magical" nature of the city and on Vidyaranya's pivotal role in its founding.

The reasons for this transformation are readily apparent if we only view the *Rāyavācakamu*'s account in its proper guise as an integral episode within a historiographic text. Such works—most notably those of the medieval Telugu genre known as *caritramu* or "dynastic chronicle"—frequently include a narrative that accounts for the dynasty's empowerment, typically through a magical talisman granted as a boon from the dynasty's tutelary divinity. There are striking similarities between the structure of our text's Vidyaranya story and examples of such empowerment narratives, suggesting that the author of the *Rāyavācakamu* was guided in his redaction by a concern to produce a comparable narrative of dynastic empowerment for his text.

As an example, we may consider the empowerment narrative from Ekamranatha's prose *Pratāparudracaritramu,*[35] a Telugu work of the early sixteenth century. In a manner characteristic of the *caritramu* genre, the work traces the fortunes of the dynasty of the Kakatiyas (who ruled over the Telugu country between the mid-twelfth and the early fourteenth centuries), combining genealogical passages giving only the barest synopses of individual reigns with detailed narratives covering the activities of the more important rulers. Of the text's extended narratives, one of the most crucial is the account of the legendary Madhava Varman, who is considered in this text to be the true founder of the dynasty. After recounting the details of

Madhava Varman's birth, the narrative goes on to explain how the young boy was able to found a dynasty as a result of boons received from the goddess Padmakshi:

> One day, in his haste to go and play with his schoolmates after their lessons in the Padmakshi temple, young Madhava Varman forgot his slate and books. Unwittingly leaving them near Padmakshi's image, he left the temple and closed the door, and then lost himself in his games with his friends. It was not until after he had gone home and finished his bath and his dinner that he realized he had forgotten his books and slate. Since he would need them later on that evening for his lesson with Madhava Sharma, who would no doubt chastise him for his negligence, he decided to go back and get them. Even though it was nighttime, he slipped out by himself and headed for the temple.
>
> There at the temple, the goddess Padmakshi was sitting in state on her throne, attended by a horde of terrifying demons—there were spirits and ghosts, goblins, *śākinis* and *ḍhākinis,* vampires, and *brahmarakṣasas.* Without feeling the least bit of fear for this dreadful host, Madhava Varman walked right up to the goddess and picked up his books and slate.
>
> The goddess was surprised to see the boy standing there so fearlessly and decided to test him to see just how brave he really was: in an instant she assumed her most hideous and frightful form. But the boy just stood there, not the least bit frightened to see her like this, and instead he only folded his hands and began to sing her praise. He prostrated himself before her feet and lay there without standing up. Seeing this, the goddess' heart began to overflow with feelings of affection for the boy, and she said, "Stand up, dear boy. I appreciate your display of courage and devotion! Ask for a boon, whatever you may please."
>
> Madhava Varman had learned from his mother of his father's death at the hands of the lord of Cuttack, and so he asked the goddess, "Please grant me the ability to vanquish the lord of Cuttack and to get our royal herds back."
>
> The goddess replied, "So be it." She presented the boy with a divine sword and shield and proclaimed, "With this sword you shall repel all the enemies who attack you, and by the power of this shield neither swords nor arrows shall reach you. With them you shall rule for two thousand months." Then, pointing out the mouth of a nearby cave, she added, "Go westward into that cave. After walking for some distance, you will come out of the cave and find yourself in a beautiful place. From that time until sunrise tomorrow, an entire army will issue forth from the cave to serve you."

> Padmakshi continued, "With this divine sword and shield, your family will occupy the throne for one thousand years. So go and rule the earth, and do not forget to honor cows and brahmans and to offer worship to Uma and Maheshvara and Lakshmi and Narayana!" (Ramachandra Rao 1984, pp. 10–11; translation mine)

Madhava Varman follows the goddess' instructions and assembles his army and, after celebrating his coronation, goes off to attain victory over the king of Cuttack. As the goddess has ordained, the dynasty of the Kakatiyas endures for exactly one thousand years from the date of Madhava Varman's coronation.[36]

The similarities between this story and the *Rāyavācakamu*'s account of Vidyaranya are indeed striking. In fact, the Madhava Varman story offers a precise structural parallel for each element and motif of the *Rāyavācakamu* account that lacks a counterpart in the standard Vidyaranya tradition. Thus, the magical, talismanic nature of the City of Victory in the *Rāyavācakamu* (the city will be unassailable through the power of Matanga's curse; it is destined to last for 360 years and serve as the capital of a dynasty of thirty kings), although alien to the standard Vidyaranya tradition, finds its perfect counterpart in Madhava Varman's divine sword and shield (the bearer of the sword and shield is unassailable; through the power of these weapons, Madhava Varman's family will rule for one thousand years). Similarly, in the *Rāyavācakamu*, the city is bestowed as a divine gift on Vidyaranya only after he has passed a test (Vidyaranya prostrates himself before the vile form of Vyasa's apparition; Vyasa reveals Vidyaranya's fate and blesses him); while this motif is underdeveloped in the *Vidyāraṇya-kṛti* account,[37] a close parallel is found in Padmakshi's testing and rewarding of Madhava Varman (Madhava Varman prostrates himself before the terrifying form of Padmakshi's apparition; Padmakshi grants him the sword and shield as a boon). Clearly, the author of the *Rāyavācakamu* has adapted the traditional story of Vidyaranya and the founding of Vijayanagara so that it serves as an account of dynastic empowerment for his text: just as Padmakshi's divine sword and shield empower the dynasty of the Kakatiyas, so does Vidyaranya's city empower the line of thirty kings who will rule from its throne. The two gifts differ only in form while serving identical functions: each is a talisman that bestows protection on its "bearer" and in so doing empowers his dynasty to rule until the term of its power is exhausted.

Apart from their obvious differences in scale, there are yet other major differences in nature between the City of Victory and Madhava Varman's sword and shield. While Padmakshi bestows her gifts as finished products, Vidyaranya must still build his city before he can hand it over to the kings it will empower. Moreover, in contrast with the portable sword and shield, which remain equally effective wherever they happen to be carried, a city is by its very nature confined to a single location. In fact, the *Rāyavācakamu* further underscores the importance of this distinction by insisting that the city's power ultimately derives from its specific siting. Vidyaranya cannot build his city just anywhere; he must first find an appropriate mythogeographic spot capable of generating protective power and channeling it into his foundation.

Since it is a site of supernatural power that is being sought, it is hardly surprising that Vidyaranya identifies it, not through any natural indications, but by means of a mysterious omen:

> He then climbed the Matanga hill and scanned the four quarters, looking for a square plot of ground on which to found his city. Just then a hare came out of a cave in the hill and began to chase a dog that had been watching a herd of cows nearby. Vidyaranya noticed this with great surprise. "In this world," he wondered to himself, "it is the rule for dogs to chase hares, but nowhere have I seen a hare chasing a dog. Might it not be due to some special power that this place possesses?"

His suspicions are soon confirmed by the testimony of some local residents, but it is the form of the strange omen that first signals the suitability of the site and suggests the specific nature of its unique powers. Interestingly, this omen of a hare chasing a hound (or hounds) is a constant element in traditional accounts of the city's founding, occurring in the *Vidyāraṇya-kṛti* (as noted above) as well as in other sixteenth-century sources ranging from local inscriptions to the Portuguese chronicle of Nuniz (Heras 1929, pp. 1–11). Moreover, the same omen (or a variant form, such as a hare chasing a tiger) occurs as a common motif in the foundation stories of other South Indian capital cities; the ancient capital of the Hoyshalas, for example, is called Shashakapura, "City of the Hare," and is said to have been founded by the dynasty's progenitor on a spot where a hare had chased a tiger.[38] The significance of the omen cannot be fully understood without recognizing that it is in fact one of a pair of omens that serve, not merely to identify potent sites, but, more important, to determine whether their power is better suited for application to spiritual or worldly ends. The site itself is signaled in either case by an omen involving a disruption of the natural predatory order, while the particular nature of the site is revealed by the specific form of the disruption. Thus, sites destined to serve for the cultivation of spiritual power *(brahma)* are revealed by omens in which the predatory order is completely *suspended,* suggesting the practice of renunciation *(tyāga)* on which the attainment of spiritual power depends. An example is provided by the story of Shankara's founding of the monastery *(maṭha)* at Shringeri, related in the various Sanskrit *Śankaradigvijayas.* In the course of his wanderings through South India, Shankara comes to a riverbank, where he witnesses a frog sitting quietly beneath the raised hood of a cobra, who shelters it from the sun; recognizing the place's spiritual power, he proceeds to found his *maṭha* there. In contrast, sites destined to serve the end of worldly power *(kṣatra)* are signaled by omens in which the predatory order is not suspended but actually *reversed.* In the story of Vijayanagara's founding, the hare chasing the hound signals the very different order of power that this site possesses—a power that augments the physical strength and courage of its inhabitants, thereby enabling them to overcome their natural enemies. It is thus clear to Vidyaranya that this is a site ideally suited for the pursuit of *kṣatra*—the kingly ideal of rule, force, and active conquest—and, accordingly, for the foundation of his city.

Having determined the suitability of the site, Vidyaranya is yet curious to learn the precise nature and reasons for its power. He calls the local elders, who come and enlighten him:

> "According to the sacred traditions of this place, it's impossible for anyone—no matter how strong he might be—to harm the weak here

> because of the curse of the great sage Matanga. A long time ago, the monkey princes Vali and Sugriva lived in Kishkindha. They had a quarrel among themselves, so they started fighting. During that war, Sugriva couldn't face Vali and fight with him anymore because Vali was such a great, strong fellow. So Sugriva ran away and came to this Matanga hill, and he stayed here on top of it. Vali came chasing right behind him, but the great sage Matanga had cursed Vali a long time ago so that he couldn't climb up this hill. And ever since that time, no strong fellow—whether animal or man—has been able to do his strong man's business up here! Anyway, whenever Sugriva couldn't fight anymore with Vali, he would come up to this Matanga hill. So you see, no matter how strong someone is when he comes to this place, he ends up powerless to do anything. He can run away all right, but he can't stay and face up to the fight! Who knows, it seems that, whether you're an animal or a man, if you stay up here, then it's impossible for your enemies to get you!"

The story to which the local elders allude is a well-known episode from the *Kiṣkindha-kāṇḍa* of the epic *Rāmāyaṇa*. Vali, the monkey king of Kishkindha, had invited the curse on himself through his carelessness in a fight with the buffalo demon Dundubhi. After struggling with the demon for many hours, he finally emerged triumphant and slew his enemy. But, rather than resting content with victory, Vali went on to pick up Dundubhi's body and throw it in the air, sending it crashing to the ground several miles away: "From the titan's jaws, shattered by the violence of the fall, blood spouted forth and the drops were carried by the wind to Matanga's hermitage. Seeing that rain of blood, the Sage, displeased, reflected: 'What perverse wretch has dared to spatter me with blood? Who is this evil, perfidious and vile creature, this madman?' " Realizing that it was Vali who had been the perpetrator, Matanga pronounced his curse: " 'May he never come here! If that monkey who, with a stream of blood, has desecrated this wood where I have built my retreat, ever sets his foot in this place, he will die!' " (Shastri 1957–1959 2:192, 193).

The elders of the place, however, have begun their explanation to Vidyaranya with a subsequent event, referring to the battle between Vali and his younger brother, Sugriva. Owing to a complicated series of events, Sugriva had challenged his elder brother's right to the throne of Kishkindha, and the two were soon led into a bitter and vicious battle. When Sugriva was no longer strong enough to face his more powerful brother, he came running to the top of Matanga's hill for refuge; but, as the elders go on to explain, Vali was powerless to climb the hill for fear of the sage's curse. What they do not explain is the final, well-known outcome of the story, which takes Sugriva far beyond this safe but inglorious stalemate: Rama comes and befriends him and, after slaying Vali, proceeds to install Sugriva as the rightful heir to Kishkindha's throne.[39]

When Sugriva thus turns the sage's curse to his own benefit, he unwittingly begins a process that transforms the curse from a specific negative power keeping Vali away into a more general and beneficent power making the sage's mountain a safe haven for the pursued. The elders are clear and insistent in their interpretation of the curse's power: "Ever since that time, no strong fellow—whether animal or man—has been able to do his strong man's business up here! . . . no matter how strong someone is when he comes to this place, he ends up powerless to do anything. . . . Who knows, it seems that, whether you're an animal or a man, if you stay up here, then it's impossible for your enemies to get you!" With the combined testimony of both a supernatural omen and local tradition, Vidyaranya is now certain of the site's suitability. He proceeds to build his city, confident that it will indeed have the power to protect its kings and empower their rule throughout the 360 years of its destined existence as a "cosmic" city.[40]

Apart from the story of Vidyaranya and the city's foundation, there is yet another episode in the text that affirms the fundamental importance of the City of Victory as the source of its ruler's authority and power. The episode begins when Krishnadevaraya secretly leaves the city one night in order to hide from his ministers (chap. 3). He does this to assert his independence and express his dissatisfaction with the way the court is coming to be run almost totally by ministers and subordinates: " 'They think of me merely as their agent for bearing the burden of the Lion-Throne,' thought the king to himself. 'In fact, everything is coming to be run by these ministers! Who even bothers to listen to me? Why, if I were ever to demonstrate my authority and attempt to act independently, everything would come to a standstill simply because the ministers would disapprove.' " In order to express his independence, the king decides to leave the city in secret and go to the Pallikonda Ranganatha temple on its northern outskirts.

When the chief minister Appaji discovers the next morning that the king is absent, however, the story takes a decidedly different turn. The issue of the king's independence fades to insignificance in the face of the far more urgent problem of the king's absence from the city. When Appaji learns from the palace guards that the king has gone out the night before and never returned, he is alarmed and worried, not for fear of the king's personal, bodily safety, but rather because of the political crisis that his absence poses. As he later explains to the king when he has found him, " 'When the harem guard women and doorkeepers said that your lordship had gone out as if to inspect the city but hadn't yet returned, I was upset to say the least. . . . Your lordship, is it proper that you should leave the city and come here like this? If your subordinates had heard of this, the city would be lost.' " In this context, "the city would be lost" is Appaji's way of politely implying that one or another of the king's ambitious subordinates or feudatories would take the opportunity to usurp the throne. The sense of Appaji's argument is that, as long as Krishnadevaraya is personally in the city, it is he who is its possessor and king. But, in order to remain as king, he must keep the city in his possession by occupying it: should he leave the city while other powerful men are yet inside, they will have the opportunity to seize the City of Victory together with the kingship it confers.

This does not imply that the king is doomed perpetually to remain a prisoner in his own capital; to the contrary, throughout most of the latter part of our text, Krishnadevaraya is away on a campaign against the Muslim kings of the Deccan and the Gajapati in Orissa. But there is no danger of losing the city on these occasions, for the precise reason that they are military campaigns and therefore all potential usurpers—the feudatories and powerful military officers—are likewise absent from the city, fighting by the side of their king. Moreover, as a precautionary measure, Krishnadevaraya has left his loyal minister Saluva Timmarasu in the capital "with a small force of horsemen to protect the city of Vijayanagara" before departing on the campaign. In light of the present episode, it is clear that the horsemen are left to protect the city as much from unloyal subordinates as from outside enemies.

To return to Appaji's dilemma, he is worried now because the king has *not* left the city in the proper way: he has gone out by himself, leaving an entire host of potential usurpers behind in the City of Victory. But, fortunately for Krishnadevaraya's kingship, Appaji, the most excellent and capable of ministers, immediately finds a stratagem to avert disaster. First, in order to prevent anyone from realizing that the king is absent, he commands the loyal palace guards to explain that the king has a headache and has not yet risen, should anyone come to the palace to inquire. Then he sends loyal spies out to search for the king, and, after just a short time, one, having been successful, returns and informs Appaji of the king's location. Finally, and most important, he sends word to all the feudatories present in the city, summoning them to "come quickly with all their forces" since the king has "decided to go hunting." As soon as the lords and their armies have assembled, Appaji marches them out of the city gate, leaving the capital "empty" and safe until Krishnadevaraya's return. Krishnadevaraya has attempted to demonstrate his independence, but the episode proves that he is anything but independent. The king's authority depends not only on wise and loyal ministers like Appaji but also, and even more fundamentally, on his continued possession of the City of Victory that empowers him.

By its repeated insistence that power and authority derive ultimately from the city, our text thus offers further support to current interpretations that view the Vijayanagara capital as, according to John Fritz, "a necessary component of the system that constituted the authority of its rulers." As Fritz has rightly argued, "The capital was not merely a setting for ritual or a precipitate of social action; rather urban form at Vijayanagara embodied the principles and relationships that constituted the authority of the king. King and god were the focus of the city: they paid homage to each other, and by radiating their energies outward they gave form, harmony, and plenty to the empire" (1986, pp. 44, 53). But our text makes it clear that it is not just the *form* of the city that is constitutive of this authority but rather the proper conjunction of form and *siting*.

Form alone remains an abstraction that can be reproduced and imposed on any new site, but the specific potency of a site is something that simply cannot be transferred elsewhere.

The course of history after 1565 further confirms this notion and testifies to the unique inimitability of the city of Vijayanagara. Indeed, even at the end of the fifteenth century, when the usurpation of authority first by the Saluvas and then, just a decade later, by the Tuluvas offered opportunities to move the center of power to a more secure location such as Chandragiri, this option was not taken for the simple reason that the city was not just the "center of power" but the *source* of power. In Burton Stein's felicitous phrase, "the political capital had become political capital" (1989, p. 71). It was doubtless in recognition of this fact that, after the decisive battle of Rakshasa-Tangadi in 1565, the victorious armies of the Muslim kingdoms of the northern Deccan seized the fallen city of Vijayanagara and remained there for six months, systematically destroying the palaces and other visible symbols of the empire's authority in the hopes of ridding themselves of this powerful foe once and for all. When the Aravidu house in turn usurped the Vijayanagara throne in the aftermath of the city's destruction, the throne they inherited had thus come to possess "neither a capital nor even a fixed territory" (Stein 1989, p. 122). Ruling alternately from Penugonda and Chandragiri, the Aravidu rulers struggled desperately to convince their subordinates that they were truly the kings of "Vijayanagara," and the fact that, from the 1570s on, they wistfully referred to these capital cities as "Vijayanagara" in their inscriptions[41] suggests that they were as deeply aware as their subordinates were of the crisis engendered by the destruction of the City of Victory. But the city was not to be revived through the mere power of its name.

Demons of the Kali Age

Of the five Muslim powers that would in 1565 join together to crush the Vijayanagara capital, the three kingdoms of Bijapur, Ahmadnagar, and Golconda figure in the *Rāyavācakamu* as enemies conquered by Krishnadevaraya. Two entire chapters of the work are devoted to these Muslim kingdoms and their "Turk"[42] lords: chapter 4 consists of descriptions of their capitals and court routine, and chapter 6 recounts the particulars of Krishnadevaraya's victorious battle with the armies of these three kingdoms.

The *Rāyavācakamu*'s account of this battle is one of the sections of the text that has attracted the most attention from historians, but discussions of this section have inevitably ignored the integral relation between chapter 6 and the chapters that immediately surround it. Chapters 4 and 5 present the spies' reports about the Muslim and Gajapati kingdoms, and chapter 7 narrates the continuation of Krishnadevaraya's battle campaign and his victory over the Gajapati. When these four chapters are viewed together as the unit they properly constitute, it becomes clear that they in fact serve a far more significant purpose than simply recording the course of one of Krishnadevaraya's military exploits. On a deeper and more important level, this portion of the text serves to articulate a complex cultural polemic against the alien civilization of the Muslim "Turks."

It is important to recognize that this polemic is an expression of the author's own cultural milieu, not of the earlier period of Krishnadevaraya's reign that is represented in the text. It is true that an earlier tradition of historiography had commonly portrayed Vijayanagara as the "last bastion of Hindu orthodoxy," a military state established to protect the South against the "onslaughts of Islam" (see, e.g., Sewell 1962, pp. 1–4), but the accuracy of this interpretation has been called into question by more recent scholars, who argue that such a view of the Indian past is too heavily colored by the experience of modern Hindu-Muslim communalism.[43] As Romila Thapar has rightly stressed, the rulers of Vijayanagara were "not concerned with stirring up anti-Muslim sentiments, as might have been expected of Hindu revivalism at that period. The Hindu kingdoms did not form an alliance against the Muslims, and the kings of Vijayanagara did not hesitate to attack Hindu kings wherever they felt them to be an obstacle" (Thapar 1976, p. 324).

Recent archaeological and epigraphic discoveries at the site of the Vijayanagara capital have only lent further support to this anticommunalist critique, by attesting to the presence of clearly defined Muslim quarters within the walls of the city's royal center (Michell 1985b) and even to the importance of Islamic stylistic forms in the elaboration of the distinctive Vijayanagara style of courtly architecture (Michell 1985a, 1991a, 1991b). While there is thus little evidence of any communally defined Hindu-Muslim antagonism in the Vijayanagara period proper (i.e., up to 1565), the present text provides unmistakable evidence that an anti-Islamic polemic was indeed taking shape in the South by the closing years of the sixteenth century. This incipient anti-Islamic orientation can be readily understood as a by-product of the destruction of the City of Victory: the text's anti-Islamic polemic is the expression of a natural antipathy for the agents responsible for this culturally disruptive act.

As we shall see below, this polemic is not, strictly speaking, communally conceived; it is directed against the "Turakas," not as members of a heretical religion, but as *mlēcchas* or barbarians, the representatives of an alien, foreign civilization. There is only one moment when a specifically religious judgment is passed against them, and that is when the brahman-caste ministers of the three Turkish kings all pause to bemoan the misery of their servitude: "Our lords are drunkards [*madya-pānulu*] who have no faith in gods and brahmans [*dēva-brāṃhmaṇa-viśvāsamu lēvu*]. They are barbarians [*mlēcchulu*], cow killers [*gō-hiṃsakulu*]." Indeed, one wonders whether the author was even cognizant of the fact that these barbarians possessed their own formal religion. Two brief passages imply that the Turks have their own distinct "patron god" (*pāliṭi-dēvuṃḍu,* an indigenous Hindu concept), somewhat generically and noncommittally named as Kartaru, "the Creator,"[44] and there is a single reference to "writings of the Mullahs" *(mullā-śāstra)* and to fakirs *(phakkīrulu)* who interpret these writings in order to predict the future. Other than this, however, there is no mention of any belief or practice that is recognizably Islamic. Clearly, it is the Turakas' ordinary personal and cultural behavior that is being targeted for criticism, not the formal beliefs and practices of their Islamic religion.

What is relevant here is of course not the fairness or accuracy of the *Rāyavācakamu*'s characterization of the Turks but rather the nature of this polemic and the particular formal structures that shape it. We shall see that the author's strategy has been to define the Turks through three sets of structural oppositions, operating on three distinct yet interrelated textual levels. First, on the surface plane of the narrative itself, the Turks are compared with the Hindu

Gajapati and found to be deficient in terms of *dharma*, the acceptable modes of social and personal conduct. Second, on the deeper level of the conceptual geography that informs the text, the kingdoms of the Turks are collectively portrayed as an inhospitable zone occupying the no-man's-land between the borders of the three *dharmic* kingdoms of the "Three Lion-Thrones." Finally, on the third and deepest level, the opposition between the *adharmic* "Turks" and the *dharmic* kings of the Three Lion-Thrones is represented in terms of an old, traditional mythical paradigm: that of the conflict between the gods and the demons. Let us consider each of these levels in turn.

The Narrative Surface

There are a handful of instances within the text when one of the characters emphasizes the *dharmic* inferiority of the Turks by explicitly contrasting them with the Gajapati (or some other *dharmic* king). In one such case, for example, when Krishnadevaraya's minister Appaji asserts that "the Gajapati is indeed a great man," he emphasizes this point by adding, "He's not like the Turks—he has faith in gods and brahmans." While explicitly articulated comparisons like this are few in number, the message of the text is yet unmistakable on account of the formal plan of its narration: thus, from the fourth chapter on, the narrative unfolds through two sets of paired chapters, the first of each pair outlining the Turks' behavior in a given situation, the second holding up by way of contrast the counterexample of the Gajapati's behavior in the same situation. The first pair of chapters (chaps. 4 and 5) presents the two exemplars in peacetime, characterizing their respective court routines and daily behavior, while the second pair (chaps. 6 and 7) portrays the two as they function in war when attacked by the text's hero, Krishnadevaraya. The rhythmic symmetry of two such alternating cycles serves to heighten the reader's perception of the Turks' *adharmic* nature, bringing it into a much sharper resolution than would be possible from a sustained focus on the Turks alone.

In chapter 4, the kingdoms of the Turks are described to Krishnadevaraya by spies who have just returned from Bijapur, Ahmadnagar, and Golconda.[45] According to the reports of these spies, the Turks are violent barbarians, rash in their behavior, and totally unrestrained in their interactions with others. Their kingdoms are ruled by fear since anyone who opposes them is cruelly subjected to horrendous torture. As Arava Rama and Fakir Gopaji report from Ahmadnagar and Golconda,

> "One day, we saw an officer giving orders for punishments in front of the audience hall. People were being sliced in two at the waist or slowly cut apart with saws; others were tied up in gunny sacks and beaten with iron maces. Some were being flogged with strings that had sharp pieces of horn tied at the tips, while others had heavy stones tied to their feet and were then left to sit astride a ruined wall. Some were tied up in bundles and left to die in the hot sun. Some had their feet, hands, ears, or noses cut off."

It is not just criminals or political opponents who are tortured in this way; to the contrary, the Turks are so vicious that they even torture their own revenue officers to ensure regular payments:

> "Some [of the revenue officers] were even being crushed to death under the feet of elephants. Some of the [other] frightened officers immediately made payments to the palace on witnessing these varied and horrendous acts of torture, and they were released with their lives. But there were others, however, who for some reason were simply unable to pay, and they were tortured to death right there in the middle of the street."[46]

Not only are the Turks excessively violent, but they are additionally portrayed as weak in character. They are sadly lacking in the proper kingly virtues of dignity *(gaṃbharamu,* from the Sanskrit *gaṃbhīra)* and courage *(dhairyam),* and, in contrast, they conduct their affairs in a state of mental confusion *(buddhi-cancalatvam).* At one point, for example, the minister Appaji comments on the report from Bijapur,

> "You know how a dignified and courageous king would act in such a situation [i.e., having heard the rumor that Krishnadevaraya is planning an attack]. If something alarming should be reported from one of the quarters, he does not worry about it immediately. But, within a few days, he will start a rumor to the effect that the feudatory ruler of the province in that quarter will be paying an inspection visit, and that

gets the local commanders going, securing the walls and bastions and setting in provisions and supplies. *That* is the courageous way of making preparations and assembling one's forces. No, what the Turks have done makes it clear that they are acting not out of courage but from a state of mental confusion."

In another context, after the report about Ahmadnagar and Golconda has been made, one of Krishnadevaraya's commanders comments on how the Turks' carelessness and confusion is manifested even in battle:

"You see, my lord, when the Turks set out for the battlefront, they don't proceed cautiously, gauging themselves with the opposing force. Instead, they just advance obstinately. If it so happens that they outnumber and defeat the opposing force, then, no matter how fast the other soldiers flee, the Turks will keep coming and massacring them. If, on the other hand, the opposing force stands firm, then they beg their commanders to let them go back. When the strategists back at the palace get word of this, they decide that fighting a battle is not the right thing to do under the circumstances, so they order the forces to be recalled, and you can be sure that those men retreat as fast as they can. And, believe it or not, when the message that they should return reaches the battlefront, they don't even stop to consider the disgrace that they will cause their ruler by retreating."

Why are the Turks such pathetic characters? The text is clear and unequivocal in its answer: it is the Turks' love of wine and opium that condemns them to live in this unenviable state. As the ministers Ayyamarasu and Kondamarasu proclaim in a memorable speech, there is no end to the Turks' debauchery:

"What are the Turks but drunkards and opium eaters! It's because of their intoxication that they are always in a state of fear like this. Whenever they've been drinking, they don't even know their own bodies, so naturally they haven't the faintest idea of what they're doing. If someone happens to come in their way, they simply chop him to pieces. . . . When they finally come back to their senses, they pause for a moment and reflect, 'Well, this is just the nature of our race, now isn't it? The brahmans, on the other hand, they aren't like us—thanks to their diet of rice with salt and *sambar*, they don't suffer from pride and malice.' "

When two new spies return from the Gajapati kingdom and begin their report in chapter 5, the moral darkness of the Turkish kingdoms suddenly yields to the light of day. The reports on the Turks had concluded with Appaji's observation that the kingdoms of the Turks must be like the very domains of Yama, god of death; in contrast, the report on the Gajapati kingdom opens with the spies eagerly praising the beauty and prosperity of the Gajapati's city by comparing it to Dwaraka, the ideal, mythical capital of Krishna. There is no violence or punishment in that kingdom because the Gajapati rules not by force but by *dharma,* the magical power that comes from living in accordance with what is right and just. As is explained earlier in the text by the ministers who instruct the young Krishnadevaraya in the matter of ruling the kingdom, a king's success depends entirely on his ability to live according to *dharma.* "If the king acts in accordance with *dharma,*" they explain, "the rains will fall at least three times in every month, causing the earth to produce abundantly. If the palace then takes the taxes that are its due without being unjust, the palace will prosper, and cash will flow into the treasury in great quantities." The Gajapati kingdom is evidently an example of the successful realization of this principle: the spies dwell on the Gajapati's *dharmic* activities—ranging from ritual observances in the temple to performances of religious donations—and there is not a single instance where punishment is described. So great in fact is the Gajapati's moral power that he does not even need to punish would-be traitors, a point made by the relation of an incident in which a corrupt priest has been bribed by some enemies to poison the Gajapati. As the priest is offering the poisoned holy water to the king, the latter notices his hand shaking and confronts him:

> "Finally the priest broke down and confessed, telling the full details of what the enemy kings had done. To the priest's utter astonishment, however, the Gajapati did not even become angry. Instead he only said, 'Give me that poisoned water.' He took it from the priest and began reciting a verse:
>
> Enemy becomes friend,
> poison harmless water,
> and wrong becomes right—

When Jagannatha is on your side,
even adversities turn to favor.

As he finished the verse, he raised the poisoned holy water to his lips and swallowed it—it was digested with no problem."

Unlike the Turks, the inhabitants of the Gajapati kingdom are distinguished by their strength of character and self-possessed manner. The Gajapati himself is of course praised for his excellence—he is "a great man" *(puṇya-ślōkuṃḍḍu)* according to Appaji, and Krishnadevaraya marvels at "the Gajapati's excellence of character" *(guṇātiśayamulu)*—but even his subordinates and subjects share in these qualities. It is the select group of feudatory retainers known as the Sixteen Patras (lit., "Worthies") who best exemplify the valor and resolve of the inhabitants of this realm. In stark contrast to the Turks, the Sixteen Patras have confidence *(kaḍaka)* in their abilities and boundless loyalty to their lord, so there is never any chance of their deserting or fleeing in the thick of battle.[47] How is one to account for the tremendous differences between the Gajapati's realm and the kingdoms of the Turks? We may recall Appaji's statement mentioned above, in which he praises the Gajapati and explains, "He's not like the Turks—he has faith in gods and brahmans." To be sure, while the Turks pass their days in dissipation and disorder, the Gajapati regulates his life with brahmanical ritual and devotion to the god Jagannatha.

In this regard, it is highly significant that the spies begin their report on the Gajapati kingdom with an account of the king's daily ritual routine: he wakes before dawn, looks at two brahmans to ensure that the entire day will be auspicious, bathes, applies his devotional marks, performs his own private worship of the planets and his chosen deity Jagannatha, goes to Jagannatha's temple and presides over a public worship attended by all the *sthānāpatis* residing in the capital, performs the ritual of "worshiping the feet" of a brahman, retires back to the palace to eat the morning meal with his family, and only then does he start the business of the day by convening the court (see chap. 5). Even his meals are ritual occasions, as we see from the description of his breakfast with his family. So great is the Gajapati's faith in Jagannatha that he is willing to leave everything in divine hands, as in the incident of the attempted poisoning just mentioned. A similar example of the Gajapati's faith occurs when the representatives of the Turks warn him that Krishnadevaraya is planning to attack; he is unshaken and merely replies, "We have nothing to fear—our divine protector Lord Jagannatha is here to take care of everything."

Ultimately, however, the purpose of this glowing report of the Gajapati kingdom is not to acclaim the greatness of the Gajapati but rather to emphasize the meanness of the Turks. The Gajapati is held up not as the final example of the kingly ideal but merely as an example of a good and acceptable king against which the Turks' departure from the norm can be measured. In the end, both are foes to be conquered by Krishnadevaraya, the text's real hero and kingly model. Krishnadevaraya embodies the ideal of the Chakravartin, the world-emperor, who demonstrates his superior virtue by conquering all other kings and uniting the various known regions of the world into one imperial realm *(eka-cakramu)*. As the soothsayers of the Turks rightly predict,

> "A king has been born in Karnataka who is an emanation of Vishnu. This kingdom of yours—as well as the Ashvapati and Gajapati kingdoms—all are to be conquered by that king! He will plant his pillar of victory, and, on his return, he will go to worship Kalyana Venkateshvara, the 108 Temples of Vishnu, the Seventy-two Temples of Shiva, and the Eighteen Goddesses. He will go to Setu, where he will worship Ramanatha and wash his sword in the sacred waters at Dhanushkoti. Then for sixty-four years he will be unopposed as he rules the entire realm from the Lion-Throne of Karnataka."

Although in the end both the evil Turks and the righteous Gajapati share in the common fate of being conquered by Vijayanagara, the narration of Krishnadevaraya's campaign is presented in two separate parts—the battle with the Turks in chapter 6 and the invasion of the Gajapati's kingdom in chapter 7—thus preserving the clear distinction between these two different classes of enemy. *Adharmic* kings like the Turks are dealt with in a manner quite distinct from that employed against a *dharmic* enemy like the Gajapati, so this last pair of chapters serves to underscore the difference and inferiority of the Turks already introduced in chapters 4 and 5.

Against the Turks, the king decides to employ an outright attack —the method of *daṇḍa* or "the rod," as it is called in the *Nīti-Śāstra* literature.[48] He sends an advance party into Golconda's territory to loot and pillage in preparation for the battle, and then, after first turning south to quell some of his own ambitious feudatories, he marches his army north to the Krishna River, where it forms the border between Vijayanagara and Golconda. By the time he arrives, he learns from his spies that the Turks have already crossed the river and are apparently preparing to mount their own offensive against Vijayanagara since they have already set up the symbolic battle tent that proclaims their intent to fight to the finish. Krishnadevaraya is outraged, but one of his commanders—Pemmasani Ramalingama Nayadu—bravely offers to counter this move of the Turks' by going with his men to infiltrate their camp and cut the ropes of their battle tent. The description of the ensuing battle is one of the most exciting moments in the text and succeeds in evoking a convincing image of the violent horror and confusion of battle. After a fierce bout of fighting, Pemmasani Ramalingama Nayadu succeeds in cutting the tent ropes, and Krishnadevaraya takes advantage of the attendant confusion to attack the Turks' camp, driving them back to the river, which—almost miraculously—has just started to flood. Pinned between the advancing army and the raging torrents of the river, the Turks panic: "Some jumped headlong into the river, and about half of them drowned in the swirling waters; another group just stood dumbfounded on the southern bank. The elephants were by now happily drinking in the middle of the river, and not one of them could be persuaded to head for shore, so their drivers panicked. Thinking it unsafe to remain in the middle of the river any longer, they dismounted, only to be swept away with their lives."

The account of the Gajapati campaign is equally engrossing, but for very different reasons. The Gajapati, we recall, is "not like the Turks": not only does he have his "faith in gods and brahmans," but he and his men possess as well all the warrior's virtues that were lacking in the Turks. This makes him a much more formidable enemy, against whom the employment of *daṇḍa* carries no guarantee of certain results. Krishnadevaraya comes to realize this the hard way: after successfully taking one after another of the Gajapati's forts in the Krishna-Godavari delta region, he is spurred on by his success to ignore his minister Appaji's objections and march right into the heart of the Gajapati's kingdom in order to attack the king himself in his capital. When the fortunes of war begin to turn against the invader, his minister finally persuades him to put aside *daṇḍa* for the more efficacious and sophisticated strategem of *bhēda*—the method of sowing dissension within the enemy's ranks (see Zimmer 1951, pp. 118–123). The tension and suspense build as Appaji implements his plan: a letter is drafted, as though to the Gajapati's Sixteen Patras, welcoming their offer to betray their lord and hand him over to Krishnadevaraya for the staggering price of the king's own personal jewels. A party is sent with the letter and sixteen boxes of jewels, as though to the Patras, but they are captured by the suspicious Gajapati as intended. Shocked to "realize" that his most trusted men have betrayed him, the Gajapati flees the capital to escape the fate that he mistakenly believes to be awaiting him. The next morning, Krishnadevaraya is able to march unopposed into the Gajapati's capital, taking it without so much as firing a single shot.

What happens next only further highlights the distinction between the Gajapati and the Turks. Whereas the Turks had been violently defeated and forced to flee ignominiously back to their capitals, the defeated Gajapati is treated with the proper respect due a worthy, *dharmic* enemy. After Krishnadevaraya has finished planting his "pillar of victory" at the Gajapati's capital, he summons the Gajapati's representative and declares his friendly intentions: " 'I want you to realize that I have come solely for the sake of increasing my glory, not with any desire of annexing your kingdom. The Gajapati kingdom I leave for the Gajapati. I shall return now to my own territory.' " The Gajapati is informed and summoned back to the capital, where he graciously receives Krishnadevaraya and even goes so far as to present him his daughter in marriage. Krishnadevaraya sums up the mood by rhetorically asking his new father-in-law, " 'Is there any real difference between you and me?' "

The Conceptual Geography

The conceptual geography of the text revolves around the notion of the "Three Lion-Thrones" *(mūḍu-siṃhāsanālu)*, occupied by the three *dharmic* kings known as the Ashvapati (Lord of Horses), Gajapati (Lord of Elephants), and Narapati (Lord of Men).[49] A number of passages in the text make it clear that the "Ashvapati" is the Mughal emperor of Agra[50] (the significance of this seemingly anomalous identification will be discussed momentarily), the "Gajapati" is of course the Gajapati king of Orissa, and the "Narapati" is the ruler of Vijayanagara. The kingdoms of these Three Lion-Thrones are of vast extent, together accounting for almost the entire Indian subcontinent. Thus, the Ashvapati rules in the north "from Sindh to the Godavari," the Narapati in the south "from Kerala to the Krishna," and the Gajapati in the east "from Jagannatham [i.e., Puri] to Bidar."[51] The only part of the known subcontinent not occupied by one of the Three Lion-Thrones is the tract in the Deccan lying between the Godavari and the Krishna rivers, stretching from the western coast across to "Bidar".[52] It is this no-man's-land between the three great powers—referred to as "the borderlands" or "the boundary regions" *(sarudu-sthalālu)*—that has been occupied by the Turks. And, just as the major part of the subcontinent is divided between the Three Lion-Thrones, so too are the "borderlands" divided between the "Lords of the Three Clans" *(mūḍu-tegala-vāru)* of the Turks into the three separate kingdoms of Bijapur (ruled by the Adil Shah), Ahmadnagar (ruled by the Nizam Shah), and Golconda (ruled by Qutb al-Mulk) (see map 1 and fig. 5).

Although the Kings of the Three Lion-Thrones fight among themselves from time to time, it is ultimately the antithetical relation between the two geopolitical triads that constitutes the more important theme in the *Rāyavācakamu*. The Three Lion-Thrones are represented as great and prosperous kingdoms, each striving to manifest its imperial destiny by ritually conquering the other two, while the kingdoms of the Three Clans are petty, little kingdoms ruled by bickering lords who can hope for no greater end than their own survival.[53] The Three Lion-Thrones enjoy boundless prosperity because dwelling within the boundaries of each kingdom there is a great god who attracts the gifts of countless pilgrims, which thus cause the kingdom as a whole to prosper: Vishnu resides at Venkatachalam (i.e., Tirupati) in the Narapati kingdom, Jagannatha at Shripurushottamam (i.e., Puri) in the Gajapati kingdom, and Vishvanatha "along the banks of the Ganges" at Kashi in the Ashvapati king-

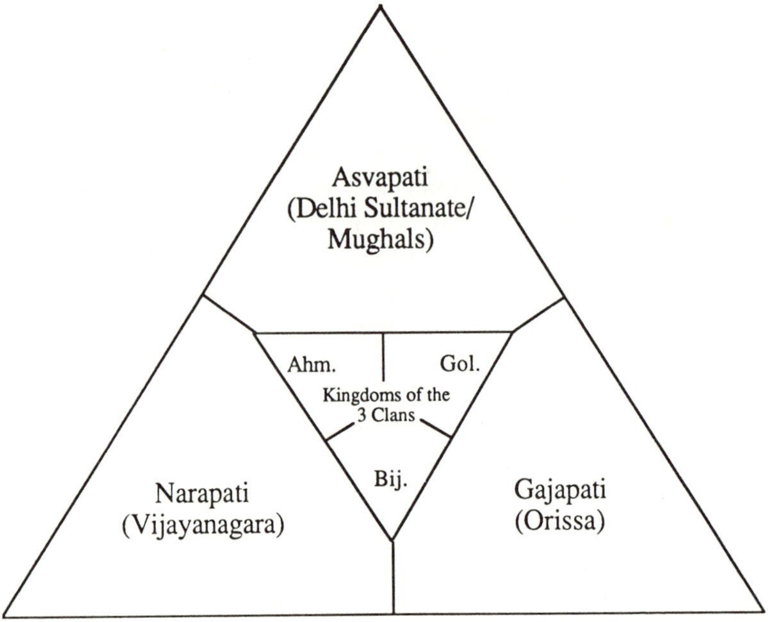

Fig. 5. Schematic representation of the *Rāyavācakamu*'s political geography—the kingdoms of the Kings of the Three Lion-Thrones and of the Lords of the Three Clans.

dom. The kingdoms of the Turks, on the other hand, do not enjoy this level of divine favor: there are no great gods gracing the territories of Bijapur, Ahmadnagar, or Golconda.

The existence of the Three Lion-Thrones is taken completely for granted, as if the known world has always been carved up between three worthy powers and thus stands in no need of explanation, while by contrast the kingdoms of the Three Clans are recognized as recent upstarts whose origins must be accounted for. As explained by one of Krishnadevaraya's commanders, it was "a fellow named Barid of Bidar" who first conquered some territory and forts in the borderlands: " 'His hawk keeper came to be known as Nizam Shah, his water-pot bearer became known as Adil Shah, and the man who was in charge of keeping the dogs became known as Qutb-al-Mulk. Each of the three was given charge over a province: the Adil Shah ruled Bijapur, the Nizam Shah Ahmadnagar, and Qutb-al-Mulk Golconda. When he gave them charge of these provinces, Barid of Bidar declared, "Your stewardship will last for one hundred years." ' " The point of this account is not merely that the kingdoms of the Turks are of common, base origin (their first kings having been servants in charge of keeping the hunting animals and "water pot"[54] of another king) but, more important, that they are ephemeral, recently created polities, destined to last for only a limited period of time. In contrast to the "eternal," uncreated kingdoms of the Three Lion-Thrones, these kingdoms are known to have been created within the recent past.

It is this contrast between ancient, legitimate kingdoms and recent, usurping upstarts that accounts for the apparent anomaly of the Mughals' inclusion among the Kings of the Three Lion-Thrones. Given the length and imperial nature of their reign—particularly when taken together with the preceding period of the Delhi sultanate (as our author does)—the Mughal Ashvapatis can by definition be nothing other than legitimate rulers. The author thus casts them in the same mold as the "Hindu" rulers of Vijayanagara and the Gajapati kingdom: that of the *dharmic* king who represents legitimate royal authority. Once the Ashvapati is presented in this role, he must be provided with all the proper attributes that accompany it —thus his relationship with the Hindu god Vishvanatha, who makes his kingdom prosper, and, as we shall see below, his identification as an emanation *(aṃśa)* of one of the great gods of Hinduism. The fundamental distinction operating here is not between Hindus and Muslims but rather between legitimate *dharmic* rulers and undeserving usurpers of royal authority.[55]

The Mythical Paradigm

So antithetical in nature are the Kings of the Three Lion-Thrones and the Lords of the Three Clans that the author is able to portray their relationship in terms homologous with the relationship between the gods *(devas)* and the demons *(asuras)* of Hindu myth:

> Kings of the Three Lion-Thrones : Lords of the Three Clans : : *devas* : *asuras*.

The unceasing war between gods and demons *(devāsura-yuddha)* is in fact the central theme of Hindu mythology; not only is there a distinct cycle of myths devoted specifically to this conflict, but it also serves as a general backdrop against which many individual myths of Shiva, Vishnu, and the Goddess unfold (see O'Flaherty 1975, pp. 270–300; and Long 1975). As common offspring of the creator god Prajapati, the gods and demons are brothers, but the two are soon differentiated by their opposing predilections: the gods for *dharma,* the demons for *adharma.* As time passes, the demons periodically gain the upper hand in this conflict, and thus a special effort on the part of the gods is necessitated to restore the balance in their favor. The conflict between the Kings of the Three Lion-Thrones and the Lords of the Three Clans replicates this mythical pattern: like the gods, the Kings of the Three Lion-Thrones are good and ultimately successful because of their devotion to *dharma,* while the Lords of the Three Clans, like the demons, are ultimately doomed to failure because of their devotion to *adharma.* Curiously, the text seems to imply that the Kings of the Three Lion-Thrones and the Lords of the Three Clans are, like the gods and the demons, on some distant level related. As the Gajapati's ambassador Brahmapantu asserts to the ministers of the Turks, the lords whom they serve are "the kindred of the others," that is, of the Kings of the Three Lion-Thrones. The two different orders of kings are thus not ultimately different by nature but have become enemies only through their opposing orientations toward good and evil, *dharma* and *adharma.*

The homology is gradually constructed by means of repeated appeals and allusions to two specific myths that express the *devāsura-yuddha* archetype. The first and most important for our text is the myth of the slaying of the Demons of the Three Cities *(tripurāsura-saṃhāra;* see fig. 6).[56] The myth is nicely summarized by one Tatkalikamati, an adviser at one of the Turkish courts:

> "When the mighty Demons of the Three Cities received a boon from Lord Shiva, they begged that their cities should be able to fly about wherever they desired and be unconquerable at the hands of any one of the gods, demons, or others. Once in every twelve years, the Three Cities would all come together for three and three-quarters hours to join in consultation, and then they would go off as usual to wander around at will.

Fig. 6. The slaying of the Demons of the Three Cities, ca. seventeenth century, painting from *maṇḍapa* ceiling, Virupaksha Temple, Hampi. (Photo Dee Foster, Vijayanagara Research Project.)

"But, as you know, things went on like this only until the time had finally come for the lords of those Three Cities. The earth-goddess went to Brahma and Vishnu and complained that she could no longer bear the weight of those unrighteous Demons. Lord Brahma took pity on her and said, 'It is impossible for the Demons of the Three Cities to be vanquished by any one of us alone. But there is a way. You, god-

> dess, become the chariot, and the four Vedas shall become your horses. Mount Meru will serve as the bow and the cosmic serpent Shesha as the bowstring. Vishnu who lies on the Ocean of Milk shall become the arrow, and three-eyed Shiva himself will be the archer. Together, we shall bring the Three Cities crashing to the ground, and thus will those demons go to their destruction!' "

The favorable outcome of the story is too well known for Tatkalikamati to need to proceed any further in his account; rather, at this point, he shifts back to the present in order to address his real purpose: " 'In the same way, if the Kings of the Three Lion-Thrones ever appear together to attack our 'Three Cities' of Bijapur, Ahmadnagar, and Golconda, then we shall be in grave danger indeed—that much is certain!' " Just as the Three Cities of myth are unconquerable by any one god alone but can easily be destroyed when the gods all join together, so is Tatkalikamati warning his fellow advisers at the Turkish courts that they must guard themselves against a joint attack by the forces of the Ashvapati, Gajapati, and Narapati.

Not only does this myth offer an appropriate analogy for the overall nature of the situation, but, moreover, many of the precise details fit as well. The Three Cities of the Demons correspond to the " 'Three Cities' of Bijapur, Ahmadnagar, and Golconda." And the three chief gods of the myth—Brahma, who suggests the plan; Vishnu, who serves as the fatal arrow; and Shiva, who takes the role of the archer—correlate exactly in number with the Kings of the Three Lion-Thrones. Although the correlation of the Kings of the Three Lion-Thrones with the three great gods is only hinted at in this speech, there is yet another point in the text where it is clearly and explicitly stated that "those Three Lion-Thrones in fact exist as emanations [*aṃśa*] of the gods Brahma, Vishnu, and Maheshvara [i.e., Shiva]," and there are still other instances throughout the text where one or the other of the Kings of the Three Lion-Thrones (most often Krishnadevaraya) is flatly stated to be an *aṃśa* of one of these gods.[57]

The second mythical structure used to characterize the relation between the Three Lion-Thrones and the Three Clans is that provided by the myth of Vishnu's avatars. Here it is not the specific myth of any one avatar that is employed but rather the general mythical pattern that underlies them all: whenever the demons gain the upper hand and threaten to disturb the cosmic balance by overburdening the earth-goddess with the weight of their *adharma,* Vishnu incarnates himself in some form to conquer the demons and relieve the earth of her burden. Here the correlation is not made as directly and thoroughly as in the previous example, and, additionally, its application is more restricted in that it serves to characterize only Krishnadevaraya in his dealings with the Turks rather than all three of the Lion-Thrones as a whole.

The first part of the comparison is advanced by an implication contained in the statement of the inhabitants of Ahmadnagar and Golconda about their rulers: " 'These barbarians give no thought to their unrighteousness, their ruthlessness, their demonic acts. Will the earth-goddess be able to bear it much longer?' " The analogy is completed by the prediction offered the Turks by their soothsayers: " 'A king has been born in Karnataka who is an emanation of Vishnu. This kingdom of yours—as well as the Ashvapati and Gajapati kingdoms—all are to be conquered by that king!' " Although not presented in as explicit terms as was the case with the Tripura myth, the suggested analogy is nonethless unmistakable: just as Vishnu has incarnated himself in the past to relieve the earth of her demonic burden, so too is he present now in the form of Krishnadevaraya to conquer the unrighteous and demonic Turks—the "demons of the Kali age" *(kaḷi-yuga-rākṣasulu),* as they are called at another place in the text.

These myths are appealed to not just as colorful metaphors serving merely a rhetorical purpose; to the contrary, they perform a central and integrating function within the overall discourse of the text. These myths are nothing less than the structuring paradigms that govern the selection, arrangement, and interpretation of the data presented; it is they that provide the author with the a priori cognitive structures needed to discover meaning among the infinite and otherwise intractable mass of data and events that constitutes the past.[58] Since the situation the author has chosen to describe is morally similar to that in the general *devāsura-yuddha* archetype, and since the Tripura myth offers additional features that provide specific correspondences with other accepted paradigms (the three gods with the Three Lion-Thrones, e.g.), the author's perception comes to be unconsciously guided by this paradigm. Thus, from among the total array of known and relevant contemporary states that he might record, he is predisposed to single out just six for special attention and to divide these further into two opposed groups of three so as to reflect the moral opposition expressed in the Tripura myth between the Three Cities of the demons and the three chiefs of the gods.[59]

We have seen above that it is the long and imperial reign of the Mughals (as successors to the Delhi sultanate) that explains why they are differentiated from the "Turks" and seen instead as *dharmic* kings; ultimately, however, it is the paradigm of the Tripura myth—reinforced, of course, by the convergent paradigm of the Three Lion-Thrones—that demands that a third *dharmic* power be represented in the first place. After Vijayanagara and the Gajapati kingdom, it is only the Mughals that provided a great enough power to fill the third position, and thus the *dharmic* Mughals are comfortably accommodated into the tripartite scheme as the incumbents of the Ashvapati throne. Similarly, it is the Tripura paradigm that has guided the author in representing the Turks by means of the political triad of Bijapur, Ahmadnagar, and Golconda. Even though there were in fact two other important contemporary Muslim kingdoms in the Deccan—Bidar and Berar, the former of which the author even mentions in passing—the triadic paradigm cannot accommodate five states, so only the three preeminent ones are singled out for representation.

Ultimately, the author has appealed to the specific myths in question because of their powerful explanatory function: as well-known conceptual patterns, they provide a means not only of selection but also of grasping the unfamiliar and transforming it into something recognizable and therefore meaningful. Islam had been present as an important force in South India for nearly three centuries by the time of the *Rāyavācakamu*'s composition, but until the middle of the sixteenth century it had never seriously threatened the survival of the preexisting South Indian social order, and, accordingly, it was for the most part ignored.[60] It was only when the representatives of this new cultural force eventually succeeded in undermining one of the key economic, political, and symbolic foundations of the traditional social order—the City of Victory itself—that an ideological crisis was engendered. With the Deccani kingdoms' eradication of the last symbol and source of imperial authority in South India, it became clear that the alien cultural order of Islam was a phenomenon that had to be squarely faced. But because the older civilization had entered a stage in which it approximated a culture of the "closed" type—a culture, that is, that sees itself as belonging to a universe in which truth has existed in fullness from the beginning of time, with no possibility for further addition or revelation[61]—it was powerless to create the new categories necessary for the comprehension of this unprecedented phenomenon. The only possible way of coming to terms with the new experience was by interpreting it in light of the previously existing categories and paradigms provided by myth. By appealing to well-known categories of demonic personalities and behavior, it was possible for the author of our text to deny the newness of the Turks' alien civilization and their abhorrent social norms and, instead, to succeed in recognizing them as "the demons of the Kali age."

A Note on the Translation

The text used for this translation of the *Rāyavācakamu* is that of C. V. Ramachandra Rao (1982), recently published by the Andhra Pradesh Sahitya Akademi. This edition is based on Ramayyapantulu (1933)—which is a reprint in book form of Ramayyapantulu (1914)—from which it differs only in the provision of some additional clarificatory punctuation and the correction of the several typographical errors contained in the earlier edition.

It should be noted that the division of the text into chapters is a feature that is not found in either the original manuscripts or the published editions. The manuscripts themselves are neither punctuated nor subdivided into sections of any sort, while Ramachandra Rao's edition divides the text into twenty-six parts by the use of descriptive section headings (ultimately derived from Ramayyapantulu's marginal headings in the 1914 edition). Since these headings tend to fragment the text and obscure its underlying plan, I have preferred instead to divide the work into seven longer "chapters," which I believe are more faithful in reflecting this internal structure.

Many authors have commented on the difficulty of the *Rāyavācakamu;* it is certainly true that its unusual language and style present a host of difficulties to challenge the translator. The text is written, not in the standard dialect of mainstream classical Telugu literature, but rather in the contemporary spoken dialect that was current among Telugu speakers in the Tamil country at the close of the sixteenth century.[1] Accordingly, the reader of today is often left totally in the dark as to the meaning of certain words that in modern Telugu have become obscure or obsolete. Compounding these problems is the fact that the author writes in a highly involved and complicated style, typified by long sentences in which the subject is often only implied and in some cases even undergoes repeated shifts. Despite these specific problems, however, the overall sense of the narrative is generally clear, and thus it is usually possible to deduce the likely meaning of any problematic word or passage from its context. In those cases where serious doubts or problems of interpretation yet remain, I have chosen the interpretation that seems to me most plausible and discussed the matter in the notes to the text.

In the interest of producing a translation that reads smoothly and is readily accessible to specialist and nonspecialist alike, I have regularized spellings, eliminated variant forms for names, and, above all, tried to avoid an overabundance of untranslated Telugu and Sanskrit terms. Where a Sanskrit verse or phrase is quoted in the text, it is given in transliterated form before the translation in order to signal its identity as Sanskrit rather than Telugu. Diacritical marks have not been used except in italicized technical terms and titles of literary works. Elsewhere, a simplified system of transliteration has been employed in which vowel length (long or short) and consonant class (in the case of retroflexes and dentals) are not indicated and according to which *ṛ* is represented by *ri*, *c* by *ch*, *v* by *v* or *w* depending on the context, and *ś* and *ṣ* alike by *sh*. Those interested in knowing the actual Telugu spellings used in the text are referred to the index of proper names and technical terms, where precise spellings as well as variant forms are given in standard transliteration following each entry. Textual problems, identification of historical figures, and other issues of interpretation have been dealt with in the notes; definitions of italicized terms will be found in the index-glossary.

Throughout the translation, the forms *Krishnaraya* and *Rayalu* have been used in preference to *Krishnadevaraya* since the latter form —although standard today—is not found in the *Rāyavācakamu*.

Part Two

Tidings of the King

Introduction

In words as one might hear
from the mouths of trusted men,
I set forth Vijayanagara's story
and bring tidings of its king.

Hear how Krishnaraya
preserved his people
  from foes savage and great:
ruthless Turks he reduced
with the power of his arms,
but the noble Gajapati
he conquered by cunning alone.

Clerks, fix in mind the many maxims
  Appaji told to Rayalu,
and you shall gain talent and taste
in the arts of reading and writing.

Young boys, read my words,
  and wisdom will be yours,
swim in these oceans of śāstra,
  and you shall keep to the path,
  serving your lords and slaying foes.

This is the report of his lordship's devoted *sthānāpati,* submitted with true humility, fear, and devotion, to the divine lotus feet of the prosperous king of great kings Shri Kashi Vishvanatha Nayanayya,[1] the prosperous great ruler, respected by kings, who is endowed with boundless good qualities, who is as steadfast as great Mount Meru, who is resplendent with imperishable riches. . . .

·1·

The Founding of Vijayanagara

In the city of Vidyanagara, Viranrisimharaya[1] got up in the auspicious hours before dawn. He heard people singing and reciting the *Garlands of Names of the Worshipful One*, the *Songs of Spiritual Praise*, songs of the Pandavas, songs of the goddess Bhramara, the story of the liberation of the elephant king, the *Bhārata-sāvitri*, the *Dadhivāmana-stōtram*, the story of the descent of the Ganga, the praise of the rivers, the *Bhārata* epic, the *Bhāgavata-purāṇa*, the *Rāmāyaṇa*, the *Mucukunda-stuti*, the *Akrūra-stuti*, the *Bhīṣma-stuti*, *Sañjaya's Nīti*, *Vidura's Nīti*, *Cāṇūra's Nīti*, *Baddena's Nīti*, and other such works.[2] He heard all of them: the collected stanzas on conduct and renunciation, the recitation of *purāṇas*, and the works on the conduct of kings. Then, after he had first looked at himself in a mirror, touched some beautiful maidens and a tawny wish-fulfilling cow, and gained the auspicious sight of a group of excellent brahmans,[3] he brushed his teeth and washed his face. When he had affixed his Vaishnava sectarian mark on his forehead and sipped some sacred water, he applied holy ash to himself. He called the Great Court to assemble and then seated himself there.

Sacred water and *prasād* were brought from the 108 Vishnu Temples, and sacred ash, scents, and *prasād* were brought from the Seventy-two Temples of Shiva.[4] The king rose and stepped forward, folded his hands in reverence, and accepted the offerings. Then he raised his head again to greet the priests of Vishnu and Shiva who had come from those distant places, requesting them to make themselves comfortable on seats befitting their honored positions.

When the king asked the priests of Vishnu if all was well and in order at the Eight Self-Manifested Temples such as Shrirangam, Shrimushnam, Venkatachalam, Shalagramam, Totadri, Naimisharanyam, and Pushkarakshetra, they replied that, thanks to his lordship's boundless majesty, the young officers appointed to assist the priests at the various temples were running matters so well that nothing further was needed and that, at the 108 Vishnu Temples, all the daily rituals were being properly carried out. The Shaivite priests reported that, at the "Panchabhuta" temples dedicated to Shiva in his forms as the five elements earth, water, fire, air, and space—namely, Ekamranatha, Jambunatha, Arunachaleshvara, Kalahastishvara, and Chidambaram—as well as at the rest of the Seventy-two Temples of Shiva and at the seats of the Eighteen Goddesses, all was prosperous, and the daily rituals were being carried out as they should be. When he heard this, the king was greatly pleased, so he presented the priests with gifts of land.

Next he summoned Dharmasanam Dharmayya, the minister of religious gifts,[5] who accordingly came forward and stood before the king. While the king listened, Dharmayya reported, "In perfect accordance with your lordship's orders, no one has caused either problem or misfortune for the residents of the brahman villages in the Dravida realm, the Andhra country, the Hayana country, Morasa-nadu, Melnadu, Karnataka, Ghattamsima, Chera, Chola, Pandya, Magadha, Malayala, and the other various localities. The inhabitants of these brahman villages are devoted to the performance of the daily rituals; to the recitation of the *Ṛg-*, *Yajur-*, *Sāma-*, and *Atharva-vedas;* to the study of the six *śāstras;*[6] to the regular performance of the five sacrifices;[7] and to showing hospitality to guests. Fully devoted to their scholarly study, they are living comfortably in their villages."

Next the king summoned his military commanders, who came forward and beheld the royal presence. They stood before him and humbly submitted their report: "In all the forts throughout the kingdom of the Lion-Throne—in the hill forts, the forest forts, the island forts, and the forts on open ground[8]—the guards, the fortifications and moats, and the locks and seals are all in a state of readiness, thanks to our lord's majesty. As for the political situation in the realms of your feudatories, there have been no unusual developments."

After that the inspector Jangayya came and prostrated himself before the king. He stood up again, and, folding his hands together, he reported to the military commanders that all his inspectors were being extremely vigilant, and that they were watching carefully both night and day by concealing themselves in the city of Vidyanagara and in the surrounding hamlets, and that he had thus learned that the members of the eighteen castes and all the other inhabitants of the city were always enjoying the greatest pleasure, and that they were always celebrating some festival or another and decorating their houses with garlands of fresh leaves. The military commanders listened to this report and then passed it on to the king.

At that point someone announced, "The banners of the gods Vithala and Virupaksha have been raised! It is time to proceed to the festival of the chariots!"

The military commanders, who were standing by the king, told the messenger that the king would be coming along soon, and then they sent the fellow off, telling him to come back and inform them once the gods had been seated on their chariots.[9]

Afterward, the nine chief accountants of the royal palace were summoned. The accountants came, and, after they had gone over all the figures for the eighteen ports, the king listened as they read to him in private all the documents and letters that had come from all the quarters.

Then he had his generals and ministers come, and for a short time he met with them in private audience. When that was over, he came back into the full court and summoned all the members of the assembly.[10] The Great Court convened for several hours, and, while he sat there, Sons and Sons-in-Law of the palace,[11] nobles and chiefs, lords, Poligars, Amaranayakas, friends, dependents, scholars, royal priests, teachers, temple priests, ascetics, soothsayers, physicians, horsemen, elephant drivers, troop leaders, Rajas, bards and panegyrists, lecturers, Pathan horsemen, knowers of the *śāstras,* specialists in dramaturgy and rhetoric, masters of wisdom, veena players, and the rest of the Seventy-two Officers[12] came and served him.

After the soothsayers and prognosticators had presented a discourse to the military commanders on what was fated and what was not, on what had happened, what was going to happen, and what was happening now, the king asked them, "Before the city of Vidyanagara was built, where was Vidyaranya Shripada?[13] What was the cause of his coming here? And once he had come, how was the city built?"

In order to answer the king's question, Mullandradindima Pumbhava Sarasvati, who knew the *Sayings of Vidyāraṇya* and the work called *Vijñānēśvaram,*[14] addressed the king as follows:[15]

"At Mukambika, Jnanendra Sarasvati accepted Vidyaranya into his hermitage and gave him instructions in the divine wisdom. Having entered the life-stage of renunciation, Vidyaranya became like one who looks on gold as dross. He cut off desire and anger and cast away envy and pride. He looked on even enemies as friends and regarded those who had cursed him as if they had blessed him. The earth itself was his bed, and the simple food he won as alms satisfied him like heavenly nectar. His clothes were the red rags of a mendicant. Totally devoted to the mastery of perpetual concentration on the ultimate *brahman,* he wandered about quietly, never staying longer than one night in any village, thus complying with his teacher's instructions.

"Owing to the force of some merit he had earned in previous lives, it so happened that, at whatever house he would come to in any village, they would give him the most exquisite rice pudding for alms. Taking the food, he returned to his guru Jnanendra Sarasvati and placed it before him. Jnanendra Sarasvati took one look at the food and reprimanded him, 'Simple food gained as alms is good enough for mendicants like us. Certainly rice pudding such as this is inappropriate! Must you bring such food, which is fit for a king?'

"Vidyaranya replied, 'It's not as if I had wanted rice pudding and asked especially for it! But for some reason, at whatever house I went to in any village, this is the way they gave me alms. When my luck is like this, what else am I to do?'

"When Vidyaranya had explained the matter, Jnanendra decided to check up on him to see if what he said was indeed true. The following day, the guru sent his other disciples to follow Vidyaranya on his rounds. As they followed him, they saw that, sure enough, at each place that he stopped he was being given rice pudding together with every other kind of delicacy imaginable. They returned and told their guru Jnanendra all the details. 'I can't blame him for reaping the fruits of merit sown in previous lives,' thought Jnanendra to himself. 'There is simply no way for him *not* to experience this good fortune.' Nonetheless, he called Vidyaranya and commanded him firmly, 'Go on pilgrimage to the Ganga, and stay there until you have attained liberation.'

"Thus commanded by his preceptor, Vidyaranya began his circumambulation of the earth.[16] He had passed through the city of Viratapura and was on his way to the Varata country when, at the bank of the Varaha River in the vicinity of the primordial mountain Adiparvata, he noticed a brahman who had taken up residence as a forest dweller beneath a sacred-fig tree, where he was devoting himself to the recitation of the *Ṛg-*, *Yajur-*, *Sāma-*, and *Atharva-vedas*. Vidyaranya approached the brahman, asked him his name and lineage, and inquired about the circumstances that had brought him here. Being a truthful man, the brahman replied, 'My name is Shingiri Bhatlu.[17] In the days when Rama was ruling the earth, that great king performed ten Horse Sacrifices and the Sixteen Great Donations. At that time, there was no one he could get to perform the King-in-the-Balance Donation, in which the king makes a gift of his own weight in gold. Therefore, Rama came to me and, saying, "Bring the sacrifice to fruition!" appointed me officiant for the King-in-the-Balance Donation.[18] After carrying out the ceremony, he showered me with gifts, and ever since I have been living in this sacred-fig forest.'

"Now this brahman happened to know all about what was fated and what was not, what had happened in the past, what would happen in the future, and everything that was happening now. If you are wondering how that was so, then just listen to what he went on to say to Vidyaranya. 'As for you, you are the disciple of Jnanendra, and your name is Vidyaranya. You have been sent by your guru, who has ordered you to bathe in the Ganga and dwell there by the river until you have attained liberation. But you can do much more than just remaining there idly. In Kashi you shall behold the sage Vedavyasa,[19] the goddess Annapurna, the wide-eyed goddess Vishalakshi, and the lord of the universe himself, Vishvanatha.[20] By their grace you will return and come to the banks of the Pampa River,[21] where you will cause a city to flourish. You will perform the coronation for a king named Harihara,[22] and, afterward, you will be happy with all the wealth you desire.'

"When Shingiri Bhatlu thus revealed to Vidyaranya his fate,

Vidyaranya was surprised and thought that the sage must actually be some kind of brahman-caste demon[23] to know all that. Nonetheless, without any fear, he thought of how to reply. 'But Vyasa certainly won't deign to appear before my eyes,' objected Vidyaranya. 'How am I to gain sight of him?'

"Shingiri Bhatlu replied, 'I will make sure that you can see Vyasa. If you do as I tell you, then not only will you gain success in your task, but my desires will be fulfilled as well.'

"Vidyaranya declared, 'Then let me fulfill your desires.'

"Singiri Bhatlu said, 'All right, I will explain it so that it will appear as clear as a berry lying in the palm of your hand.'

"Vidyaranya was very pleased and said, 'Please do, tell me how I am to cause Vedavyasa to appear.'

"Shingiri Bhatlu began, 'If you promise to return from Kashi, I will explain everything. Listen carefully to all that I am about to say. Once you have gone to Kashi, Vedavyasa will appear. At noon, he will come up to the bank of the Ganga. He will be carrying a yoke with wine pots on his shoulder and wearing a leather cap, leather-tasseled sandals, and a black sash. Four dogs will be following at his sides, like the four Vedas.[24] In this vile form, he will come and set down his yoke on the Manikarnika Ghat. Then he will bathe in the river, and, no sooner than it takes to milk a cow, he will come back to the steps and climb out. Once he is standing there, you must immediately go up to him, and, without the slightest hesitation, you must prostrate yourself before him and hold on tight to his feet. He will no doubt entreat you in the manner of a low-caste person, saying, "Please stop, sir! You, a great ascetic, groveling in front of me, a vile wretch! Stop!" But, no matter how much he implores you, do not let go! If you keep grasping tight, he will eventually take pity and bestow his grace on you.'

"After Shingiri Bhatlu had finished speaking, Vidyaranya left and went on to Kashi. At Kashi, he hid himself at the Manikarnika Ghat and waited. Sure enough, at noon, he saw Vedavyasa coming, in just the outfit that Shingiri Bhatlu had described. Vidyaranya leapt out and threw himself prostrate on the ground. He touched Vyasa's feet and then his own eyes, in order to purify his vision with the dust of the sage's holy feet. Then he just remained there, full of devotion.

"Vedavyasa looked at the mendicant and wondered how the fellow had known his true identity. When, by looking with his eye of wisdom, he saw what had happened, he spoke to Vidyaranya. 'Shingiri Bhatlu told you, didn't he! That's how you knew who I really was. All right, if that's the case, then well enough; Shingiri Bhatlu has been my friend for a long time. But, poor fellow, staying in that sacred-fig forest without decent food and a proper place to sleep, he must be suffering great hardships indeed!

" 'Now listen. You will found a city in Karnataka. The auspicious glances of Lakshmi, the goddess of fortune, will continue to fall on that city for 360 years. You must be preceptor to the occupants of the Lion-Throne there for as long as the city exists. Tell those kings that, in order to make Shingiri Bhatlu happy, they must every day feed one thousand brahmans,[25] giving them full meals with rice pudding and all manner of other delicacies. In that city there will flourish a line of thirty kings who will become renowned for their fame, and that will be the cause.'

"When Vedavyasa had spoken, he showed his grace by teaching Vidyaranya the secrets of several mantras, and then he disappeared.

"Vidyaranya was overwhelmed with joy and proceeded to bathe in the Ganga. Then he went and received the auspicious sight of the lord of the universe Vishvanatha and of the wide-eyed goddess Vishalakshi. Then, after first proceeding to Gaya and Prayag to visit the gods in their temples and bathe in the holy waters, he started his return journey.

"When he came again to the place where Shingiri Bhatlu was living, he told him all the details of his trip to Kashi. When he related the matter of what Vedavyasa had ordered him to do, Shingiri Bhatlu was quite pleased. He said to Vidyaranya, 'If through the grace of Lakshmi you are to found a city and establish a line of kings there, then I too will come to that city to bless those kings and take away their misfortunes. Tell them that, in order to make me happy, they must make perpetual and abundant food donations both night and day in the feeding houses of that city and also at the sacred Vishnu Temples, at the temples where Shiva resides in his five elemental forms, and along the banks of the great rivers Ganga, Yamuna, Sarasvati, Godavari, Sindhu, Narmada, Kaveri, Tamraparni, and the rest. We shall go to Vidyanagara and stay there constantly, blessing the kings!'

"Then he sent Vidyaranya off.[26] Vidyaranya went to the Kashmir tract in the northern country, where he learned all the *śāstras* from one Mandala Mishra. One day, when he was supplicating the goddess Lakshmi in accordance with the teachings of the *Cintāmaṇi-mantra,* the goddess appeared before his very eyes. She commanded him, 'Ask for whatever boons you may desire.'

"He replied, 'I am to found a city in my name. If you reside there, then, for as long as you do so, all the inhabitants of the city will live in comfort, and for that reason my name will enjoy everlasting fame. It is a general rule that, so long as a person's name remains known in this world, he will enjoy the pleasures of heaven, obtain wealth, and enjoy increase of sons and grandsons.[27] Therefore, my wish is for you to remain forever in the city that I will build.'

"The great goddess showed him her grace, saying, 'I will come and reside there as you have wished. Now proceed on your way without turning back and looking at me.[28] I will be following behind you.'

"Vidyaranya did as she commanded and left the Kashmir country. He came to Ujjain, and then to Kolhapur, and, as he was on his way from there to Kishkindha, he stopped to bathe in the Tungabhadra. Then he came to the bank of the Pampa River and worshiped the goddess Pampa and her consort lord Virupaksha.

"He then climbed the Matanga hill and scanned the four quarters, looking for a square plot of ground on which to found his city. Just then a hare came out of a cave in the hill and began to chase a dog that had been watching a herd of cows nearby. Vidyaranya noticed this with great surprise. 'In this world,' he wondered to himself, 'it is the rule for dogs to chase hares, but nowhere have I seen a hare chasing a dog. Might it not be due to some special power that this place possesses?'

"He sent someone to call the youths and the elders who lived in those parts, and, when they came, he asked them about the incident. They replied, 'According to the sacred traditions of this place, it's impossible for anyone—no matter how strong he might be—to harm the weak here because of the curse of the great sage Matanga.

A long time ago, the monkey princes Vali and Sugriva lived in Kishkindha. They had a quarrel among themselves, so they started fighting. During that war, Sugriva couldn't face Vali and fight with him anymore because Vali was such a great, strong fellow. So Sugriva ran away and came to this Matanga hill, and he stayed here on top of it. Vali came chasing right behind him, but the great sage Matanga had cursed Vali a long time ago so that he couldn't climb up this hill. And, ever since that time, no strong fellow—whether animal or man—has been able to do his strong man's business up here! Anyway, whenever Sugriva couldn't fight anymore with Vali, he would come up to this Matanga hill. So you see, no matter how strong someone is when he comes to this place, he ends up powerless to do anything. He can run away all right, but he can't stay and face up to the fight! Who knows, it seems that, whether you're an animal or a man, if you stay up here, then it's impossible for your enemies to get you!'

"Vidyaranya was amazed by their story. 'Then this place is imbued with the power of a great sage,' he reflected to himself. At length he decided, 'I must found my city in this place.[29] Among the three kingdoms of the Ashvapati, the Gajapati, and the Narapati,[30] it is the Narapati who is by all means the greatest. Thus I must found my city as a favor for the kingdom of the Narapati.'

"Vidyaranya thought, 'To ensure that the city will never experience instability, the gnomon must first be set up at an auspicious moment. Then the *vāstupuruṣa* must be established.[31] Next, after the site has been prepared for the city, the plans for the palace, the temple, the fortification walls, the bastions, and the nine gates[32] can be laid out. Then the buildings proper can be constructed, and then finally the treasuries can be arranged.'

"Together with a disciple who had studied with him and was a master of the four Vedas and Shankara's philosophy, Vidyaranya sat down and began planning. They set the time for the foundation at an auspicious moment—favorable by both astrological and other factors[33]—which would come on a Saturday, the bright full moon day in the month of Chaitra, in the cyclic year named Prabhava,[34] in the 1,127th year of the Shalivahana-Shaka era.[35] In order to set up the gnomon on the night of the new moon coming in the dark fortnight, Vidyaranya called together experts in the *śāstras,* mantra specialists, and soothsayers. First, in order to prepare the north-south alignments, they sighted the constellation Trishanku in the south and the pole star Dhruva, and then, ceremonially sprinkling water three times,[36] they planted the gnomon. Next, in order to mark east and west, they sprinkled water and planted gnomons. They made the *vāstupuruṣa* with sixteen *maṇuvus* of gold[37] and deposited it in a pillar made from the solid heartwood of a tree. They dug a pit so that the pillar would stand in water all the way up to its head.

"Vidyaranya told his disciples, 'When the precise auspicious moment comes, I will blow a conch-shell trumpet. Immediately on hearing that sound, you must perform the foundation.' So saying, he sent his disciples to their respective places and then waited anxiously so that the precise moment should not be missed.

"Just then, it so happened that a mendicant *jangam* priest came by on his alms rounds and blew his conch-shell trumpet to announce his presence. Hearing the sound and thinking that it was their guru blowing his conch, the disciples implanted the *vāstupuruṣa.* But then, right after that, they heard a second conch-trumpet blast. Wondering why their guru had blown the conch a second time, they went to where Vidyaranya was and asked him about it. With his eye of wisdom Vidyaranya realized that a *jangam* had blown a conch trumpet and that the disciples, mistaking that for the signal, had gone ahead with the foundation, thus missing the auspicious moment. The result, he realized to his great sorrow, was that the city had received an unstable foundation. Instead of lasting in fame for 3,600 years as he had hoped, the city would last for only 360 years, all because of the error committed by his disciples. Vidyaranya went on and completed the establishment of the *vāstupuruṣa,* reflecting all the while that things had indeed turned out exactly as Vyasa had predicted.

"From that time until the present, twenty-nine kings have enjoyed the city for three hundred years. Accordingly, there are still sixty years left for the city and its Lion-Throne to stand."

Thus did the brahman finish his story.

·2·

The Coronation and Education of Krishnaraya

After hearing the story of the city's foundation, Viranrisimharaya turned to his military commanders and said, "Indeed, the time has come to pass this diadem on to Krishnaraya. Besides, I am growing old, so it is only fitting that officers should be appointed to perform Krishnaraya's coronation so that he may begin to rule the kingdom."[1] So the king found an auspicious time and presented his signet ring to his successor.

All the officials and military commanders came together for the occasion. There were the ministers[2] Ayyamarasu, Kondamarasu, Bacharasu, Allamarasu, Viramarasu, and Appaji; the commanders[3] Lakkana Dalanayakulu, Ellana Dalanayakulu, Apparapilla, and Mannarupilla; the clerk Rayasam Ramachandrayya, the treasurer Bokkasam Bhaskarayya, and the petitioners Avasaram Venkatayya and Triyambakayya; the officials Lakshmipati Pradhani and Tipparasu; the commanders Dalavayi Lingarasu,[4] Arviti Bukkaraju, Saluva Makaraju, the chief of Shripati, the chief of Budahalli, the chief of Nandyal, the chief of Avuku, the chief of Toragallu, Rachuri Timmaraju, Sangaraju, and the chief of Velugodu,[5] Peddasani Akkappa Nayudu, the Kamma nobles, and the Tuluva nobles; as well as such scholars of the city as the master of the four Vedas Ramadikshitulu, the master of poetry in eight languages Krishnavadhanulu, the scholar of etymology Venkataramashasturlu, and the master of a thousand things at once Prabhakarashasturlu;[6] not to mention the astrologers, great poets, and other people both young and old—all of them together helped give Krishnaraya the ritual bath at an auspicious moment, just as it is prescribed in the *śāstras*. Then they had him sit on a gold seat on the ceremonial platform, where he performed the ten donations, the sixteen great donations, and other meritorious acts such as donations of mountains of gold, silver, jewels, and pearls, donations of tens of millions of cows, and grants to establish a thousand families. Water was brought in golden vases from the four oceans and again from all the great rivers, such as the Ganga, Yamuna, Sarasvati, Narmada, Sindhu, Kaveri, and Tamraparni. Then, at the precise auspicious moment—the air resounding with the tones of the eighteen royal instruments[7]—a group of brahmans anointed the king with those waters as they chanted Vedic mantras. Immediately afterward, they showered him with gold and with quantities of the nine precious gems, and then they dressed him in fresh clothes, draped him with a yellow shawl,[8] and perfumed him with the finest scents, such as sandalwood, red sandalwood, musk, and excellent civet oil.

After Krishnaraya had sent them all back to their residences, he called his Sons and Sons-in-Law, his relatives, attendants, and friends. He seated them all in a line and joined them for a feast. When the meal was over, he washed his hands and rinsed his mouth with scented water, and then he put on a pair of wooden sandals and took one hundred steps while reciting the *Shorter Rāmāyaṇa.*[9] When the ceremonies were all finished, he seated himself on a multicolored carpet and summoned Appaji and the other ministers and commanders. This is what he said to them:

"Ever since Viranrisimharaya undertook the responsibilities of the Lion-Throne, my brothers Achyutaraya and Chandramauli[10] and I have never been present at the court. Now that you have called on me to bear the burden of the kingdom, it is for you to instruct me in the matters of ruling. In what way is the occupant of the Lion-Throne to act? How should he protect the people? How is he to deal with his attendants? How is it that he acquires *dharma?* How is he to manage expenditures? In what way does he conquer his enemies, and how does he sustain his allies? How does he protect his intimate friends? What are the ways in which he should honor those who take refuge in him and serve him? Who are the people worthy of serving as his bodyguards? How is he to know all the ways of thinking about money and expenditures? How does he acquire everlasting fame? You know all this and more about royal conduct, is that not so? Please instruct me in detail!"

When the king had spoken, Appaji, Ayyamarasu, Kondamarasu, Bacharasu, and several other ministers replied, "What your lordship has just spoken of is indeed the business of proper royal conduct. All these aspects of conduct, a good sense of discrimination, thorough discharging of all affairs, skillfulness,[11] and consultations with ministers—these are the means of achieving total rule." Thus they began to instruct the king in the matters of royal conduct.

"First of all, you should know that the King of the Lion-Throne is none other than an emanation of Vishnu. If you ask how that is so, there is the statement of Lord Krishna himself: '*Narāṇāṃ ca narādhipam*[12]—and among men, know me to be the king.'

"Then there is a verse on royal conduct:[13]

> With the radiance of youth and precious gems,
> the fresh scent of oils and flowers,
> and the loyal service of great men—
> such a man will be called king.[14]
>
> For a man who is loved by the goddess Shri,
> a hero as radiant as the mine of virtue—
> seek no farther than the Lion-Throne
> and the person of the king.

"The occupant of the Lion-Throne should understand the seven-limbed state[15] comprising king, minister, ally, treasury, country, fort, and army. He should know the group of seven gifts of honor, which are palanquin, fine clothes, ornaments, vehicles, royal favors, camphor, and *pān*. He should know the seven techniques for dealing with an enemy,[16] namely, conciliation, sowing dissension, bribery, attack, deceit, overlooking transgressions, and trickery in war. And there are seven royal vices,[17] as enumerated in this verse:

> Women, dice, drink, the hunt,
> arrogance in words, harshness in war,
> and wasteful spending of money—
> these seven do not befit a great king.

If you are wondering what these really mean, *women* is to be understood as indulging in the company of women; *dice* is of course gambling with dice; ***drink*** means the imbibing of alcohol; going hunting is clear enough; ***arrogance in words*** is taken as cursing and censuring others; the next one means undertaking a war without just cause; and, finally, the last one means inappropriate spending. These seven vices should be renounced.

"There are many other things that the king should do. He should:

—beget the 'sevenfold progeny,'[18] which are a son, a treasure, a temple, a garden, an irrigation tank, a literary work, and a village established for brahmans;
—surround himself with the sevenfold assembly,[19] which includes poets, scholars, *purāṇa* reciters, epic bards, jesters, and singers;
—know the seven constituents of the body:[20] blood, flesh, fat, the vital humor, bone, marrow, and semen;
—bear on his sturdy shoulders the entire circle of the earth, which is surrounded by the seven oceans of salt, sugar, alcohol, ghee, curds, milk, and pure water;
—unleash the splendor of his fame to roam at will through the seven continents known as Jambu, Plaksha, Kusha, Krauncha, Shaka, Shalmali, and Pushkara;
—know the greatness of the seven great mountain chains Himavanta, Malyavanta, Nishadha, Vindhya, Pariyatraka, Gandhamadana, and Hemakuta;
—cause all to see the ascetic power of the seven great Sages Kashyapa, Atri, Bharadvaja, Vishvamitra, Gautama, Jamadagni, and Vasishtha;
—know which are the seven worthy gifts,[21] that is, turbans, earrings, necklaces, clothes, conveyances, scents, and *pān;*
—distance himself from the fourteen defects of kings, which are lack of belief in the Vedas, lying, being in an unreceptive state of mind, incoherent talk, anger, anxiety, procrastination, not making the acquaintance of wise people, lack of interest in monetary affairs, useless worry, not doing that which must be done, not keeping secrets, not employing auspicious means, and falling prey to vices;
—increase his wealth by means of cowherd villages and pleasure gardens, merchant traffic on land and sea, and forts, protecting them through the mere glance of his eye, which reduces his enemies to dust;
—offer compassion and protection to the crippled, the blind, the dumb, the deaf, the maimed, and others who wander homelessly;

—welcome and protect the terror-stricken enemies who come seeking refuge;
—know the secrets of the *tarka-, vidyā-,* and *artha-śāstras,* dealing, respectively, with logic, wisdom, and the principles of war;[22]
—show expertise in the riding of chariots, horses, and elephants and in running nimbly on his feet;[23]
—know the threefold duties of liberality, righteousness, and doing good to others;
—know the three powers coming from material resources, good counsel, and personal bravery;[24]
—know the three ways of enemy, ally, and neutral powers;
—know the threefold powers of creation, maintenance, and destruction;
—observe the threefold *sandhyā* worship,[25] at morning, noon, and evening;
—perform the fire offerings in the three sacrificial fires, namely, the *āhavanīya, gārhapatya,* and *dakṣiṇāgni;*
—know the three ways of the Wind, which bring cold, torpor, and fragrance;
—savor the three types of *pān:* that made with cardamom, sandalwood, and areca nuts, that made with white leaves, and that made with a lime paste ground from pearls;
—know the three universal qualities of clarity, activity, and inertia;[26]
—know the characteristics of the three types of heroes[27] in literature: the highest, middling, and lower;
—become an adept in the four goals of life: duty, material success, pleasure, and final release from bondage;
—examine with care the four types of religious texts, which are Veda, *śāstra, purāṇa*, and Epic;
—study diligently the four collections of the Veda: *Ṛg-, Yajur-, Sāma-,* and *Atharva;*
—know and protect people in all the four stages of life: student, householder, forest dweller, and mendicant;
—maintain an army composed of the four divisions of chariots, elephants, horses, and foot soldiers;[28]
—know the four psychological constituents[29] mind, intellect, ego, and consciousness;
—observe the four daily acts of personal tidiness: shaving, anointing the body, brushing the teeth, and dressing in clean clothes;
—become attractive through the four means of clothes, ornaments, scents, and flowers;
—know the fourfold ways of love, including flirting, enchantment, using aphrodisiacs, and pining;

—know the characteristics of the different types of erotic heroes, classified as *bhadradanta, kūcimāra,* and *pāñcāla,* and of their male confidants, known as *viṭa, vidūṣaka,* and *pīṭhamardana;*[30]
—know the characteristics of the four different types of women,[31] classified as *hastini, cittini, śaṅkhini,* and *padmini;*
—know the four stages of maturation, which are childhood, adolescence, youth, and old age;
—know the characteristics of the four types of go-between: the adultress, the clever woman, the family woman, and the gossip;
—know the five types of sense data: sound, touch, color, taste, and odor;
—exercise caution in the use of the five sense organs: the ears, skin, eyes, nose, and tongue;
—know all about the matters of alienation of friends, gaining friends, war and peace, loss of gains, and rashness;[32]
—know the almanacs relating to beginnings, means, people, things, wealth, divisions of place and time, agriculture, revenge, and peace and act in accordance with them;
—come to the realization that he is composed of the five elements earth, water, fire, air, and space;
—know the seats of the five vital airs[33] known as *prāṇa, apāna, vyāna, udāna,* and *samāna;*
—avoid the five arrows of the god of love, which are made of lotuses, Ashoka flowers, mango blossoms, jasmine, and blue lotuses;
—know the five great classes of musical sounds,[34] namely, those produced by blowing, by plucking, by striking, by bowing, and by the human voice;
—know the five types of food,[35] that is, those that are ingested by munching, chewing, licking, slurping, and drinking;
—be a connoisseur of the six flavors: pungent, bitter, salty, sour, sweet, and astringent;
—know the six activities of a king,[36] which are peace, war, marching, neutrality, dual policy, and alliance;
—listen to the histories of the Six World Emperors Harishchandra, Nala, Purukutsa, Pururava, Sagara, and Kartavirya;
—listen to the stories of the Sixteen Exemplary Kings Gaya, Ambarisha, Shashi, Bindu, Anangu, Prithu, Nrigu, Marutta, Bharata, Rama, Dilipa, Shibi, Rantideva, Yayati, Mandhata, and Bhagiratha;
—be familiar with the six philosophical schools of the . . . , . . . ,[37] Jains, Kapalikas, Buddhists, and Charvakas;
—investigate the six *śāstras*[38] of Vedanta, Vaisheshika, the Bhatta school, the Prabhakara school, and the Purva- and the Uttara-Mimamsa;

—surround himself with wealth and grain, buildings and conveyances, relatives, servants, maidservants, and other such people;
—enjoy the eight pleasures of food, clothing, scents, flowers, *pān*, devoted women, trusted friends, and a comfortable bed;
—suppress the eight varieties of pride, namely, pride of rank and family, of appearance, of learning, of resolve, of strength, of youth, and of kingdom;
—anoint himself with perfumes made of the eight scents, which are musk, camphor, sandalwood, civet oil, red sandalwood, rosewater, superior civet oil, and *śrīgandha;*
—be an expert in the eight matters of warriors,[39] such as handling the reins, giving and receiving honors, arranging the hair, handling weapons, and stopping the arrows and spears thrown by other heroes;
—show skill in manifesting the sentiments[40] of love, heroism, compassion, wonder, humor, terror, disgust, and violence;
—be a connoisseur of the nine precious gems: pearls, rubies, diamonds, lapis lazuli, agate, topaz, sapphires, coral, and emeralds;
—possess the nine treasures of the God of Wealth,[41] namely the *padma-, mahāpadma-, śaṅkha-, makara-, kacchapa-, mukunda-, nanda-, nīla-,* and *kharva-nidhis;*
—know the definitions of the eight syllabic groupings used in poetic meters,[42] called *sa-, na-, ya-, ma-, bha-, ra-, ta-,* and *ja-gaṇas;*
—know the differences between the twenty types of rhyming or *yati,*[43] known as *svara, pluta, ubhaya, hṛdyanusvāra, vikalpa, prāgbhava, saṃśaya, prabhu, vibhāga, kāku, ādēśa, nitya, ārya, akhaṃḍa, varga, cakkaṭi,*[44] *ekkaṭi, sarasa, lāṭa,* and *vakuḷa;*
—know the eighteen types of description[45] used in poetry, including descriptions of the season, of the hero, of the hero's prosperity, of the forests, of the mountains, of passionate love play, of water play, of drinking the nectar of the beloved's lips, of the king, of the city, of the hero's son, of consultations, of a messenger, of a wedding, and so on;
—be skilled in the eight languages, which are Sanskrit, Prakrit, Shauraseni, Magadhi, Paishachi, Chulika, Apabhramsha, and Telugu;
—avoid committing the ten literary inelegancies of breaking the internal rhyme, violating the meter, repetition, hesitation, circumlocution, violation of conventional vocabulary, use of obscene colloquialisms, and so forth;
—be skillfull in employing the nine sentiments and the many figures of speech so as to produce verses that are in proper meter and abound in smooth descriptions;[46]
—search out and patronize good poets who can teach poetry, drama, and poetics through both definition and example;

—know the secrets of the ten stages of love,[47] called looking, worrying, grieving, sighing, praising, losing all sense of shame, losing appetite, developing fever, stammering incoherently, and attempting suicide;
—be able to distinguish between the sixteen stages of death,[48] which are trembling, feeling pain, losing all concern for personal tidiness, becoming contentious, worrying, wasting away, becoming sorrowful, languishing patiently, forgetting where one is, forgetting who one is, giving up eating, becoming hot with fever, falling silent, the departing of half of the soul, and returning to the five elements;
—know the secrets of the sixteen parts of the body, namely, the toes, the feet, the heels, the knees, the tongue, the thighs, the navel, the belly, the breasts, the chest, the neck, the lips, the cheeks, the eyes, the forehead, and the head;
—know the sixteen arrows made of the flowers of the white lotus, water lily, mountain jasmine, mango, nutmeg, Alexandrian laurel, mimosa, Ashoka, *viruvāji,* jasmine, golden jasmine, *kētaki, vāvili,* red lotus, heavenly laurel, and banana;
—know the four types of bows, which are made of buds, of sugar cane, of vines, and of flowers;
—stay out of range of the Love God, who strings these four bows with the four different bowstrings made of black bees, *kurivēlu,* buds, and vines and then aims the sixteen arrows at the sixteen parts of the body;
—search out and patronize experts in the sixty-four sciences;
—punish the wicked and protect the good.

Your majesty should realize that there are yet many other principles of royal conduct; we have mentioned only some of them."

When Appaji, Ayyamarasu, Kondamarasu, Bacharasu, and the other ministers had finished their discourse, Krishnaraya looked at them and said, "Indeed, you know the past, present, and future and matters that require great foresight. You know what is fated and what is not. No wonder you have been able to explain all these principles of royal conduct with such clarity! Now we ask, how are we to attract income to the palace, so that it comes like bees to the flower, drawn by the scent in the wind?"

The assembled advisers replied by explaining, "If the king acts in accordance with *dharma,* the rains will fall at least three times in every month, causing the earth to produce abundantly. If the palace then takes the taxes that are its due without being unjust, the palace will prosper, and cash will flow into the treasury in great quantities."

In illustration of this principle, they recited a verse:

> "To acquire wealth:
> make the people prosper.
> To make the people prosper:
> justice is the means.
> O Kirti Narayana!
> They say that justice
> is the treasury of kings.[49]

"If someone who harms innocent people or animals goes unpunished, the king's righteousness and power as well as the merit he has acquired will be lost. This is a well-known fact, and there is a story about it.[50] At the time when the Dvapara age had ended and the Kali age had just begun, the great king Parikshit had been anointed as king, just like you. As everyone knows, the *dharma-śāstras* undergo a decline over time, so that, while they are complete with four quarters or 'legs' in the Krita age, they have only three legs in the Treta age, two legs in the Dvapara age, and but one leg in the Kali age. At that time, the god Dharma took the form of a cow, and, because it couldn't support itself on its one remaining leg, it lay near Parikshit's city, overcome with grief. 'In the olden days,' the cow lamented, 'when King Yudhishthira[51] was protecting *dharma,* I was so happy! But alas, now that the Kali age has begun, three of my legs have become *adharma,* and only one leg of *dharma* remains, so I can no longer even stand up.' It so happened that the great king Parikshit chanced to come out from someplace nearby in order to inspect the city and saw the cow. Noticing that the animal could not stand up and was so distressed that the tears flowed from its eyes, the king wondered if someone might have harmed the innocent creature. When he asked the cow about it, she retorted harshly, 'Why do you ask? Can you possibly do anything to help?' Parikshit replied, 'I only asked on your account. Besides, I am not the kind of person who would ask just for the sake of politeness. If you belittle my sincerity and disregard what I might be able to do for you, the loss will be yours, will it not?' And then he recited a verse,

'A second-rate king
   who does not punish
   the wretches who hurt innocent animals

will lose his life,
   his place in heaven,
   and all his riches.
This much, my dear, is certain.'

He went on to introduce himself, 'My name is Parikshit. I am the son of Abhimanyu and the grandson of Arjuna.'

"At that point, the wish-fulfilling cow revealed its true form and said, 'And I am the god Dharma. I grant you the boon that all men shall obey your command and that, for as many days as you rule, you shall protect *dharma* so that it walks on all four legs, making it impossible for the evil of the Kali age to overtake it.' So saying, the god disappeared. Thus it was that king Parikshit banished the evil of the Kali age to the place where it belonged. King Parikshit became strong and lived happily for his full span of one hundred years, ruling so that his subjects never feared the calamities of death, thieves, and drought but were instead surrounded by wealth and stores of grain, just as it was in the reign of Rama. And you, our Lord, should protect *dharma* and rule the kingdom in precisely this same way."

When Rayalu had duly heard all these principles of conduct from Appaji and the others, he said, "Up to this point, Ishvara Nayaka, Narasa Nayaka, and Viranrisimharaya have ruled the kingdom.[52] Now, I must go and see all the kingdoms, forts, lands, citadels, temples of Vishnu, sacred places, and feudatory kingdoms that have been under their power." The ministers considered the king's statement and said, "That is appropriate indeed. Yes, the king should go and inspect in person the realms ruled by his predecessors. If you merely stay where you are, then you won't be able to learn anything about the business of the kingdom. You should go and let your subjects behold you. To impress your enemies and feudatories, you should go together with your terrifying army to inspect the eight directions and make your fame shine."

Krishnaraya was pleased to hear them speak thus and so resolved to go and see all the realms of the vast earth. But first he decided to send out spies, so that they could find out everything about the various lands and about the behavior of the local lords and chiefs, about their strengths and weaknesses, about the various villages, hamlets, and towns, about what the people both learned and simple were saying, and about what was going on in the citadels and come every day and secretly report to him what they had learned. He found people who were fast of foot, strong in mind, able to speak many foreign languages and to disguise themselves in numerous ways, and told them to discover the secrets of others and then come back and report to him. He sent them to Bijapur, Ahmadnagar, Bidar, Rajahmundry, Arangam, Chennapatnam, Shrirangapatnam, Chadarangapatnam, Shrirangam, Madurai, Rameshvaram, Ummattur, Shivasamudram, Penukonda, Golconda, Gurramkonda, Melnadu, Morasa-nadu, Ghattamsima, the Tamil realm, Malayala, Kochchi, Konkan, Kerala, Viratapura, Varatadesha, Magadhadesha, Matsyadesha, Vidarbhadesha, Kambhojanagara, the Kashmir tract, the city of Delhi, and to other places; to Tuluva, Haima, and the other southern kingdoms; to Chandragiri, Gandikota, Cuddapah, Nandyal, Bellamkonda, Raichur, Mudgal, Nidgal, Mysore, and other cantonments. As the spies wandered about in the towns, they kept their ears open for news of people who were becoming unruly or showing signs of going over to the cause of enemies. Whenever they heard news of such things, they informed the people in question that they had their orders to put a stop to such behavior. They would tell the people that they should behave themselves and not violate the orders of the palace, and, from then on, such people would become afraid to do any wrong. Thus did the king conduct his affairs so that everyday life was pleasant for all his subjects. All the city's streets and lanes were safe, and none of the people ever had to worry about being accosted while they were out and walking around.

·3·

Krishnaraya and Timmarasu

At night, after finishing his daily activities and dismissing his court, Krishnaraya would go out in secret to inspect the city. Once he had acquainted himself with everything that was going on, he would come back to the palace at the break of dawn to lie down for a little while. At sunrise, he would get up again, brush his teeth, and wash his face, and then, after he had applied his devotional mark and sipped some sacred water, he would come into the Great Court. Calling to mind all the things that he had seen and heard during the night while on his secret inspection round, he would look at Inspector Jangayya and ask him what had transpired during the night. The king would listen carefully as Jangayya gave his report, and, if all was in accordance with what he had himself seen, he would remain happily quiet.

On one occasion, however, the inspector happened not to cover everything. The king got angry and chastised him for not knowing about a dispute that had occurred during the night at a given house number in such and such row of a certain street in one ward of the city:[1] "How is it that you do not know about this! But then how can I blame you? No," added the king sarcastically, "you are doing an excellent job in your inspectorship, and I am doing a perfect job of ruling the kingdom!"

At that the inspector grew terribly frightened. In order to make the city more secure, he went day and night with neither food nor drink. He posted men in the streets and ordered them to come and report to him at frequent intervals. At first he wondered if someone might have come to Rayalu in secret to inform the king of the incident, but, when he considered the matter further, he realized that Rayalu must have gone out to inspect the city and witnessed the event himself, for it was clearly not just something that he had merely heard of. Once Jangayya had come to this conclusion, he ordered watchmen to conceal themselves diligently, saying that Rayalu was in the habit of going out to inspect the city at night and that thus they should stay in the streets with caution, not asking anybody anything and not allowing any troubles to occur.

That evening, as soon as Rayalu had gone back into the palace after dismissing the court, Jangayya went in person with his closest friends and retainers to wait by the audience hall. There they waited until two hours after the palace had been locked and sealed, keeping their eyes on the place from which Rayalu would emerge as if setting out for a pleasure stroll. Finally, Rayalu came cautiously out and looked around. When he noticed Inspector Jangayya, he called him over and said, "I am going out now for my nightly inspection of the city. You and your trusted men may follow at a distance, but don't let yourselves be seen." For the rest of the night Inspector Jangayya fearfully followed right behind Rayalu as he inspected the city from street to street, and then only after the king had returned and gone back into the palace could Jangayya return in peace to his own home. After Appaji and the other ministers learned of the incident, they became very cautious both day and night whenever they happened to be engaged in confidential discussions in their respective houses.

As things went on in this way, Krishnaraya would customarily pass the morning hours by listening to people recite verses on royal conduct. It so happened that, one day, Padyaniti Chandrayya[2] wasn't able to come to the gathering, so he sent his son to the palace instead. The son came and recited works on royal conduct such as *Sañjaya's Nīti, Vidura's Nīti, Cāṇukya's Nīti,* and *Bhartṛhari's Collection of One Hundred Verses on Nīti.*[3] Rayalu listened attentively as Chandrayya's son recited without getting so much as a single verse wrong. Suddenly, the king was struck by a verse from *Baddena's Hundred Verses:*

> If his army is greater
> than the forces of his feudatories:
> then alone will a king have strength

and place those feudatories
far from the power to command,
O Badde Narendra![4]

When Chandrayya's son had read this verse, Rayalu told him to read it again two or three times, and thus the king fixed the verse in his mind.

One day, Rayalu summoned the accountants in his service and asked them, "How many lakhs are yielded by the provinces subject to the Lion-Throne of Karnataka? How many hill forts, forest forts, island forts, and forts on open ground are there in the kingdom? How many citadels are there? How many cities and villages are there, and what is the extent of the cultivated lands? How much is in the palace treasury in the accounts for the various forts? I want you to prepare detailed figures for our holdings in cash, precious ornaments, and the nine jewels; for the amount of deposited treasure;[5] for the accounts relating to the district temple superintendents; and for the palace's salaried forces, including elephants, horses, and their attendants; and then submit your report."

When the king had summoned the nine treasurers and commanded them in this way, their leader Allalanatha, who was keeper of the small treasury,[6] replied apologetically, "All these days, Viranrisimharaya was never one to inquire into the details of the accounts. But, now that my Lord has shown an interest in these matters, I will be glad to go and prepare the figures you have requested and report them to you tomorrow." So saying, Allalanatha went off and calculated carefully all day and all night, and then the next morning he came back and submitted his financial report:[7]

"When Vidyaranya founded this city, the amount of treasure that he buried[8] for use by the occupants of the Lion-Throne was 995.6 million in cash, with an additional 40 million in precious ornaments and 60 million in jewels. In addition, there is the sum of 195.6 million in cash, which represents the amount deposited into the treasury by the previous kings after balancing the amounts expended in running the Lion-Throne against the tax revenues that were generated.

"Aside from this, there are the current assets of the Karnataka kingdom, standing at 108.4 million. From this sum, however, 6 million has been given away in the form of land grants for the maintenance of gods and brahmans, grants of rent-free lands, and grants for the support of monasteries,[9] so that leaves a balance of 102.4 million.

"In this kingdom, the rate[10] for the maintenance of armored horses is 100 *ghettis*[11] per month per horse, which comes to 100,000 *ghettis* per 1,000 horses, or a total of 2,400,000 for 24,000 horses. For elephants, the rate is 1,000 *ghettis* monthly per elephant, or, for 120 elephants, 120,000 *ghettis,* which comes to 1.2 million for a total of 1,200 elephants. For foot soldiers, the rate is 2 *ghetti varāhas* monthly per soldier, which comes to the rate of 2,000 *ghettis* per 1,000 soldiers, and thus a total of 400,000 *ghettis* monthly for 200,000 soldiers. On the basis of this calculation, the districts around the strong forts of Adoni, Cheyyeti-durga, Gutti, Gandikota, Chandragiri, Gurramkonda, Maddur, Somagiri, Trishirapuram, Kunnattur, and Penukonda, around the military commanders' forts at Nandyal, Shrirangapatnam, Ummattur, Vallamkota, Madurai, Palyamkota, and Dindikal,[12] and around the forest forts of Satyavedu, Kottikal, Dankinikota, and Naranavanam have been designated as estates for rule by the Amaranayakas. The income from these estates is sufficient for the maintenance of the 24,000 horses, 1,200 elephants,[13] and 200,000 foot soldiers with which they serve you. Although the Amaranayakas have occupied these estates in accordance with our figures, they have nonetheless failed to provide the correct number of elephants, horses, and foot soldiers.[14] This is certainly worthy of your majesty's consideration."

When he had heard the report, the king ordered the accountants to consult the palace register and then write out a detailed report specifying the exact numbers of elephants, horses, and foot soldiers that each Amaranayaka was required to provide.

The king was disturbed by the fact that the officers hadn't reported so much as a single elephant, horse, or attendant in the direct employ of the palace. He turned toward Appaji, Ayyamarasu, and the rest of the ministers and asked them, "Do you have any suggestions as to what else needs to be done?" The ministers all remained silent until finally Saluva Timmarasu spoke up. "Rest assured!" he said hesitatingly to the king. "We will run things to your satisfaction! Your lordship need not so much as speak a word."

When Timmarasu had spoken, Rayalu was annoyed. "They think

of me merely as their agent for bearing the burden of the Lion-Throne," thought the king to himself. "In fact, everything is coming to be run by these ministers! Who even bothers to listen to me? Why, if I were ever to demonstrate my authority and attempt to act independently, everything would come to a standstill simply because the ministers would disapprove."[15]

He gave the matter much thought, and then one night he left the palace as if he were going out on his inspection of the city, but sneaked off instead to a temple that was located several leagues[16] north of the city. He called the priest and asked for some water. The priest brought the water, and Rayalu brushed his teeth and washed his face, put on his devotional mark, and sipped sacred water. Then he had the priest bring him some cakes that were the sanctified remains from the Lord's food offering; he ate these and then sat down to relax.

Meanwhile, back in the city, Saluva Timmarasu came at dawn to the palace as usual and inquired whether Rayalu had arisen yet. The spies, harem guard women, cook women, and doorkeepers who were standing watch there said, "Last night Rayalu went out to inspect the city, and he hasn't come back yet." Appaji immediately ordered them, "If anyone else comes and asks, tell them that Rayalu has a headache and hasn't gotten up yet." Forthwith, he went to the entrance of the audience hall and sat down there. He sent spies off in the eight directions, telling them to search all the streets and then come back and report to him in private. The spies went off and searched in all the eight directions.

Before long, one of the spies returned and secretly told Saluva Timmarasu, "The king has gone by himself to the Pallikonda Ranganathaswamy temple several leagues north of here, and there he sits, gazing toward the city."

Appaji sent written messages to all the nobles and lords, and to the Amaranayakas, telling them that Rayalu had decided to go hunting and that, accordingly, they should come quickly with all their forces. They all hurried and prepared themselves. As soon as everyone had assembled—all the horsemen, elephant riders, foot soldiers, retainers, nobles, and lords who happened to be in the city—the force sallied forth with Timmarasu at the head. Once they had gone the distance of no more than one bow shot, Timmarasu got down from his palanquin and ordered all the foot soldiers, horses, and elephants to fall into formation and wait. He himself walked on some distance with a few of his own retainers; then he stopped and told them to wait while he continued on alone.

As Timmarasu came walking out of the fortification walls, Rayalu saw him coming. The king pulled his shawl over himself and lay down, pretending to be asleep. Appaji approached Rayalu and saw that he was sleeping, so he folded his hands respectfully and stood there waiting. Rayalu continued with his ruse for a while, until finally he stirred and sat up as if he had just awakened. He looked at Appaji and exclaimed, "Appaji! What brings you here?"

Timmarasu prostrated himself before the king. "Your lordship," he began explaining, "when you went out last night as though to inspect the city, how was I to know that you had actually come here? This morning I went to the palace as usual and asked if you were up yet. When the harem guard women and doorkeepers said that your lordship had gone out as if to inspect the city but hadn't yet returned, I was upset to say the least. Immediately I sent spies out to search in every direction, and soon one came back and told me that you were here. As soon as I heard this, I knew that I could not let the news become public! So I sent messages to all the nobles and lords, telling them that they should come quickly with all their forces since the king was preparing to go hunting. To those who were near at hand, I said that the king had ordered me to summon them when he was ready to go hunting and that, accordingly, it was time for them to set off. In this way, I got them out of the city and hastened here. Your lordship, is it proper that you should leave the city and come here like this? If your subordinates had heard of this, the city would have been lost! If the swordsmen were to hear of it, what a disgrace it would be! It is most inappropriate to do things like this. Was it advisable for your lordship to set your mind to such a thing?"

When Timmarasu had been so sensible in informing the king of the fearful things that might have happened as a result of his action, Rayalu sarcastically replied, "With such great men as you to carry the burden of the Lion-Throne, how could such things possibly ever happen? Indeed, you are so capable that you can pluck a mere piece of grass and turn it into Mount Meru![17] And then you can make Mount Meru move around like a piece of grass! I ask you, who else is capable of performing such feats?"

Saluva Timmarasu rejoindered, "I must admit that it is just as you say. But why? Because it is your lordship who has entrusted me with the affairs of the throne. If you really think about it, I myself am nothing more than a worthless piece of grass. Now everyone values a sapphire, which, if it is genuine, attracts grass when it is rubbed. But, if the sapphire despises the grass and thus fails to attract it, then it is not a fine sapphire and will have little value. Just like that, a servant is elevated to greatness only through the majesty of the lord who rules him. Similarly, it is only the lord who is surrounded by great servants who will gain fame and renown."[18] After this double entendre, he added, "Come, let's go back to the city."

"No," said the king, "I have serious doubts as to the quality of my sovereignty. Is there anyone who submits to my will? What am I to say to all the people who do not obey me? Why, I am not even worthy of punishing them! How is a king to rule the earth if he lacks the simple power to command? How is he to uphold what is right, how to punish the wicked and protect the good? If I cannot resolve this dilemma, I am better off staying here than returning to the city."

Saluva Timmarasu replied, "What your lordship says is absolutely true. Yes, that would be the proper course of action. Now, if your lordship will only tell me what you would like to do in this instance, then, with your lordship's authority, I will carry out the plans to your satisfaction."

The king said to Appaji, "Since you have made me a supreme monarch, you must implement my wishes in a manner befitting my status. Lately, I have been listening to verses on royal conduct. Just the other day, I heard a verse that struck me as exceptionally profound, and, ever since, I have wanted nothing more than to put that teaching into action. I have concluded that I must gather a force that is greater than that of all my feudatories and thus check the power of the Turks. I realize quite well that nothing will be possible without a standing, salaried army, so let us now acquire such a force, complete with elephants, horses, and foot soldiers, and then I shall return to the city."

Saluva Timmarasu replied, "Your lordship hardly needed to go to such lengths for such a small matter. Why, if it pleases you, I shall assemble the elephants, horses, and foot soldiers at this very moment. Then you may return to the city in triumph with your own complete army. Now just wait while I assemble a force of elephants, horses, and soldiers for the direct service of the palace." Then and there, Appaji summoned the nobles and lords, the Amaranayakas, the horse troops, and the Seventy-two Officers and told them to come to the court. He called the accountants of the militia and asked them the number of Amaranayaka elephants, horses, and foot soldiers that were in the service of the Lion-Throne.

The accountants reported, "The Amaranayakas are required to provide 24,000 horses, 120 elephant units,[19] and 200,000 foot soldiers. To maintain this force, they rule *amaranāyakaṃ* estates with a collective yield of 48 million per year—calculated from a monthly rate of 4 million."

When the accountants had made their report, Appaji said to them,[20] "Hurry and take a count right now of all the *amaraṃ* elephants, horses, and foot soldiers. If you find that any of them come short, note the number missing, and figure the amount due for the missing units. Keep in mind that ten years have passed since Viranrisimharaya's accession. When you have calculated the total cash due, get them to pay up immediately."

The accountants followed Appaji's command and went out to count the cavalry and foot soldiers. The horses fell short of the figure by half, and the foot soldiers fell short by a quarter, so they ordered the Amaranayakas involved to hand over the amount due immediately. The Amaranayakas requested that their transgression should be forgiven this time since their reputations had otherwise been unblemished for quite some time. "We have been experiencing hardships lately," they explained, "and there is really no way that we can pay the amount due. But, if you will let us continue running our districts as usual, we will set a price on the elephants and horses that we presently have and offer them to the palace instead. We will just have to get some more for ourselves later."

Appaji agreed to their proposal. The Amaranayakas proceeded to determine the number of elephants and horses that would be equal in value to the sum they owed. They decided that 500 elephants, 12,000 horses, and 100,000 foot soldiers with their commanding officers should be sufficient for them to regain their good terms with the palace. So they led those elephants, horses, and foot soldiers up to the king and presented them to him. "If it pleases you," they said, "accept these in lieu of the sums we owe."

The king was amazed at this accomplishment of Appaji and could not help but praise him. "Who else but you has the power to make possible the impossible?" He presented his minister with the seven worthy gifts: a cap, an ornamental shirt, a necklace, a pair of pearl earrings, a yellow shawl, fragrant musk, and *pān*. Then he ordered the elephant drivers of Tulu to be in charge of the new palace elephants and placed the horsemen of Kabbili, Morasa-nadu, and Tulu in control of the newly acquired palace horses. When that was done, the king mounted the elephant named Masti Madahasti and climbed into its howdah of gold. He called to Saluva Timmarasu and told him to take the seat behind him. Followed by his entire army, the king marched into the city of Vijayanagara.

Later on, after he had sent Appaji and the others back to their houses, he told his intimates of the episode. "Is there any other minister in this world who is like my Appaji Saluva Timmarasu? Just look at what can be done when you have a minister like Appaji! I tell him that we must assemble a salaried force within one day or else I will not return to the city, and he patiently replies that he will assemble it right then and there. In no more than the wink of an eye, he has produced 500 elephants, 12,000 horses, and 100,000 foot soldiers, saying, 'Do with them what you will.' When I beheld that, I was truly amazed. Just before, I had told Appaji of my desire to launch a campaign against the Turks and had told him that we would have to assemble horsemen and elephant drivers for Karnataka. But no, that is not enough for him! By the mere glance of his eye, he acquires 12,000 horses for the royal troops and enables us to assign them to the horsemen of Kabbili, Tulu, and Morasa-nadu!"

As the king went on and on in his praise of Appaji, his officers began to make provisions for the 12,000 new horses and the 500 new elephants. They set wages for the men who rode and drove them and assigned a servant to each. In each of the stables, they posted a staff of four grooms-in-charge, six clerks, sixteen workers, and six Gollas to guard the money bags, in order to ensure that the horses would be properly taken care of and fed with hay and horse gram. Additionally, a new accountant was appointed to oversee the flow of funds from the treasury to cover these daily expenses and to guarantee that this huge staff of people should receive their correct monthly salaries.

"Indeed," rejoiced the king, "today at last my kingship has been set on firm ground."

And there is one final point. When the Amaranayakas determined the value of their 500 elephants and 12,000 horses to present to the king, there was not a single one among them who thought the valuation unfair. To the contrary, all were in full agreement about the value of what they gave. On average, the value of the elephants was set at 6,000, which works out to 120,000 per 20 elephants and comes to the sum of 3 million for the total of 50 elephant units. As for the horses, they agreed on 200 *varāhas* per horse,[21] which comes to 200,000 per 1,000 horses and 2.4 million for the total of 12,000 horses. Thus it was that, in the mere wink of an eye, the elephants and horses brought the palace an income of 5.4 million.

"With incomparable men like Appaji, indeed anything is obtainable!" concluded Rayalu. At that, the minister Ayyamarasu said, "The occupant of a Lion-Throne of course possesses countless women and jewels. But there is something even more important than that to a king, as it is said in a verse on royal conduct:

> Sad the king
> who thinks women can be wives
> or stone jewels serve as precious gems!
> Hear me, Badde Narendra—
> Earth is the wife
> wise men the gems.[22]

"In other words, if a king can only find a perfect jewel of a man, then he will be able to gather the nine jewels and collect entire armies. Thus, you must certainly not consider Appaji to be an ordinary minister—for he is indeed an extraordinary minister! He alone is capable of accomplishing the impossible! And what makes him so special? Well, all men are men; they all have two arms and two legs. But, even so, one can distinguish superior, average, and inferior ones among them. Now how is that? Why, the superior ones stand out from the rest on account of their greater qualities! In the same way, all the five metals may appear comparable, but of course gold is better than all the rest put together. Why? Because, when you put it to the touchstone, gold shines all the brighter! In this same way, Appaji must be recognized as the greatest of men because of his superior qualities. As a final example, there is the verse:

śateṣu jāyate śūraḥ   sahasreṣu ca paṇḍitaḥ /
vaktā śatasahasreṣu   dātā bhavati vā na vā //

One in a hundred is born a hero,
and scholars come one in a thousand.
When it takes a hundred thousand to produce a great orator,
where can a generous man be found?

According to that maxim, one in a hundred will be a hero, one in a thousand a scholar, and only one in a hundred thousand will be a minister who can speak eloquently in the assembly. Then will there be even one generous man in the whole country? Indeed, how could it be possible for everyone to have Appaji's qualities?"

·4·

Reports of the Turks

When Ayyamarasu had finished speaking, he and the king then began to discuss private matters. Suddenly, Marichi Ramayya hurried in to announce that the king's spies had just returned from Bijapur. The spies were ushered forward, and this is the report that they submitted to Krishnaraya:

"We went to Bijapur and inspected the city and its suburbs, the fort and its bastions, the horsemen, elephant riders, elephants, horses, and foot soldiers, and all the Amaranayakas in their service. Then, as we approached the palace gate,[1] we noticed that all the viziers and lords had gathered together with Dondo Pandita and the other ministers in the audience hall before the hall of justice.[2] They were joined in their discussions by Mukunda Pandita and the other ministers of Qutb-al-Mulk of Golconda. The chief minister of Bijapur opened the discussion: 'Ever since Krishnaraya has been installed on the Lion-Throne of Karnataka, he has been determined to launch a campaign against us Turks and has been making every effort toward that end. This much is clear from the detailed written reports we have been receiving from our agents in Vijayanagara. This is particularly disturbing because, in the opinion of young and old alike, among the three kingdoms of the Ashvapati, the Gajapati, and the Narapati, it is the Lion-Throne of the Narapati that is by far the greatest and outpowers the other two.' At this, Muddo Pandita of Golconda was outraged and said, 'Nonsense! As far as the Lion-Thrones are concerned, all three are perfectly equal. Is there any such thing as relative superiority among them?' Someone else joined in by saying, 'The Nizam Shah's horsemen and elephants perform well enough in battle, but, since he is weak in the area of forts and resources, you must admit that it would be difficult to call him great.' At that, Muddo Pandita of Golconda quipped back sarcastically, 'Why not? Is that any reason to think in terms of inferiority and superiority?'

"While they were thus arguing back and forth at each other, Brahmapantu, who represented the Gajapati king Bahubalendra,[3] calmly began to speak his unbiased opinion: 'You should realize that those three Lion-Thrones in fact exist as emanations of the gods Brahma, Vishnu, and Maheshvara. Just as there are differences between those gods, so too among the horses of the Ashvapati, the elephants of the Gajapati, and the Karnataka Lion-Throne of the Narapati, it is the Narapati, the "Lord of Men," who is superior. Why? Just recall the statement of Lord Krishna himself: "And among men, I am the Lord of Men."[4] This is why the Karnataka kingdom is so blessed with villages gifted to gods and brahmans and with sacred pilgrimage centers, rivers, and lakes. But that is not the only reason. Vishnu himself is there in person at Venkatachalam! Since the Lord Vishnu himself lives in that kingdom, he attracts all the elders and wise men, the brahmans and ascetics, the heads of famous monasteries, and even the very kings of the other kingdoms, who all go there to present their gifts to him! And that is why the master of Karnataka's Lion-Throne is such a celebrated man. After that it is the Lion-Throne of the Gajapati that comes second because Jagannatha has manifested himself in that kingdom. And then third comes the Ashvapati, who occupies the kingdom of the god Vishvanatha, who lives on the banks of the Ganga. Finally, there are the three kings whom you serve—the Adil Shah, Qutb-al-Mulk, and the Nizam Shah—who occupy the northern borders of Karnataka. They are kindred of the others, but can one rightly consider them the equals of the lord of Karnataka?'

"Dondo Pandita, Muddo Pandita, and Dado Pandita all three were great ministers and could see the truth of Brahmapantu's words. 'Yes,' they admitted to themselves, 'our lords are drunkards who have no faith in gods and brahmans. They are barbarians, cow killers. And, since we are in their service, we have little chance to think objectively and offer real advice. Instead, we must say what they want to hear, or else we lose our posts. Yes, Brahmapantu's point is well taken.'

"After a few moments' silence, they resumed their deliberations.

'At any rate, if the king of Karnataka comes and crosses into our border districts, it will indeed be horrendous both for the Gajapati and for us. A stratagem must be found to prevent that at all costs! Our border forts must be readied with provisions and supplies, and we must man them with a strong force of elephants, horses, and foot soldiers.'

"Once they had finished their deliberations, they informed the Adil Shah of their decision. When he heard their plan, he only became furious and began to shout. 'Has the king of Karnataka already come and crossed the Tungabhadra? Your fears are baseless! Just think—so far Ishvara Nayaka, Narasa Nayaka, and Viranrisimharaya have all ruled in Karnataka without causing any trouble for us. Will the reign of Krishnaraya be any different from theirs?'

"Dondo Pandita and the others wisely replied, 'The policy of kings is never as straightforward as it may seem. As long as fate has yet to unfold, who knows what path divine providence will eventually favor? The Nizam Shah and Qutb-al-Mulk both realize this, so, when they heard the reports that had been sent from Vijayanagara, they immediately went into consultation with their ministers. Indeed, they have since sent messages to the effect that they have secured their borders and are waiting with great caution. Even Brahmapantu has advised his lord Bahubalendra to stock the mountain forts along his borders with supplies and provisions, and they have in fact already been reinforced with fresh elephants, horses, and riders. For our part, we should send provisions and troops to Shankaranayadu of Ikkeri Basavapatnam and other such princes and to Boyi Ramappa[5] so that they can reinforce the border districts under their control.'

" 'Then send them as you say,' the king recanted, swayed by their advice. 'And see to it that the fort and bastions of Bijapur are made fast, and make sure that the necessary provisions and supplies are distributed.'

"Thus, for the past eight days, the servants of the royal gateway have been overseeing the placing of cannons, mortars, and rockets and the setting of rake stones, boulders, spikes, tiger heads, and horse trippers outside the fort to prevent any horses from entering.[6] They have sent spies in all directions and ordered them to return daily to report whatever they hear. And they have sent sixty spies to the city of Vidyanagara alone. So, as you can see, everyone in the country of Bijapur is thinking of nothing but military planning and preparation. Even the people who live in the border tracts have heard of the matter, and they too have begun sending their own troops to Bijapur."[7]

Rayalu, Appaji, Ayyamarasu, and Kondamarasu had listened intently as the spies described all that they had seen and heard in Bijapur. "So," declared the king, "it seems that the *sthānāpatis* of Bijapur, Ahmadnagar, and Golconda have sent back reports concerning the developments that they have witnessed here, and that is why those kings have grown so cautious. The Adil Shah's ministers have decided on a plan of action to recommend to their lord, and that is why he has sent provisions and supplies to all the border tracts. How well prepared they are—just look at their strength and resources!"

Rayalu turned to the spies, gave them gifts, and then ordered them to return to Bijapur and continue bringing back reports of everything that happened from day to day. Then Rayalu sent away the servants who were nearby so that he could consult with Appaji and his other advisers. Here are the details of their discussion:

Rayalu said to Appaji and the others, "The Turks have heard of my resolve to launch a campaign against them, and now they have already begun to mobilize their own forces. But how are we to take their actions? Are they in fact bravely planning their own offensive, or are they merely cowards taking care to protect themselves?"

In answer to the king's question, Appaji and the others said, "You know how a dignified and courageous king would act in such a situation. If something alarming should be reported from one of the quarters, he does not worry about it immediately. But, within a few days, he will start a rumor to the effect that the feudatory ruler of the province in that quarter will be paying an inspection visit, and that gets the local commanders going, securing the walls and bastions and setting in provisions and supplies. *That* is the courageous way of making preparations and assembling one's forces. No, what the Turks have done makes it clear that they are acting not out of courage but from a state of mental confusion."

Ayyamarasu and Kondamarasu agreed. "Yes indeed—what are the Turks but drunkards and opium eaters! It's because of their intoxication that they are always in a state of fear like this. Whenever they've been drinking, they don't even know their own bodies, so naturally they haven't the faintest idea of what they're doing. If someone happens to come in their way, they simply chop him to pieces. Indeed, they act like the demons of the Kali age. When they finally come back to their senses, they pause for a moment and reflect, 'Well, this is just the nature of our race, now isn't it? The brahmans, on the other hand, they aren't like us—thanks to their diet of rice with salt and *sambar,* they don't suffer from pride and malice.' Because they think in this way, they appoint only brahmans to serve the palace,[8] and then these brahmans do all the governing for them. Yes, it is solely on the advice of these brahmans that they appoint their commanders—called *nāmjād*—and make all the arrangements for governance. In fact, it is only through the good sense of these brahmans that they have been able to keep their kingdoms in order—things have gone however these advisers have steered them. If these advisers ever disagree among themselves, their lord threatens their lives—not realizing that it is his own position that he is really threatening! Naturally, the advisers of the Three Clans are always anxious to put aside their differences and reach a consensus so that they may proclaim what is to be done. Thus you can see that the Lords of the Three Clans are not their own masters[9] but are totally dependent on the advice of their ministers. They are unlike your lordship, who has the benefit of both his own initiative and the advice of others. Indeed, there is no equal for your lordship's manner of deciding policy.

"If all three of the Turk kings agree to unite in a single campaign against you, they would be able to muster 150,000 horses, 1,500 war elephants, and 300,000 foot soldiers. In order to defeat them, all you would need is a force that is twice that size. Would it ever be possible to gather that many horses in Karnataka?—hardly. Nor would it be necessary, as long as you use a force that is balanced between all three divisions. So take 12,000 salaried horsemen and 24,000 Amaranayaka horsemen, 50 salaried elephant divisions and 120 Amaranayaka elephant divisions, 300,000 salaried foot soldiers together with replacements, and 500,000 *amaraṃ* troops. If you assemble your force on this scale, then what can the Turks' campaign possibly amount to?

"On account of his own boldness, on account of his being favored by the gracious glances of the goddess of fortune, and on account of divine favor, our Rayalu will certainly be victorious. Indeed, as the elders are fond of saying,

Yato dhairyastato lakṣmīḥ yato lakṣmīstato hariḥ /
yato haristato dharmaḥ yato dharmastato jayaḥ //

Where there is boldness, Lakshmi will be found;
and where Lakshmi is, Vishnu will follow.
Wherever Vishnu is, there will be *dharma;*
and where *dharma* is found, victory will surely be seen.

You see, in the end, it is boldness that is more important than anything else, and you are clearly a bold man. Because of this, any action that you undertake will prove successful. Mere numbers of elephants, horses, and foot soldiers are not the cause of it. It is only through divine favor that kingdoms and continents can be ruled. Thanks to their possession of the divine command wheel, the first Six World Emperors were able to rule the seven continents without even moving from where they were. After them, there were the Sixteen Exemplary Kings who ruled the earth. Your lordship is graced with the favor of lord Venkateshvara, just as they were."

After considering the statements of his ministers, the king gave his order to Appaji and the others: "Let us proceed exactly as you have advised."

The king then inquired whether any more spies had returned with reports from distant places. Someone informed him that Arava Rama had just returned from Ahmadnagar and Fakir Gopaji from Golconda. The king dismissed those who were waiting on him and summoned the spies forward to tell what they had found out about those places.

"From the time we left Vijayanagara," they replied, "we hurried through numerous villages and towns until we finally reached Ahmadnagar and Golconda. At the various border points, they were interrogating all the foreigners, travelers, and people from other parts. Whenever they would find people who didn't have the proper papers, they would confront them and demand, 'Where are you coming from! To whose side do you belong!' Only after receiving a satisfactory answer would they send the frightened people on their way.

"Once you get to the city and have seen the outlying suburbs, you must get someone who knows you to vouch for you if you wish to enter the citadel. This acquaintance must declare that you are a friend or relative and that he agrees to be held responsible for any trouble you should cause while inside. Then they will give you a badge to wear on your head and send you on in—all you have to do is show that badge to the people at the gate, and they let you pass. As you are moving around inside the citadel, you must show this seal whenever you encounter one of the watchmen they call *kotwāl.*

"After wandering about inside the citadel for so many days, when you are ready to return to your own district, you must go and meet the first officer to get clearance. He takes his seal and stamps it onto your pass; you must show this seal to the watchman—the *kotwāl*—and then to the guards at the gate of the citadel. Only then will they permit you to leave.

"Thanks to our skill and resourcefulness, we were able to get through many such difficult moments and to explore that city carefully. One day, we saw an officer giving orders for punishments in front of the audience hall. People were being sliced in two at the waist or slowly cut apart with saws; others were tied up in gunny sacks and beaten with iron maces. Some were being flogged with strings that had sharp pieces of horn tied at the tips, while others had heavy stones tied to their feet and were then left to sit astride a ruined wall. Some were tied up in bundles and left to die in the hot sun. Some had their feet, hands, ears, or noses cut off. And this was not the end of it! They were going so far as to torture their own revenue officers in imaginative ways—some were even being crushed to death under the feet of elephants. Some of the frightened officers immediately made payments to the palace on witnessing these varied and horrendous acts of torture, and they were released with their lives. But there were others, however, who for some reason were simply unable to pay, and they were tortured to death right there in the middle of the street. The leaders and officials happily swore and cursed as they watched these atrocities.

"As soon as the torture was finished, the officers began assembling in front of the palace hall. They all salaamed when the principal chief and a few retainers appeared to them from on top of the hall. When he had finished with this appearance and was going back to the palace, the chief went along raised walkways that had been erected. He stood there in that raised position, looked down on the people crowding the surrounding courts, and ordered that they should be given the usual gifts and honors, each in his proper turn. Since there were stores of cash and gifts, sashes and tunics, turbans and turban bands, all right there in the various surrounding courts, the servants went and brought them immediately. They stood in front of the principal chief and distributed them to everyone. It seemed that everyone was present at court, but, no matter how many came forward, the chief ordered them all to be given food, and so each was given food. Then the chief went back into the palace.

"Some officials began to read out the reports that had come in from the four quarters, while the *nāmjāds* who commanded the elephants and several divisions of foot soldiers listened intently. When they had finished, the lords then began deliberating together, and this is what we were able to overhear:

" 'So Vijayanagara wants to attack Bijapur, Ahmadnagar, and Golconda. If they come and attack with their 300,000 horses, 1,000 elephants, and some number of foot soldiers, then fighting with them will be bad news indeed. For it seems certain that the king of Karnataka would not come alone from the south but that the king of Agra in the north and the Gajapati in the east would also show themselves. We serve none of those hostile Kings of the Three Lion-Thrones, the Ashvapati, Gajapati, and Narapati! As long as those Three Lion-Thrones haven't set their sights on us, we in the kingdoms of the Three Clans have been able to occupy and rule the boundary regions, surviving merely by the strength of our necks. But if they decide now that they are ready to fight with each other over our lands, and if for that reason they send us messages telling us to present ourselves for battle, it will be impossible for us to fight with them! It was only by fate—or perhaps by the power of Kartaru, our chief's patron god—that we came to be nobles and have dominated these borderlands for these sixty years. As long as there have been no kings for these lands, the Adil Shah, Qutb-al-mulk, and the Nizam Shah have taken the name. The king of Agra rules from Sindh to the Godavari, the king of Karnataka from Kerala to the Krishna, and the Gajapati king from Jagannatham to Bidar. As for us, we have the unconquerable forts in between that have not fallen to the Kings of these Three Lion-Thrones, and thus we have been able to grow like the Three Cities of legend. So perhaps there is nothing to fear.'

"As they were thus discussing things among themselves, a fellow named Tatkalikamati spoke up and addressed the rest. 'What you have said about the Three Cities is exactly right. When the mighty Demons of the Three Cities received a boon from Lord Shiva, they begged that their cities should be able to fly about wherever they desired and be unconquerable at the hands of any one of the gods, demons, or others. Once in every twelve years, the Three Cities would all come together for three and three-quarters hours to join in consultation, and then they would go off as usual to wander around at will.

" 'But, as you know, things went on like this only until the time had finally come for the lords of those Three Cities. The earth-goddess went to Brahma and Vishnu and complained that she could no longer bear the weight of those unrighteous demons. Lord Brahma took pity on her and said, "It is impossible for the Demons of the Three Cities to be vanquished by any one of us alone. But there is a way. You, goddess, become the chariot, and the four Vedas shall become your horses. Mount Meru will serve as the bow and the cosmic serpent Shesha as the bowstring. Vishnu who lies on the Ocean of Milk shall become the arrow, and three-eyed Shiva himself will be the archer.[10] Together, we shall bring the Three Cities crashing to the ground, and thus will those demons go to their destruction!"

" 'In the same way, if the Kings of the Three Lion-Thrones ever appear together to attack our "Three Cities" of Bijapur, Ahmadnagar, and Golconda, then we shall be in grave danger indeed—that much is certain!'

"When Tatkalikamati had finished speaking, the other ministers all said, 'That is no doubt true! But, even so, during however many days we have remaining to us, it is still our duty to advise our lords and carry out the affairs of state. We can't just sit here doing nothing. Now, our *muqims*[11] in Vijayanagara have sent messages informing us that, ever since Krishnaraya acceded to the Lion-Throne of Karnataka, his mind has been set on launching a campaign against us Turks. The Adil Shah has likewise been warned of this by his representatives, and, accordingly, they inform us that he has sent provisions and supplies to his border posts and ordered his command posts to strengthen his borders. He himself is waiting in a state of readiness in the capital. As for our own two clans, we must find worthy men and send them to our border forts and fortresses. And let us think ahead and decide what to do in the event we hear that the king of Karnataka has gathered his army, sallied forth, marched to our borders, and set up his battle camp.'

"So, at this point, Ahmadnagar and Golconda sent out 120 spies with orders to report daily on all further developments. Thus the spies came to Vidyanagara, wearing various disguises and speaking in many different languages.

"Once they had sent the spies, the ministers resumed their discussions. Wondering who would be the victor if Krishnaraya decided to attack the Turks, they summoned brahman fortunetellers, they called for fakirs who were skilled in interpreting the writings of the Mullahs, and they sent for soothsayers who knew past, present, and future. When they had posed the question to them, the various specialists all replied, 'A king has been born in Karnataka who is an emanation of Vishnu. This kingdom of yours—as well as the Ashvapati and Gajapati kingdoms—all are to be conquered by that king! He will plant his pillar of victory, and, on his return, he will go to worship Kalyana Venkateshvara, the 108 Temples of Vishnu, the Seventy-two Temples of Shiva, and the Eighteen Goddesses. He will go to Setu, where he will worship Ramanatha and wash his sword in the sacred waters at Dhanushkoti. Then for sixty-four years[12] he will be unopposed as he rules the entire realm from the Lion-Throne of Karnataka.'

"When they heard of this pronouncement of the soothsayers, all the local people—young and old alike—said, 'Yes, it will probably turn out just like that. These barbarians give no thought to their unrighteousness, their ruthlessness, their demonic acts. Will the earth-goddess be able to bear it much longer? Who knows, it will probably end up for them just as it did for the Demons of the Three Cities!' Speculating in this way, they all started back to their homes. We took the opportunity and followed these people out of the palace quarter.

"We joined company with a group of fakirs and left the city. Before long we met up with a group of pilgrims who were on their way from the Ganga to Dhanushkoti, so we followed behind them until we crossed the waters of the Krishna River and came to Karnataka. We removed our disguises and finally reached the city."

After the two spies Arava Ramudu and Fakir Gopaji had finished relating all that they had seen and heard in Ahmadnagar and Golconda, Appaji, Ayyamarasu, and Kondamarasu said to Rayalu, "Those Turkish domains sound like the kingdom of Yama himself, the god of death! Can anyone doubt that their cities are just like that and that the people who live there are the very messengers of death! Yet these men have gone to such places to gather their information! Yes, by the greatness of their king, they have gone to the cities and kingdoms of the barbarians and have passed through lands of a hundred different languages! They have had to rub shoulders with the likes of minstrels from Maharashtra, Gujarat, and Kanauj! They have endured all sorts of hardships to wander off to those cities. Their greatness of character is clear—would it even be possible for the weak spirited to go and come back?" Thus they praised the palace spies. Rayalu was so pleased that he gave them presents worth 500 *ghețțis*. Then he dismissed them, telling them to continue wandering about the various cities as usual and to report on developments from day to day.

Rayalu dismissed everyone else and then turned to his ministers: "You heard the reports of what's happening at Bijapur and at Ahmadnagar and Golconda. The people of those two houses have certainly grown suspicious—just look at the precautions they are taking. What do you think is really the cause for their fears?"

The ministers said, "Until now, there had never been any rumors of Vijayanagara planning to attack the Turks. Without any threat from your predecessors on the Lion-Throne, the Turks just went on happily minding their own affairs. But, now that your lordship has risen to the Lion-Throne, you have acted in ways that clearly display your munificence and power. Do you expect that these enemies of yours should not take notice and be concerned? What do you expect when every day you treat the *muqims* of the Three Clans so politely? They are intelligent men. You can be sure that they report back to their rulers and say, 'Lord, the occupant of the Lion-Throne in that city gives both wages and gifts to those who serve him. Whenever his *sthānāpatis* return to the court from afar, or if someone comes with a written report—or even if someone gives some information verbally—he walks right up to the person and honors him with presents of betel nuts and leaves. And, ever since that lord ascended the throne, what does he give to his standing army, to his cavalry troops?[13] Why, he orders them to be given cash from the treasury itself, and thus has he established a salaried force. If a lord who enjoys *amaraṃ* tenure dies, he annexes his district. He gives gifts and honors not only to his own servants but to the servants of other places as well, giving them appropriate amounts of cash. And he has nothing but friendly things to say about the Lords of the Three Clans.' The servants of the Lords of the Three Clans have been staying here in Karnataka for many days, and, moreover, since they have been studying works on royal conduct, they are growing wiser, and this is reflected in the reports they send."

Rayalu replied, "I just do not understand their reaction. I am not the kind of king who gets angry and shouts at people this way and that. Instead, I politely engage them in pleasant conversation and speak in such a way as to show respect and honor for their rulers."

Ayyamarasu said, "But that's precisely the point. Whenever your lordship speaks in a polite manner, that itself is sufficient cause for your enemies to worry. Why? It's just as it has been said in the verse on royal conduct:

> Is it really courtesy
> when a great man speaks politely?

Is it courtesy
  when a bow bends down at the tip—
    then jumps back up
    and looses a shaft
    that slays the man before it?[14]

Following the logic of this verse, the servants of the Three Clans grow suspicious when they reflect on all that they have seen and heard. They have read *Cāṇukya's Nīti,* so naturally they write their reports in the cautious way they do. The people back there read these reports, and then the ministers inform their king that they have studied the reports and concluded that this is the plan that should be implemented. That appears to be the cause of their preparations to fight with us."

When Ayyamarasu had finished talking, Appaji and the rest of the ministers excused themselves and withdrew. Then the king summoned 'Ain-ul-Mulk, Ankusha Rao, Rana Jagadeva, Ganuti Timmappa Nayadu, Rachuri Rami Nayadu, Pemmasani Ramalingama Nayadu, Hande Malla Rao, and Boyi Ramappa, who were his Sons of the Eating Dish from the Eighteen Districts;[15] he also called the military commanders Apparapilla, Kupparapilla, Saluva Nayadu, Komara Timmappa, Sangaraju, Chervapradhani, Tipparasu, Ayyappa Nayadu, Kotakam Vishvanatha Nayadu, Chevvappa Nayadu, Akkappa Nayadu, Krishnappa Nayadu, Velugoti Yachama Nayadu, Kannada Basavappa Nayadu, Saluva Makaraju, Matla Anantaraju, Timmaraju, Viramaraju, and others; he summoned the Reddi princes Bommi Reddi, Naga Reddi, Basuva Reddi, and others; he called for the Kamma Nayakas led by Vithalappa Nayadu; he called for his Sons and Sons-in-Law, for the government officials, and for all the other Amaranayakas.[16] He asked them all how they were and then asked, "How many elephants, horsemen, foot soldiers, and retainers do you have?"

At that, the *sthānāpatis* who served Vithalappa Nayadu, together with a kinsman of Parashurama Nayadu, a man named Virabhadrayya, who was one of the *sthānāpatis* of the Amaranayakas, and Dalapati Rayadu all came forward and together said to Rayalu,

"After your lordship established the salaried army, the various people of the *amaraṃ* districts have reassembled horses and elephants, horse riders and elephant drivers, foot soldiers and retainers, all according to the figures established by the palace. Things are not as they used to be! Now they keep themselves prepared for whatever royal tasks your lordship may wish to undertake at any time. As you have seen fit, you have sent accountants to count our forces. And, whenever these officers have come and taken count, it has turned out that the Amaranayakas have maintained even more than the amounts assessed by the palace—ten extra elephants, 100 extra horses, and 1,000 extra foot soldiers. Since they have subsisted all these days on your lordship's wealth, they have become perfectly willing to provide what is needed for the palace's undertakings."

Rayalu was extremely pleased to hear this. He then held full court with all his Amaranayakas. He addressed 'Ain-ul-Mulk and Ankusha Rao, "You used to live in Bijapur and have spent many days there. In fact, we have even heard it said that you were lords there long before the Adil Shah came to power. You also know about the circumstances of their neighbors to the north and east, the Nizam Shah and Qutb-al-Mulk. Tell us, then, just how was it that they rose to power?"

Here are the details of 'Ain-ul-Mulk's reply to Rayalu:[17] "There was long ago a fifteen years' war between the sultan of Delhi—who is one of the Kings of the Three Lion-Thrones of the Ashvapati, the Gajapati, and the Narapati—and Prataparudra, king of Warangal.[18] At one point during that war, the supplies and provisions in Prataparudra's forts and citadels ran out, so Prataparudra—who felt that it would not be in accordance with *dharma* simply to let his subjects die—came outside the citadel to make one bold last stand. While he was fighting outside, Prataparudra was injured by the hand of the sultan, who must have been able to hit his mark through some divine favor. The sultan sounded the victory drums and marched back to Delhi with Prataparudra as his captive. When the sultan's mother heard this news, she asked her son if she might see the famous Prataparudra. He replied that she should look at him sometime while he was asleep. That very night the sultan's mother went in and looked at Prataparudra of Warangal as he slept. She soon came back and scolded her son. 'He's not a human being at all—he's an emanation of Shiva himself! Why, I saw him lying there with his trident and drum! Is it proper for you to have captured such a king as that?'

"The sultan smiled and replied, 'Because you looked at him as he slept, Prataparudra appeared to you as an emanation of Shiva, isn't that so? Well, why don't you take a look at me sometime while I'm sleeping.' That night, after the sultan had gone to bed, she went and looked, and there he was in the form of Vishnu, lying on the cosmic serpent Shesha together with the goddess Lakshmi. He had his conch, discus, and mace and was marked with the *śrīvatsa* and the *kaustubha* gem. When she saw this, she was astonished and thought to herself, 'Why, shame on you! If you're really this great a being, then is it right for you to have captured Prataparudra?'

"The next day she said to the Delhi sultan, 'You know your own greatness. If you lay out a feast and feed Prataparudra, show him respect and honor, and then send him back to Warangal, your fame will last forever.' On the advice of his mother, the sultan saw to Prataparudra's satisfaction by letting him bathe, and then he served him a meal. When he had thus shown him respect and honor, the sultan sent him back to Warangal. I am sure you have heard this story!

"Well, sometime after this, a fellow named Barid of Bidar[19] conquered some territory and took some forts, and, thus strengthened, he began to rule his kingdom. His hawk keeper came to be known as Nizam Shah, his water-pot bearer became known as Adil Shah, and the man who was in charge of keeping the dogs became known as Qutb-al-Mulk. Each of the three was given charge over a province: the Adil Shah ruled Bijapur, the Nizam Shah Ahmadnagar, and Qutb-al-Mulk Golconda. When he gave them charge of these provinces, Barid of Bidar declared, 'Your stewardship will last for one hundred years.' Among the three, the Nizam Shah is the eldest, then comes the Adil Shah, and last is Qutb-al-Mulk. So it was in this order that they received their thrones and were given gifts and honors such as betel nuts and leaves. These three houses have good horses by the thousands and a hundred elephant divisions. It is not, however, a kingdom that employs foot soldiers, nor are there any Turks there who have the experience of having served our side. Since here in Karnataka we use a four-limbed army—which includes foot soldiers—the people of that land just don't understand the battle techniques practiced here. For that simple reason, those Turkish lords would never be able to hold their ground before the king of Karnataka."

When 'Ain-ul-Mulk had finished telling what he knew, Ankusha Rao and Rana Jagadeva agreed, "Yes, it's just as 'Ain-ul-Mulk has said."

'Ain-ul-Mulk continued, "You see, my lord, when the Turks set out for the battlefront, they don't proceed cautiously, gauging themselves with the opposing force. Instead, they just advance obstinately. If it so happens that they outnumber and defeat the opposing force, then, no matter how fast the other soldiers flee, the Turks will keep coming and massacring them. If, on the other hand, the opposing force stands firm, then they beg their commanders to let them go back. When the strategists back at the palace get word of this, they decide that fighting a battle is not the right thing to do under the circumstances, so they order the forces to be recalled, and you can be sure that those men retreat as fast as they can. And, believe it or not, when the message that they should return reaches the battlefront, they don't even stop to consider the disgrace that they will cause their ruler by retreating. The people of Karnataka, on the other hand, they have the power of discrimination; they know the difference between what can be done and what cannot. Once the decision has been made to fight, then, even if all seems hopeless, in the thick of battle you do not lose your resolve. With a clear conscience you can go ahead and order your men to march forward and meet the foe, and all those foot soldiers will rise bravely to the task because yours is the power of a real master."

When he had said this, all the other Amaranayakas nearby agreed and shouted in unison, "Hear, hear! The man is right!"

Rayalu said, "Whether in attack or retreat, you men truly know how to fight! Whether in victory or defeat, you know that everything will be just fine! It is clear now that we must launch an attack on the Turks. All of you, go wash your hair and prepare for the march!"[20] Giving gifts of betel nuts and leaves to each, he dismissed them.

·5·

Account of the Gajapati Kingdom

A little while later, the king was talking with Appaji and his other trusted friends when the spies Vayuvegi Hanumantayya and Manovegi Purushamrigayya were ushered in. They had just returned from the city of Shripurushottamam[1] in the Gajapati kingdom. They stood before the king and submitted their report. Here are the full details of what they told Rayalu:

"Hurrying on our way from Vidyanagara, we went to the Gajapati kingdom to survey its various districts. We inspected Rajahmundry, Cuttack, and some other places; finally, since Mukunda Bahubalendra Gajapati was staying in the presence of Lord Jagannatha, we went to Shripurushottamam. It was just like the verse that describes the beauty of Lord Krishna's city:

> Whichever way you look—
> radiant assembly halls
> adorned with the glow
> of golden vases.
>
> Whichever street you take—
> doorways to homes
> decked with mirrors,
> stalks of sugar cane,
> and plantain.
>
> Whichever way you go—
> the splendor of brave warriors,
> hosts of riders,
> horses, and elephants.

Whichever direction you turn—
  wafting scents
  of camphor and musk
  from the breasts
  of doe-eyed women.

Look where you will,
it is a garden of many pleasures
made from gold and precious gems.

Such is the beauty
of a city rich and glorious.[2]

"Shripurushottamam was just such a place—the very crown of beauty! When we looked around, we saw people who had come from every quarter of the earth just to attend the great festival of Jagannatha: there were householders and mendicants, forest dwellers and students, excellent brahmans fair in limb, kshatriyas, vaishyas, shudras, and the rest of the eighteen castes. They all came to behold Lord Jagannatha. How is one to describe the greatness of Tarakabrahma Jagannatha who resides in that temple, which is a veritable Vaikuntha paradise for the Kali age! They distribute the lord's *pirasād* there without distinguishing between 'your people' and 'our people'; instead, everyone takes it together. So great is the power of Jagannatha that no one who comes to his temple even worries about purity and impurity or considers the pollution that would ordinarily come from mixing with people of other classes.[3] How is one to describe everything that was going on there, and how can one possibly do justice to the power and serenity of that place? To describe it would be impossible even for the cosmic serpent Shesha, with his thousand heads and two thousand tongues!

"Mukunda Gajapati woke up in the hours before dawn and started the day by receiving the auspicious sight of two excellent brahmans. Then, accompanied by the Sixteen Patras,[4] he went out a distance of two or three leagues to answer the call of nature. When he had come back again, he washed his face and affixed the Vaishnava sectarian mark on his forehead. He drank some holy water and then began his morning rituals by performing the worship of the planets. Then, following the methods used in the worship of Jagannatha, he performed *pūjas* involving the sixteen reverential acts, praised the god by reciting his thousand names, gave him food offerings, worshiped him with lamps and flowers, and honored him by means of circumambulations.

"By the time he emerged from the inner chambers,[5] the *sthānāpatis* of the other rulers[6] had already assembled before the temple. There were such men as Anantoji Pantulu, who represented the lord of Agra; Madhavayya, who represented Man Singh;[7] Chennagirayya, the representive of the lord of Chand; Karunakarayya, who represented the lord of Cuttack;[8] Obalayya, representing the lord of Warangal; Dhakoji Pantulu, the representative of the sultan of Delhi; Bekoji Pantulu, representing the lord of Bidar; Gopaji Pantulu, representative of the lord of Golconda; Ayyapparaju,[9] representing the lord of Ahmadnagar; Viramaraju, representing the lord of Bijapur; and Purandarayya of Burhanpur and Baboji Pantulu of Baganagaram. These and the other resident *sthānāpatis* had taken their baths at sunrise and had already performed their early morning prayers. They had put on clean *dhotis* of white silk and draped fresh shawls across their shoulders, and now they came bringing pure and flavorful food offerings with which to worship Jagannatha. Once they had all seated themselves in the hall of Lakshmi before the god's *pūja* chamber, the Gajapati king came out and made himself comfortable on a golden seat inlaid with the nine jewels. The assembled men summoned their respective *purāṇa* reciters and listened to their recitations. Then, as a group of trusted scholars chanted benedictions, the Gajapati king went forward to collect all the offerings that had been presented to the god—sacred ash, scents, pressed rice, coconuts, breadfruits, and other such things. He took the offerings with both hands, placed them reverently on his head, and brought them out to the assembly. He distributed the *prasād*—consisting of cakes, areca nuts, and betel leaves—to the *purāṇa* reciters and the *sthānāpatis* and then sent them back to their residences.

"He then summoned another brahman and began to wash his feet. He worshiped the brahman's feet in the proper way, using scents, pressed rice, and flowers. When he had finished, he presented the brahman with 100 *gheṭṭis* of areca nuts and betel leaves. Then he took the water that had been sanctified by contact with the brahman's feet and strained out the dust that had been washed off in the ceremonial act. This he applied to his own forehead; then he sipped the water itself.

"After that, he went to eat with his family and relatives. He told them all to set out their golden dishes and then gave the order for the food to be served to them where they sat, without leaving anything left over. He drew a curtain at one place near the line where everyone sat and seated himself behind it on a comfortable seat made from the nine jewels. He took his own dish, which was made from 100 seers of eighteen-karat gold,[10] and he placed a magnificent and valuable topaz in the center of it. His food was served on this dish. While he ate, he was attended by maidservants who watched carefully to make sure that, once he had mixed a curry with rice, he would not mix the same curry again and that, once he had picked up something and munched on it, he would not munch on the same thing again.[11] If, unaware, he was about to touch something a second time, they would tap his hand with a bamboo rod, and, since he was not supposed to touch anything again, he would pull back his hand before he had actually made contact with it. After he had tasted all the different dishes, he got up and washed his hands. Then he walked one hundred steps while someone recited the *Shorter Rāmāyaṇa*.[12]

"When his meal was finished, the king adorned himself with fine clothes and ornaments in preparation for the assembly of his full court. As everyone sat at the palace gateway, the Gajapati came into the single-storied audience hall[13] and seated himself. He summoned a court officer, who directed the courtiers to seat themselves according to their respective ranks. In accordance with the occasion, he began to converse with the Sixteen Patras and the foreign officers.

"Niladripantulu—who represented the Nizam Shah—and the *sthānāpatis* of the Adil Shah and Qutb-al-Mulk together addressed the king: 'According to the reports we have received, the lord of Karnataka has begun to mount an attack. He has assembled his fourfold army and marched out, and he has come to the border regions and made himself seen. Our lords have all along sent you their support, for better or for worse, and assisted you in the battles you have fought with the lords of the north and the south. You will remember, for example, that our masters all agreed to support you in your war against the king of Agra in the north because that was such a major conflict. Now this is certainly not going to be anything as serious as that; in fact, it should most likely be enough if you just stay prepared and watch carefully from your own border. Our masters the Adil Shah, the Nizam Shah, and Qutb-al-Mulk all three are strong in their border defenses, so there does not seem to be any cause for real concern. But, if things should turn out to be more serious than we have expected, be forewarned that the enemy may try to enter your territory and march as far as the outpost of Ahmadnagar, near Kondavidu.

" 'Of course, it is never pleasant to assume that one will be defeated in battle. But, if victory should happen to favor the lord of Karnataka, leaving our Lords of the Three Clans crushed in the borderlands, then your own frontier will be threatened, and a great calamity will be upon you! Therefore, we urge you to think carefully about what must be done and to take precautionary measures before it is too late!'

"When the representatives of the Three Clans had given their advice to the Gajapati king, he reprimanded them by saying, 'We have nothing to fear—our divine protector Lord Jagannatha is here to take care of everything.'

"The representatives of the Three Clans were growing impatient. 'Yes,' they replied, 'your Jagannatha is here, and the Kartaru of our own masters is there, but that has not stopped them from setting up encampments to prevent the lord of Karnataka from crossing the Krishna River. Why don't you order your officers to strengthen your own border points?'

"The Gajapati lord finally agreed, saying, 'All right, I shall do as you say.' He sent officers to the forts at Kondavidu, Udayagiri, Bellamkonda, Nagarjunakonda, Kondur, and other places, to tell the commanders that they must be ready and prepared for an attack. Then he advised the Sixteen Patras that they should likewise prepare themselves and be cautious; so they too sent extra supplies and provisions to their respective provinces and forts.

"This was not all. Mukunda Gajapati went on to give the Sixteen Patras further orders: 'I am beginning to fear for my own safety during our daily expedition to bathe in the Godavari River.[14] Given the time that it takes to get there, bathe, perform the *pūja* for Jagannatha, and return, it means that, by the time we finally reach the city again, we have spent close to six hours away from the safety of the capital. I think we should be more cautious. I want you to make sure that there is no one present within the space of one league surrounding that bathing ghat. Make it so empty that there is not a sound to be heard.'

"Starting the next day, the Sixteen Patras carried out his orders. They spread out and stationed themselves as guards to make the area totally secure. Eight horsemen positioned themselves in the area to the north of the Godavari. The Gond Forests were nearby and posed an additional threat: if the Mughal cavalry were ever to attack from that direction, it would be impossible to detect them among the shadows until it was far too late. So, in order to avert this potential disaster, four more horsemen went on reconnaissance in that direction. Two other horsemen stayed within two leagues of the spot, circling around continuously to make sure that no one else was moving about in the vicinity, and the last two riders stayed right with the Gajapati lord on the riverbank. In this way, sixteen horsemen vigilantly protected him. The Gajapati lord had his bath and performed his morning prayers, and then, after he had performed the *pūja* for Jagannatha, he immediately returned to town.

"One day, the Gajapati king came to the spot for his bath and ordered the Sixteen Patras to assume their usual guard positions. The king had his bath and then immersed himself in the performance of his rituals. The sixteen horsemen were guarding him that day in the usual way, with two riders staying by the bathing ghat, four riders moving about in the shadows of the Gond Forests, and so on.

"That day it just so happened that there were some enemy lords who had climbed a hill some distance away. When they saw the Gajapati bathing, they assessed the situation and said, 'There is the Gajapati! He has come with his horsemen for a bath in the Godavari. If we hurry and charge right now with our four thousand Turkish horsemen, we will be able to encircle him.' These four lords raised their standards, sounded their drums, and charged off in an ambush that violated all sense of propriety. Hearing the din of the charging horses, elephants, riders, and elephant drivers, the four horsemen who were riding around in that area spurred their steeds on and clashed with the attacking force. The four enemy lords and their four thousand horsemen surrounded these four horsemen, but that did not stop them from clashing with the four thousand. The four charged the group simultaneously in four different directions, striking out and cutting their foes in half, six to one blow. The horses and riders were standing in formation, four or five hundred to a line. The Patras attacked several such lines until the riders had all fallen flat on the ground, split and dismembered, and the horses had scattered and run off. The four horsemen were exhausted but were able to hold their ground.

"Meanwhile, the eight horsemen who had been riding around north of the Godavari came back and were surprised to see the fallen Turkish horses. The other four horsemen said, 'Some have perished in the fray; but there were others who simply scattered and fled when they realized they couldn't face the battle. We don't know just how many horsemen have either fled or perished.' The four battle-weary horsemen joined up with the other eight horsemen, and together all twelve rode back to find the Gajapati.

"Meanwhile, the two horsemen who had been waiting by the king happened to notice the Turks, who by now had regrouped and were preparing to attack again. The two men hurriedly rode back to the king from the east side of the bathing ghat. Just then, the Gajapati himself happened to look up and see the Mughal horses charging toward him. Immediately realizing that it would be disastrous for him to remain there any longer, he jumped on his horse, crossed the river, and rode off some distance with the Patras. But he had forgotten all about Jagannatha since his mind was on the attacking horsemen. It wasn't long before he realized his mistake. 'Now look what we've done,' he thought to himself. 'We've forgotten all about Jagannatha and ridden off without him.' He turned to look back toward the bathing ghat and saw that the enemy horsemen had led their tired and thirsty horses down to the north bank of the river to drink. He stopped in his tracks. 'I forgot to put Jagannatha back into his divine *pūja* box,' he confessed to his men. 'We've come all this way with just the empty box!'

" 'No need for your lordship to get so upset about it,' declared one of the Sixteen Patras when he realized how distressed his lord was. 'I'll go back and get him.'

"The Patra excused himself and rode back. He searched around the spot in the river where the king had worshiped, and, finding Jagannatha lying there, he picked him up and put him carefully back in the divine *pūja* box. Just as he was ready to ride off, some of the other horsemen spotted him and began to chase after him, but the Patra boldly turned and cut them to pieces. He crossed the river, rejoined the others, and presented the box containing Jagannatha to his greatly pleased lord.

"The Gajapati was pondering the pointless fray and trying to remember whether there had been any evil portents earlier that morning when the men who had just fought interrupted his revery. 'Although you did not realize it, we were engaged in a fight a short time ago, and we succeeded in killing many enemy horses and riders.' The king expressed his gratitude and presented gifts of areca nuts and betel leaves to the twelve horsemen who had combated the Mughal horsemen as well as to the lone Patra who had ridden back to get Jagannatha.

"As the party proceeded on its way back to the capital, the other three Patras were disturbed by the fact that they had not been able to join in the morning's battle. One of these three happened to be riding in front of the Gajapati when they came to a woody area and found their path obstructed by an enormous branch. The Patra coolly drew his 'death blade'[15] and hewed off the branch with a single blow. The Gajapati king was so impressed by this act that he gave presents to that Patra.

"As they rode on, the remaining two Patras grew even more upset that there had been no way for them to display their prowess. Suddenly, however, they rounded a corner and found the way blocked by an enormous branch from a tamarind tree, as big around as the height of four men combined. One of these two riders spurred his horse and leapt up into the air like a gazelle. Holding onto his horse with his thighs, he grabbed the branch of the tamarind tree in his two hands and flew on, pulling the branch out of the way. The Gajapati king watched in amazement as the man flew through the air on his horse, brandished his sword twenty or thirty times, and then landed on the ground again, still mounted. The king was so pleased that he gave gifts to the Patra.

"By the time they drew near to the Godavari, there was only one Patra left who had not yet been honored by his lord. But then the Patra found a canal blocking his path, fifteen feet deep and sixty-four feet wide. Without hesitating, he spurred his horse and leapt right over it. The Gajapati king watched approvingly and gave gifts to this last rider. Now that each man had pleased his lord, they all rode cheerfully back to the city.

"After we had witnessed all of this, we came back to the city ourselves. We looked around and saw the king's palaces, the houses of the Sixteen Patras, and their arena for sword practice. We stopped to watch the swordsmen who were practicing there—their skill is so great that neither gods nor demons would be any match for them. No doubt your majesty has witnessed the skills of incomparable wrestlers from other lands, but the Gajapati wrestlers' style is altogether unique! They don't just lift the barbells; they go so far as to lift them crosswise. And do you know what else they do? They take a two-hundred-pound dummy made out of gunnysacks, lift it as high as a man's upraised arms, and then heave it down on themselves. They catch that massive gunnysack between their legs and hold it there while hanging from a cross beam. You may be wondering why they do this. Well, sometimes in battle an enemy rider will swoop by and attempt to grab a horseman under his arm. You see, if the captive horseman puts up a good fight without letting go of his horse, then the other horseman will have to give up. These men with their armored horses do not show the least fear, not even in the midst of a raging battle. So the others try to catch them under their arms and whisk them from their mounts. It takes a lot of strength to stay mounted when the enemy does that—and of course skill and confidence as well—so that's why they practice in this way. And then there are the damask steel 'death blades'[16] they use, so heavy that they must be carried on a porter's head. Well, they can take those death blades and completely demolish a hundred-yard wall so that nothing will be left standing. With that sword they can cut through the bole of a tamarind tree just as though they were slicing a pithy banana stalk. They can even plant two crowbars in the ground and slice them to pieces with that blade! They take rods of iron out of a basket and twist four or five of them together, and then, since the blacksmiths can't get them apart, these men take them apart with a sledgehammer, beat them straight, and return them to the blacksmiths the next day. And their aim is amazing—they can take aim and break an iron cudgel in exactly the spot you tell them to. Our wrestlers could never acquire that kind of skill. Why, if they were ever to go there and watch, they'd have to return home in shame.

"We've never seen the likes of that kingdom anywhere—so strong and prosperous! And we might add that, whenever the Gajapati king presents a gift—no matter to whom—he gives an elephant, a horse, a necklace, a pair of pearl earrings, a sash, cap, and shirt, and areca nuts and betel leaves. He doesn't just dismiss them with areca nuts and betel leaves, as is the practice in this kingdom."

When the spies had finished reporting everything they had seen and heard and all the discussions they had overheard as well, Appaji spoke up. "Yes," he said to Rayalu, "the Gajapati king is a great man. He's not like the Turks—he has faith in gods and brahmans, you can be sure of that. Let me tell you what happened once. Some enemies of Mukunda Bahubalendra Gajapati once decided to bribe the priest in the temple of Jagannatha and thus win him over to their side. Every day during the worship of Jagannatha, this priest would take the holy water and *prasād* to distribute it to the worshipers, but he was not in the habit of consuming any himself. So one day the enemies instructed the priest to put some powder prepared from the root of the deadly *vatsanābhi* into the holy water before giving it to the king. The priest agreed to this treachery and mixed in the poison as directed. Perhaps it was because he was standing right there in the presence of Lord Jagannatha, but for some reason the priest became so nervous that his hands began to shake. The Gajapati noticed this and asked, 'Why are your hands trembling like that?'

"The terrified priest was too frightened even to speak. The Gajapati looked him right in the eye and demanded, 'Just why are you so frightened? Tell me the truth at once!'

"Finally the priest broke down and confessed, telling the full details of what the enemy kings had done. To the priest's utter astonishment, however, the Gajapati did not even become angry.

Instead, he only said, 'Give me that poisoned water.' He took it from the priest and began reciting a verse:

> *'arir mitraṃ viṣaṃ pathyam adharmo dharmatāṃ vrajet /*
> *anukūle jagannāthe viparīte viparyayām //*
>
> Enemy becomes friend,
> poison harmless water,
> and wrong becomes right–
> With Jagannatha on your side,
> even adversity turns to favor.'

As he finished the verse, he raised the poisoned holy water to his lips and swallowed it–it was digested with no problem. This incident has now become famous throughout the world. As you can see, he is truly a man who knows the way of God."

Marveling at the Gajapati's excellence of character, Rayalu gave thousands of bundles of areca nuts and betel leaves to the spies. He told them to continue traveling from land to land, bringing back reports of whatever further incidents they might learn. And thus he dismissed Vayuvegi Hanumantayya and Manovegi Purushamrigayya.

·6·

The Battle with the Turks

Rayalu spoke in private with Appaji, "Tell me, now that you have heard for yourself the news from all the lands—don't you think that we should go ahead and set out for battle with the Turks? The *amaraṃ* chiefs are already prepared and waiting. Why don't you call the astrologers and have them set an auspicious time for starting our march."

Just as he was told, Appaji summoned the astrologers, and they decided on the auspicious day, period, and moment at which the battle tent[1] should be set up as well as the times at which the king should march out to the encampment and enter the tent. The king was informed of their decisions, and he gave the order for the battle tent to be set up in accordance with that plan.

As they were thus preparing for their campaign against the Turks,[2] Appaji and Rayalu summoned all the Boya lords. The king gave a feast in the palace for the lords of the Eighteen Districts. After the meal, he addressed those Sons of the Eating Dish as follows: "As our first action, I want you to ride ahead into the territory of the Turks. Fan out quickly and raid all the areas within a distance of three leagues from the border. I want you to pillage those lands until there is not a single man, cow, sheep, goat, or horse remaining."[3] Then they came out from the palace together with the vanguard and all their equipment and marched to the battle tent. Standing in front of the tent, the king assembled all the other chiefs and nobles, all the horsemen and elephant riders, the hordes of officers, the vanguard, the rearguard, and the guards of the flanks, and he spoke with each in turn. He summoned the Amaranayakas of the Balavankam family, the salaried palace forces, and the nine palace treasurers, saying, "Come with all your forces and equipment."

"Take a count," he told the treasurers, "to see if the numbers of elephants, horses, horse riders, and the rest tally with the figures set by the palace, and call the hordes of suppliers—both those of the Karnataka kingdom[4] and those who are independent—and the Poligars. Make sure that all the forces are up to the figures set by the palace, and then start marching." Then he gave specific orders to the various supply officers—the accountants, clerks, butchers, grain distributors, and petitioners.

He ordered Saluva Timmarasu to stay behind with a small force of horsemen to protect the city of Vijayanagara, and then he proclaimed, "Beat the drums! Strike the tabors! Let the four quarters resound with the sounds of victory for our campaign!" He told messengers to go to the horsemen and elephant riders, to the Amaranayakas, Sons, and Sons-in-Law, to the Rajas, to the troops, and to the Kamma Nayakas and to announce to all of them that the march was starting. Then he himself went in and had his meal. After finishing, he came out and ordered the third and last drum to be beaten. He mounted his horse and started the march.

First the army went to Ummattur-Shivasamudram and attacked Ganga Rao's city.[5] They surrounded and suffocated it, capturing the place in just one day. The king left some loyal officers there and then marched on to the fort at Shrirangapatnam, where he inspected the ramparts and bastions and worshiped the Lord Adi-Ranganayaka. He continued on to Ikkeri and inspected Sukkula Nayudu's troops.

He ordered his army to march on into the borderlands of Bijapur. When the archers and soldiers stationed in the forts there saw the massive force advancing before them, they left their posts and fled, without offering the slightest defense. The king was able to occupy the forts at Raichur, Mudgal, Addanki, Adoni, and so on, even on the first day of fighting.

Rayalu posted occupation forces in all the captured forts and marched on toward the borders of Golconda. There, the horsemen of the Three Clans had already sallied forth and crossed the river, digging trenches and setting up camp on the other side. Some of the king's spies had discovered this and returned to inform the king of their strength and numbers: "The Turks have crossed the Krishna River with 100,000 horses and a thousand elephants, and they have established their camp. But you will be glad to know that our men have not been sitting idle either. They have already penetrated three leagues into Golconda's territory and pillaged all the villages lying within that zone. They have cleaned out all their grain stores, they have burned their fields, and they have entered the homes of every householder and taken all their carefully hidden savings. They have burned down entire villages, after first rounding up all the cattle, sheep, goats, and horses and selling them to our own villagers for just a single coin each. They have certainly done an impressive job of devastating that territory. And the men stationed in our forts are all ready and waiting for battle."

When he heard that the Turks had crossed the Krishna River and set up their battle tent within his own territory, Rayalu grew furious.[6] He summoned Pemmasani Ramalingama Nayadu[7] from among his Amaranayakas and said, "It seems that the Turks have already crossed the river and pitched their battle tent! This means that they are taking the offensive after all and that they intend to fight to the finish. What can we possibly do now to respond to this affront?"

Pemmasani Ramalingama Nayadu replied, "What can the Turks' campaign possibly ever amount to? By your greatness, my lord, I will go and cut the ropes of their battle tent. If you sound the battle drums and march forward at that very moment, I will see to it that the Turks of the Three Clans will scatter and flee back to their own territories, every man for himself. Besides, even if we were not able to rout them right here and now, how would they ever be able to withstand the terrible heat and thirst of summer? No, my lord—we have nothing to fear! With your leave, I shall carry out this plan."

Rayalu was exceedingly pleased to hear this idea, and so he gave little bundles of *pān* to Ramalingama Nayadu in token of his favor. Ramalingama Nayadu took leave of the king and came back outside, where he summoned all the nobles of his own Kamma caste. Raising his folded hands to greet them, he said, "All these days we have been eating and living off our wages from Rayalu. And now, the lord who has maintained us has a task he needs done! He has ordered us to go and attack the enemy who has brazenly marched on us. Look at this—he has sent me with this gift of betel nuts and leaves! The gift is yours, so I expect nothing but manliness from you. You will be the foundation and life for future generations of our Kamma caste, and you can live on forever in the praise that will always be on others' lips! So step forward, all of you who will come with me to embrace the pleasures of heaven!"

As he jumped and danced about excitedly to urge them on, eighty thousand soldiers came forward as bridegrooms for the battle. Leaving the hopes and worries of this world, they eagerly joined Ramalingama Nayadu, and, indeed, each considered himself as fortunate as if the battle he was marching off to was a waiting bride.

When the Turks learned of this, they placed sixty thousand armored horsemen around the tent, and they waited with their swords drawn. Circling around these men, they posted another ten thousand fully armored horses, and again, around these, they placed a thousand rutting elephants as still further protection. Thus did the Turks of the Three Clans guard their battle tent and wait in readiness in their respective camps.

As soon as Ramalingama Nayadu approached the people in the Turks' camp, he and his men dismounted and jumped up onto the elephants' backs with their swords and shields. They sported around on top of the elephants like lion cubs frolicking on the slopes of a mountain. They cut the maddened elephants' trunks to pieces, and they pierced the elephant drivers with their spears and made the elephants trample them to death. They lifted the mail off the horses' backs and stabbed them with short spears, hafted spears, and pig prods. They sliced them up just like cucumbers, six slices to the blow. Rather than waiting around to be subjected to this torture, the terrified horsemen who still had a chance tried to ride off in whatever direction they could. But, even so, Ramalingama Nayadu's brave men managed to fell four thousand horses so that the carnage lay as smooth and flat as a sandbar, and then they fell on the unmounted riders, who stood with their swords drawn and ready to fight. Four thousand of these riders fell in the hand-to-hand combat with six thousand of Ramalingama Nayadu's men.

Meanwhile, Ramalingama Nayadu cut the tent ropes as he had promised, and, at the very moment that the tents were flying to the ground, Krishnaraya sounded the battle drum and mounted his war elephant. With his two royal parasols and his crocodile banners, he marched forward with his force of 120 elephant units, 60,000 horses, and 500,000 foot soldiers, all keeping in tight formation.

It just so happened that, at that same moment, both banks of the Krishna River began to swell up in flood. The elephants of the Turks were exhausted from the battle and the heat and had built up a tremendous thirst, so no sooner had they sensed the cool breeze that was coming with the rising water than they began to run for the river. Many of the Turkish horsemen realized that, if the river were to flood and cut off their supplies, it would no longer be possible for them to fight from this side, so they immediately turned around and followed the elephants. The three chiefs of the Turks hurriedly discussed the situation with their advisers. "Now this is a fine fate!" they exclaimed in panic. "The river is swelling up, and here we are with our camp set up on this side. If the river cuts off our supplies from the rear, we'll never succeed in fighting from this position. Let's hurry and cross back over the river and retrench ourselves on the other side!"

But, just as the armies of the Turks were ready to cross, the river filled completely in a rushing torrent. Rayalu took advantage of their plight by attacking from the rear. The Turks panicked and tried to flee: some jumped headlong into the river, and about half of them drowned in the swirling waters; another group just stood dumbfounded on the southern bank. The elephants were by now happily drinking in the middle of the river, and not one of them could be persuaded to head for shore, so their drivers panicked. Thinking it unsafe to remain in the middle of the river any longer, they dismounted, only to be swept away with their lives. As for the leaders of the Three Clans of Turks, they climbed from the elephants' backs into boats and headed for the safety of the northern bank. Once there, they took stock of the situation and concluded that it would be inappropriate to remain and fight at this time. So they gathered the survivors and rode off hurriedly in their respective directions, to Bijapur, Golconda, and Ahmadnagar.

Krishnaraya came up to the bank of the river and ordered his men to round up all the elephants and horses that the Turks of the Three Clans had left behind. "All these tents, banners, and kettledrums have fallen to us in the very first battle," said the king, "so round them up as well."

The king and his ministers turned and looked toward Mukku Timmayya[8] and the other great poets and asked, "How would you describe today's victory?" Timmayya replied with a verse,

"Krishnaraya the Man-Lion!
You slew the Turks from afar
  by the mere power of your great name.
O Lord of the elephant king!
At the mere sight of you
  the great host of elephants hurried away in fear."

·7·

The Gajapati Campaign

After Mukku Timmayya, Alasani Peddanna, Madanagari Mallayya, and all the other poets[1] had finished praising him, the ministers Appaji, Ayyamarasu, Kondamarasu, and Bacharasu addressed the king in voices of praise and suggested, "This time—thanks to the full flooding of the Krishna River—we have been able to defeat the barbarians and force them to retreat to their respective places. Once the waters of the river subside, we should continue forward in our campaign against them.[2] But, in the meantime, during these two months of Ashadha and Sravana, let us take the forts and strongholds of the Turks that lie south of the river as well as the garrisons and forts of the Gajapati. Then we will be free to march all the way up to Ahmadnagar."

"Your suggestion sounds quite sensible," replied the king. "And besides, were we to continue now and march against the barbarian kingdoms north of the river, then the forts in the Gajapati's territories would pose a threat to our success: surely the people manning those forts at Udayagiri, Kondur, Kondavidu, Bellamkonda, Nagarjunakonda, and Vinukonda would block the flow of supplies and equipment we would need for our campaign. We must not allow that to happen! Yes, let us first capture all those various provinces and post our own men in their forts. Then we can be sure that our supplies will move freely."

The elders with him considered the matter and soon agreed that the campaign should be continued in this manner. So the king called to all his horsemen and troops, all his chiefs and nobles, and gave them the orders to begin marching. He summoned the men who played the tabors, kettledrums, and horns and ordered them to sound the drums. As they began performing the *pūja* of the war drums, the thundering din that arose was almost unimaginable. Here is a verse to describe it:

> With an impetuous thirst for conquest,
> the lord of the world sounds the drums,
> striking terror in the hearts of his foes.
>
> As the drums' roar convulses the earth,
> surging waves pound the ocean's shores.
> Entire mountains are swept away,
> and the three worlds, unanchored,
> start to spin and reel.
> It is like the roar of towering thunderheads
> at the coming of the rains
> or the resonant bursting of the cosmic egg
> at the birth of time itself.[3]

When all the soldiers had assembled their gear and prepared themselves for the march, Rayalu mounted his horse and marched forward at the head of his well-armed force. He marched through Gutti and Gandikota on his way to Udayagiri, where his force stopped and scaled the walls of the fort known as Hurmattu. The people inside the fort fought for all they were worth, but, in the end, they were unable to withstand the barrage of canonballs, so they announced their intention to surrender. The armies of the king held their fire while the enemies left the fort, and then the king went up into the fort to look around. He was quite surprised to see that they had surrendered even though they still had so many supplies left. He left the fort in Kampanna's charge[4] and marched on to Kondur, where the people fled from the fort as soon as they heard the sound of the battle drums. The king entered the fort, inspected it, and left someone in charge.

The king marched on toward Kondavidu. The people manning the smaller forts there beheld the army advancing on them like the ocean pounding at the shore, and, when they saw the great clouds of dust rising up from the soldiers' feet and eclipsing the rays of the sun, they ran out of their forts in terror. Others fled in fear of the blaring horns that announced the advancing host. In this way, all the men manning the local forts and strongholds in the district of Kondavidu were easily driven away from their posts and ran off to join their chiefs.

Meanwhile, spies came from the various areas around the forts and reported to the king that all the inhabitants of these locales were terrified to hear reports that the Boya leaders and the lords of the Eighteen Districts were advancing with an infantry force 300,000 strong and overrunning all the districts within the sphere of the forts at Kondavidu, Kondapalle, Bellamkonda, Vinukonda, and Nagarjunakonda. To protect themselves, the local people were burning their own fields and fleeing to whatever fort happened to be nearest. Encouraged by this report, the king dismissed the spies and sent them back to their stations. He marched on to Kondavidu itself and began the battle. The enemy army fought for all they were worth: whenever they were about to lose their advantage, they would hurriedly retreat back into the fort, and, in this way, the fighting raged on for a day and a half. Finally, in the middle of the second night, the fort's defenses were broken, and the next morning the king went in to inspect the place, and he decided to leave Kondayya there as officer-in-charge.[5]

As the king continued his campaign and marched on to Vinukonda, the news of Kondavidu's fall preceeded him, leading the men of Vinukonda to conclude that they did not stand a chance. They left their posts and fled even before the battle started. The king marched in unopposed and posted Bhaskarayya to hold the fort. He took his army and marched on to Bellamkonda, where the men guarding the fort took flight as soon as they heard the reports of the king's guns. He left Virabhadrayya in charge and marched on with the troops to Nagarjunakonda. The men of Nagarjunakonda employed all kinds of stratagems throughout that day and the next, but, when they were unable to do anything more, they fled to their own home districts. So the king left Ayyalayya in charge there.

Finally, the king marched on all the way to Ahmadnagar,[6] where the vanguard of his army forced its way into the outlying hamlets and wrought havoc by raping and ransacking everything in sight. The enemy horsemen sallied out from the fort and met the king's forces in battle. Within a mere three and three-quarters hours, as many as twenty-eight hundred enemy horses had been bowled over and slain, together with their riders. When the fort's commander-in-chief received this news, he began to think, "Even if we continue to hold out in the fort, it is clear that reinforcements will never be able to reach us. That would certainly make things ugly for us! Whatever happens, we might as well just go ahead and call it quits now." He lost no time in fleeing from his post, and he was followed by all his men.

The king demolished the fort and went on to plow and sow every inch of ground in the surrounding hamlets with castor beans and swallowworts. Then he departed from that place and resumed his march toward the Gajapati kingdom.

As they were marching, Appaji came and spoke with Rayalu: "You have wrought havoc throughout the kingdoms of the Three Clans by taking their forts and strongholds. Indeed, you have even sown the fields of Ahmadnagar with castor beans. You have conquered all the Gajapati's hill forts, water forts, forest forts, and forts on open ground. But let me warn you now—it would be unwise to continue any further in this campaign! You will have to cross the mountain passes, and, once you are on the other side, the Gajapati's allies will not let your supplies move through!"

Rayalu paid no attention to that sound advice and instead was only annoyed that anyone should be audacious enough to defy his wishes. He held firm in his resolve and ordered his army to press on. Sure enough, as they were proceeding through the Gajapati's passes, a man named Chitapu Khan[7] ambushed them with his sixty thousand mounted archers, letting loose a storm of arrows that fell like a monsoon cloudburst on the horsemen and foot soldiers in the passes. Everything turned to chaos, as some tried to escape from the downpour of arrows and others just stood there and bravely faced them. Some men stood dumbfounded, unable to tell which way was forward and which way back, while yet others were so overcome with fear and confusion that they frantically ran around in circles.

Since it was impossible for the whole army to face Chitapu Khan and put up a good fight in the midst of this confusion, a small force of the best salaried horsemen was sent to attack him from the rear. This force ascended hurriedly to the higher levels of the pass that rose up on Chitapu Khan's flanks and then suddenly surprised him by storming down on his rear with arrows, swords, and *barijis*. They cut Chitapu Khan's men to pieces, six to one blow.

When Chitapu Khan's force could no longer hold its own in the pass, his men broke and fled, with the king's men following in hot pursuit. These men drove Chitapu Khan all the way back to his fort, and only then did they drop the chase to return to the pass. In all, twenty-three thousand of Chitapu Khan's men and four thousand of his horses perished in that spot. Rayalu continued marching his army forward, but not without first leaving behind thirty thousand of his men to guard the passes, and then he marched down into the Gajapati's territory on the other side, completely laying the area to waste as he went. Finally, the army encamped near Potlur-Simhadri.[8]

When the Gajapati king received this news, he turned to his advisers and expressed his fears: "The Adil Shah, Qutb-al-Mulk, and the Nizam Shah all three together were unable to withstand his attack and were forced to retreat to their own lands! If those three great warriors were put to flight, then how will I, singly, ever be able to fight this mighty foe?"

His advisers replied, "Ever since the time when this territory first came under the rule of our Lion-Throne—thanks to the great valor and strength of the Sixteen Patras—the lord of Karnataka has never once invaded our territory. But you must recall that, in the days of your predecessor Pedda Gajapati, an incident occurred when the king was going on pilgrimage to Setu. As he passed on his way through Kanchi, Kalahasti, Arunachalam, Chidambaram, Jambukeshvaram, and Kumbhakonam, the soldiers and horsemen who followed in his train happened to get out of hand. Wild with the excitement of war, they ransacked some of the Shiva temples, Vishnu temples, irrigation tanks, brahman settlements, villages, and groves in the territory of the Rayas. Beyond that, they even went so far as to commit the impropriety of conquering and annexing some of those lands that were within the Rayas' territory.[9] Now, Krishnaraya has come to fulfill his divine purpose and seek revenge. He has put the barbarian Turks to the flight, and now he has invaded our territory, conquering mountain forts, water forts, forest forts, and forts on open ground. These are forts that are impossible for ordinary enemies to take even after a year's struggle, yet he has broken their ramparts and bastions and conquered them within the space of just one day! As for the remaining classes of forts—he has conquered those and reduced them to dust! Because he has been able to do all this, he can be no mere mortal—he must be an emanation of Vishnu himself!"

The Gajapati responded, "Yes, you are right. It must be because my predecessor violated the Karnataka kingdom that this strong and able king is now launching a counteroffensive against us. At any rate, let us look into our chances of success if we must fight with him."

The Gajapati summoned the Sixteen Patras, including Balabhadra Patra, Durga Patra, Bhima Patra, Mukunda Patra, Bhikara Patra, Bhairava Patra, Ranaranga Patra, Akhanda Patra, Murari Patra, Vajramushti Patra, Turagarelam Patra, Ashani Patra, Asahaya Patra, Gajankusha Patra, and Mrigendra Patra. The Sixteen Patras came and presented themselves to their lord, who told them to be seated. "Have you heard about what is happening?" asked the Gajapati. "The lord of Karnataka has marched to Ahmadnagar and destroyed it, and now he has crossed the passes and encamped in the vicinity of Potlur-Simhadri. In fact, he is only four leagues away from us at this very moment, and no doubt tomorrow or the next day his horsemen and armies will begin their attack. We will have to show ourselves at that point, but I wonder if it will really be advisable for us to leave the safety of the capital. What would you suggest?"

The Sixteen Patras replied, "This is the way we see it, our lord. It just so happened that, when the warriors of the Three Clans marched against the lord of Karnataka, they were unable to hold their own and were forced to retreat to their respective capitals. That led the lord of Karnataka to believe that he has nothing to fear from anyone, and that is why he has so audaciously crossed the Turkish territories, stormed through our border passes, and marched on our city. What we should do now is send word to the Lords of those Three Clans, instructing them to amass a strong force along their frontier to make it impossible for him to retreat. If we then march out and face him, he will be in a very hot situation indeed! Our territory extends all the way from Kalahasti to Jagannatham—who but a fool would march into such a vast area? He has truly jumped in over his head! It is clear that he is directed in this campaign, not by the sound advice of his ministers, but rather by his own vain pride. It is he who is in peril, for surely the victory will be ours. After all, they attack far from their base of power, while we stand firm on our own territory. If we encourage our people and tell them that they must stand firm at all costs and drive off these attackers, the lord of Karnataka will never be able to withstand us. He will decide to retreat, and he will be forced to go running back to his own territory. So tomorrow morning, our lord, give *pān* to the horsemen and troops and tell them to prepare themselves for battle. If you then take the royal insignia and retire to some high place with a good view, all that will remain for you to do is to sit and enjoy the spectacle. Just you watch! When the sixteen of us appear on the battlefield, the lord of Karnataka will turn and flee! We will capture his treasury, his elephants and horses, and his highest-ranking chiefs, and we shall bring them to you in person."

They continued to proclaim their valor, each in his own terms:

"I vow that I will slice them to pieces in the battle, six to the blow."

"And I will cut off the tusks of their war elephants, together with their trunks."

"And I will mow that army so it falls like a field of sugarcane at harvest."

"Yes, and if they are so proud as to try to take our country, I will catch them all and imprison them."

By the time the Sixteen Patras had finished swearing their oaths, the Gajapati was clearly relieved. "Yes, each one of you is capable of single-handedly performing many terrifying acts. So just think: if the sixteen of you descend all at once from ten different directions, it will be as terrifying as the monsoon with its thunder and lightning descending from the heavens! It will be like the raid of old on Prince Uttara's cattle,[10] in which Arjuna rode out to attack Duryodhana's men and came back not only with the recovered cattle but also with the turbans and earrings of the vanquished warriors! Your fearsome battle tactics will make the lord of Karnataka shake in terror! His men will be so confused that they won't even know their own bodies—they will have to stand right where they are, unable to move their arms and legs. Yes, you must fight like that!

"Naturally there are limits to my resources, but whatever valuables are left in the treasury, and whatever lands remain in the frontier, all this shall belong to you and to your horsemen. So I implore you, think neither of glory nor of shame, but just do what you must at the battlefront."

The Gajapati presented his Sixteen Patras with the seven most worthy gifts, of turbans, gold necklaces, pearl earrings, shirts, sashes, musk, and *pān*, all in token of his affection. "I realize that I may have had my shortcomings, and I know that I have sometimes shown my anger and disfavor. Perhaps at times I have said things that were unpleasant for you to hear. But I ask you please to forget all that now and do whatever you can to find a way to victory. We must defeat the king of Karnataka and so preserve the name of the Gajapati kingdom!"

Moved by his speech, the Sixteen Patras replied together, "Lord Jagannatha watches over everything, as you shall see for yourself tomorrow morning. We shall come at sunrise, prepared for battle, and you, our lord, must come prepared for victory."

Kamalanabhayya, the *sthānāpati* of the lord of Karnataka, had witnessed this scene from start to finish, so he immediately set about writing a painful letter to inform Krishnaraya of the enemy's strategy. He affixed his seal and entrusted the letter to a spy. "Go with the greatest possible secrecy," he instructed the man, "and put this directly into the hands of Rayalu himself when he is alone in his innermost quarters."

At the fourth hour, shortly before dawn, the spy arrived at the king's encampment and handed over the letter. As Rayalu read the letter in silence, he became deeply worried, and his mind began racing. "Their strategy totally foils our plans," he thought. "In fact, the whole campaign is quickly becoming a disaster! Damn!—this is what I get for making light of Appaji's advice. Surely we are all doomed to die in this mess since the Sixteen Patras never say one thing only to do another. No, they will certainly be able to do whatever they have promised. We have fallen into the enemy's net, and there is no way out for us now!"

Rayalu was so worried that he could not stand still, so he began pacing back and forth. When the troops beheld their king in such an agitated state, they began crowding together and whispering nervously among themselves. Disorder spread rapidly throughout the camp, and many of the men began to feel terrified. Rayalu tried to pull himself together by walking around the camp under the pretense of giving a lamplight audience to his men. Here are some of the things that he overheard his men saying here and there:

"As soon as the sun is up, the Gajapati force will fall on our camp!"

"If that's what happens, there'll be no possible way for us to withstand the attack!"

"Rayalu is the one to blame for this calamity! He jumped right into this mess without listening to Appaji!"

"If only he would listen to Appaji even now, there might still be a way to save us from this disaster!"

Panic reigned throughout the camp, among young and old, and even among the horsemen. When he realized the extent of their fear, Rayalu hurried off to Appaji's tent. Appaji noticed Rayalu approaching, and, to keep the people who were with him from realizing that the king was coming, he pretended that he was going out and told them to go back to their tents. As soon as they were gone, Appaji invited the king into a private chamber within his tent and asked him to sit down. "Something must be terribly wrong for you to come in person and call on me like this," exclaimed Appaji. "Would I not have come and reported to you if only you had summoned me? What is it?"

"Yes," the king replied, "there is indeed something terribly wrong. Here—read this letter that Kamalanabhayya has sent from the Gajapati's camp."

He handed the letter to Appaji. Appaji read it and said, "Well, what do you expect me to say? Did I not earlier fall at your lotus feet to offer my advice? Did you listen to me then? No, you just insisted on marching forward. What about the catastrophe that befell us in the Gajapati's passes—wasn't that enough for you? No, without even thinking about that, you had us march on another thirty leagues, right into the heart of the Gajapati's territory. Here we are, camped near the Gajapati's capital; he's ready to attack us, and *now* you're all worked up! Well, if you think this is anything, just wait until you see what happens tonight—now *that* will be something, like the end of time itself!"

At that, Rayalu recited the following *nīti* verse:

> "There are many who will be your friends in pleasure,
> but a minister who can turn back an invasion
> and a soldier who knows no fear in battle
> are rare even among the gods.

"As long as you are here, I know you won't let us get into trouble —isn't that so? Yes, I admit it—the reason I'm so worried and confused now is because I came here without listening to your advice. But what good can it do us now to go on discussing my faults? Just tell me a way to get out of this unfortunate mess—that's all I'm asking."

Appaji asked in reply, "Well, does my lord have any ideas?"

Rayalu said, "If they succeed in implementing the strategy that the Sixteen Patras have devised, then we will suffer much more than just physical harm—we will be thoroughly disgraced. That would bring nothing but calamity and misfortune for my subjects. Can't you see that I'm worried over the prospect of losing my power to the Gajapati?" He went on to say to Appaji, "I don't care what plan you devise. Just instruct me, and I assure you that this time I will listen carefully and do exactly as you say! Isn't there some way that we can save the trouble and the money we've invested in this campaign so far?"

Appaji recited the following poem to convey his advice:

> "When even the meanest, most implacable foe
> can be bought into friendship,
> will there be anyone in all the worlds
> who cannot be swayed to your side?
>
> It can turn enemy into friend,
> friend into servant,
> and servant into loyal son—
> Wondrous are the ways of money!

From even the worst of perils
it can lead a king to safety:
Sowing dissension in the enemy's camp
is the best expedient for a desperate king!

"This situation clearly calls for a scheme employing the strategem called 'the sowing of dissension.' But let me warn you," added Appaji. "If we are to stave off this calamity, it will be at the expense of vast quantities of priceless jewels."

"All right," replied Rayalu, "as long as we can save ourselves through one of the seven stratagems, that will be good enough. Besides," added Rayalu before leaving to head back to his own palatial tent, "the entire contents of my treasuries, my elephants and horses, all my armies and provinces, my forts with all their bastions, my villages and land—all are in your hands anyway, so use them as you will." He said this with full sincerity, really meaning what he said.

Appaji had no time to waste. He hurried to the palace tent and summoned all his trusted advisers. Ayyamarasu, Kondamarasu, Rayasam Viramarasu, Avasaram Lakshmipati, and the other ministers came together with the nine treasurers of the royal accounting office and Golla Komarasvami, the guardian of the treasury. He ordered the Gollas guarding the entrance to start rumors of secret consultations: "If Subuddhi or any of the Gajapati's other officers should happen to come, just tell them we are in a secret meeting. Don't let them come in, but don't let them go either. Tell them to wait."

Appaji began dictating an official letter for the clerk to write down: "Address this letter to the Sixteen Patras, writing out all their names in the proper order of their rank. I want you to write down what I dictate as though it is coming from Rayalu himself. Once you've got all the names and titles, begin like this:

"I have read the letters that you sent. Therein you have written as follows: 'We went to the Gajapati earlier tonight and reassured him by saying, "From the very beginning you have said so many kind things to us, shown us so much respect, and circulated such flattering news about us to the various

district forts with no other purpose than to honor us. How shall we ever be able to forget these things, even as we pass from this life into the next! It is as illustrated in the verse: With pain and difficulty, you can remove the blade of a sword that is planted in your flesh; but, try as you will, you can never remove words once planted in your heart." Now that his fears have been put to rest, we are ready to carry on with our plan. Tomorrow morning, as we march out to battle against your camp, we will seize him and hand him over to you. All we request in turn is that you give us the jewels and ornaments you wear. We would like your silver "butter-lump" necklace, the parrot necklace made of the nine jewels, your necklace of lapis lazuli, your diamond-studded gold chain, your emerald bracelet, the string of Hormuz pearls, your sapphire crown, your diamond-studded belt, your ruby necklace, your pearl anklets, your diamond armlets, your great pearl-encrusted broadsword, your lion mask inlaid with the nine gems, and your pearl ring. If you send us these and the rest of your sixteen royal ornaments, coming to a value of sixty-four lakhs, then you may rest assured that we will carry out our part of the agreement in a way that is to your complete satisfaction.' Thus you had written. I am accordingly sending you these sixteen ornaments—worth sixty-four lakhs—exactly as you have requested. Take whatever ornaments you want and enjoy them; I trust that you shall in turn honor my request and send the captive to me."

The clerk finished writing the document and affixed the names of each of the Sixteen Patras. Then Appaji had sixteen boxes made to hold the ornaments and gifts. He summoned sixteen officers and instructed them, "Entrust these boxes to sixteen men, and go with them to the place where the Sixteen Patras are camped, as if you are going to present the boxes to them." Giving the officers presents and *pān,* he continued, "If anyone should stop you while you are on your way, do not resist them. When they take you before their commander, you are to cooperate and let them find out what you are doing."

Meanwhile, Subuddhi, the officer who had been sent by the Gajapati to keep him abreast of all that was happening, learned that officers were secretly proceeding toward the Gajapati's camp with sixteen boxes, and, accordingly, he wrote a report back to his king:

"I have evidence from some spies who were on the way from the Karnataka camp to ours that there is a group of officers on the road and that they are carrying large boxes toward our camp. This appears highly suspicious—something should be done about it immediately."

As soon as the Gajapati had read Subuddhi's letter, he ordered his men to go and capture the officers and seize their boxes—which were of course full of the priceless ornaments that Appaji had packed up as though for the Sixteen Patras. They brought the captives before the Gajapati and had the boxes opened. When he noticed the letter addressed to his Patras, he ordered someone to read it out loud.

As soon as he heard the polite complimentary formulas at the beginning of the letter, his mind began racing. "The truth is out! From the very beginning, those traitors must have been taking note of each time I got angry with them. The jewels and letter are clear proof of that. I trusted the Sixteen Patras, and that's why I'm here, about to start a battle. Is there no limit to their treachery? Jagannatha, my lord! How could you lead me into such calamity? From now on I must trust no one!"

He chased away the sixteen officers whom he had captured and had them driven off far away from the city. He himself fled northward, going a distance of seven or eight leagues.

The next morning, the Sixteen Patras prepared themselves for battle and came to the Gajapati's palace. Stopping at the palace gate, they told their servants to go and tell the king to get ready to leave for the battle. Since the Gajapati had informed the guardians of the palace gate that he was leaving, they told the Patras' servants of the matter, explaining that the Gajapati had secretly fled the city in the middle of the night.

The Sixteen Patras were astonished to hear this and immediately began consulting with each other: "It would be too great a disgrace for us to go and follow him now, wherever he is. To do what he has done right before the battle stands as the clearest violation of trust. He has acted in despair, without giving the least consideration to what is in the city's best interest. Well, he will find out for himself soon enough!" So saying, they all rode home to their respective forts.

When Krishnaraya learned of this development, he had the battle drums sounded and marched into the capital. He stopped there and ordered Subuddhi's men to stand guard in pairs at the gates of the fort and at the entrance to the palace inside the city so that no one would be able to enter the palace. Then, near Potlur-Simhadri, he had a pillar of victory[11] set up. When that was done, he called Subuddhi and told him, "I want you to realize that I have come solely for the sake of increasing my glory, not with any desire of annexing your kingdom. The Gajapati kingdom I leave for the Gajapati. I shall return now to my own territory."

Subuddhi wrote a letter to the Gajapati to inform him of what Krishnaraya had said. When the Gajapati—who seemed to be a wise man—read this letter, he was overjoyed and returned immediately to his city. Once he realized that the Sixteen Patras had actually committed no wrong, he had his spies summon them back to the capital. They came and presented themselves before their king. "It is not you who have tricked and betrayed me," he said, and then he presented them with gifts and asked them to be seated. Feeling no further distrust of Rayalu, he began to speak to the king. In order to speak with words that were suited to the occasion, the Gajapati began by reciting the Sanskrit verse:

> "*naṣṭaṃ kulaṃ bhinna-taṭākakūpān*
> *vibhraṣṭa-rājyaṃ śaraṇāgataṃ ca /*
> *gō-brāhmaṇān deva-gaṇālayāṃśca*
> *yaduddharet pūrva-catur-guṇaṃ tat //*
>
> A broken family, damaged tanks and wells,
> a fallen kingdom, one who comes seeking refuge,
> cows and brahmans, and temples of the gods—
> supporting these is four times as meritorious!"

and then continued to say polite and fitting things to the king.

Rayalu then said to the Gajapati, "After all, is there any real difference between you and me?" Saying nice things in this way, he presented many fine presents and gifts to the Gajapati and gave him four ornamented garments. For his part, the Gajapati presented his daughter Jaganmohini to the king and poured water to seal their marriage.[12]

To honor his new son-in-law and his daughter, he gave them ornaments that were truly worthy of being presented as gifts. "Instead of the usual silks, scents, and treasures that are given as dowry, I give for my daughter all the kingdoms south of the Krishna River that are under my control, with all their forts, fortresses, and bastions. And the elephants, horses, and foot soldiers of those lands I give as her servants and attendants." He also gave swings and evening carriages, cattle and livestock, fine furniture, and a goose-down bed with legs of coral. All this and more he gave to his dear daughter. And of course he gave all at once all the worthy things his new son-in-law deserved. For one, he gave endless quantities of ornaments made from the nine gems, which were of unparalleled quality and were taken from his own palace treasury. He also gave a vast assortment of the nine gems, equal in value to the nine-gemmed ornaments sent by Appaji to the Sixteen Patras. He gave Chinese porcelains and Chinese silk brocades as well as ceremonial clothes made out of yellow cloth. He gave elephants and horses, swords and shields, and other such gifts as befit a king. Then he held a feast in honor of the new couple, ordering Subuddhi to sit behind them and attend to all their needs.

Rayalu was pleased beyond measure. He ordered the royal drums to be sounded and mounted his elephant. Sharing the howdah with Appaji and Subuddhi, he began his march back to his own capital.

It was not long before the three warriors who ruled Golconda, Bijapur, and Ahmadnagar heard about all this. "From now on," they declared, "it will no longer do for us to pick up our swords and oppose Rayalu. We must go see him and make peace." Walking in a properly solemn manner, they came to see Rayalu. They stopped in front of the king and salaamed politely before him seven times. In order to profess the sincerity of their desire to make peace, they presented him with the gifts they had carried all the way on their own heads and fell to worship his feet. Having developed a proper attitude of fearful respect, and having learned of the power of his munificence, they recited a verse to express their feelings:

"Our customs are crooked, from our mouths come only poison and fire!
We are vile wretches, an irascible race, blinded by pride—a fine people indeed!
O Lotus Eyed! Who can hope to change his inborn nature?
How, O King, could we ever hope to renounce our ugly ways?"[13]

They exchanged remarks back and forth, and the Turks showed their respect to Rayalu by proclaiming that, henceforth, they would no longer entertain the idea of building up their border defenses. Then they set off for their own places, without even having to be dismissed by Rayalu.

Now that Krishnaraya had attained victory over the Turks to his north, he continued on his way back to his own territory. As he was proceeding on his way to Tirupati, he received news that some people from the fort of Gulbarga had become proud and were shouting defiantly from atop the fort.[14] When he heard this news, he asked the identity of those in revolt and was told that they were barbarians. At that the king said, "Turn back; we will go and besiege the fort." They erected an escalade, and, within three and three-quarter hours, they had captured the fort. The king seized the fort's commander and left Gujjari Kalyana Rao in command with six thousand horses and horsemen under his control.

Krishnaraya arrived at Tirupati and beheld Kalyana Venkateshvara and the goddess Alamelumanga.[15] He made a gift of gold and cash and worshiped the lord by giving him all sorts of ornaments. He performed the Sixteen Great Donations there and then had a copper image made of himself, with his hands folded in respect and flanked by his queens Tirumaladevi and Chinnadevi, so that he could always remain standing there in the eastern doorway to attend on his lord. Once he had set up the image before Venkateshvara, he departed and went on to Kalahasti, where he beheld the lord and worshiped him with gifts and ornaments made of the nine gems. Then—it was in the year Shrimukha, on the seventeenth day of the bright fortnight of the month of Ashvayuja—he honored the lord with gifts of cloth and grants of entire villages and performed the Sixteen Great Donations in his presence, arranging for many sacrifices to be performed at the same time.

From Kalahasti, he proceeded to the three places that had been worshiped by the Tripuras, where he beheld the lord and beheld Vandishvara. Coming to Alagargudi, he worshiped and presented that god with gifts, including a pearl-studded crown and a brooch made of emeralds. Coming to Madurai, he worshiped Minakshidevi and Chokkanathaswami during the three sacred times of dawn, noon, and dusk and honored them with gifts and countless ornaments. To the Goddess, he gave diamond earrings and brooches made of lapis lazuli and nose rings. After staying there for a three-night vigil of worship, he went on to Shrivilliputtur, where he worshiped Sampengi Mannaruswami together with Cudukoduttunachyaru and presented them with nose rings, ruby studded waistbands, gold anklets, and image frames crowned by lion mouths and inlaid with the nine gems. He had a tank dug and gave one lakh *māḍas* to cover the construction of a stone *maṇḍapa* in the middle of the water.

He went on to Karuvanallur and beheld Kshiravarnaswami. He went to Shankaranarayanagudi, where he bathed in the sacred pool of the snakes called Nagatirtha, and then he worshiped Shankaranarayanaswami together with his consort Gometi. He went to Tenkashi, and, after bathing in the Celestial Ganga pool at Trikutachalam, he worshiped in the Painted Hall. He came to Agastyaparvatam, where he bathed in the Kalyanatirtham pool and honored Agasteshvara by having a temple gateway constructed. He went to Gajendramoksham and worshiped the lord there. He went to Shalivatapuram and beheld Lord Venuvaneshvara and his consort Kantamati. He gave some money for the construction of a hall faced with copper there and established an *agrahāram* village for brahmans, calling it Krishnarayasamudram in his own name. He paid his respects to the pontiff of the Totadri-matham and then went to Kurungudi to worship the five Nambis. He went to Kanyakumari and worshiped the Goddess, he went to Shrikanduru to worship Subrahmanyaswami and his consorts Valli and Devayana, and he went to the Nine Tirupatis, giving ornaments made from heaps of the nine gems to each of those places as befit their status.

He went to Setu, the original site of the bridge to Lanka, and worshiped Rama. He crossed the sea in rafts and washed his sword in the sacred waters at Dhanushkoti. Returning to Setu, he bathed in the sea there and then performed the King-in-the-Balance and other donations. He worshiped the deities Kashivishveshvara, Ramalingaswami, Setumadhavaswami, and the goddess Parvatavardhana. Then he bathed in the twenty-four sacred pools and gave away a crore of cows and fed a crore of brahmans. To the god, he gave three times his weight in gold, and, to the goddess, he gave all manner of ornaments and heaps of the nine gems. For three nights he remained there in worship, and then finally, after bathing in the Kotitirtham Pool, he took leave of the god who dwells there and began his return to the capital.

When he came to Gokarna, he worshiped Gokarneshvara and his consort Brihadamba. He circumambulated the Bakula grove and bathed in the Gokarna *tīrtha* and in the Mankana *tīrtha*. He gave all sorts of ornaments to the Goddess there. Coming to Shrirangapatnam, he worshipped Adi Ranganayaka.

Finally, at an auspicious moment, the king entered his own capital of Vidyanagara. He worshiped Vithala and Virupaksha and gave them gifts. He presented them with ornaments that seemed to be truly priceless and then entered the palace. There he stopped and bowed to pay his respects to his elders, before entering his court again at an auspicious moment. He summoned Appaji and his other advisers and his Sons and Sons-in-Law and held full court.

There, in the presence of everyone, he had Appaji sit on a jewel-studded carpet and showered him first with jewels and then with gold. He presented him with four ceremonial garments and gave him all sorts of ornaments, including bracelets, emerald anklets, a necklace and earrings with four pearls, a set of emerald earrings, a feather crest studded with pearls, a diamond necklace, and ruby rings. He further honored him with fine scents such as sandal, musk, and genuine civet oil. After giving Appaji all these gifts that would be wonderful to wear, he gave appropriate gifts to all the remaining people as well. Then, as instruments of all sorts sounded, he had them mount elephants and sent them to their homes.

Later, he assembled all the Seventy-two Officers, including the chiefs and nobles, the cavalry officers, lords and Poligars, Amaranayakas, the leaders of the Boyas, salaried officers, servants, accountants, the royal bodyguards, grain distributors, scholars, poets, specialists in drama and rhetoric, soothsayers, physicians, horsemen, *sthānāpatis,* dependents, and Bhagavatas, and gave them all gifts and *pān*. After speaking with them respectfully, he dismissed them.

The next day the king spent in court with a full assembly of scholars, poets, and palace officers who were skilled at telling pleasant stories. After conversing for a while with Saluva Timmarasu, Rayasam Kondamarasu, and the other ministers, the poets whom everyone considers to be the best masters of their art all looked at Rayalu and said, "Just as the fame and glory of the kings who ruled long ago are preserved for all to esteem in the literary works they commissioned, so should you commission works so that your majesty's fame and glory will endure forever." The king was very pleased by this idea, so he commissioned Mukku Timmayya, Alasani Peddanna, Madanagari Mallayya, and other great poets to compose literary works for him. When he requested this of the leaders among the poets, they answered, "As your majesty wishes." He presented them with shirts and *kuḷḷāyi* caps, necklaces and pearl earrings, bracelets, and ceremonial garments and requested them to write *Parijātāpaharaṇamu* and *Manucaritramu*.[16]

And so, my lord, I have recorded for you everything that has happened up to this point, and I will be sending you news of whatever continues to happen in the future. I remain in devoted attention at my lord's lotus feet, deserving of your protection. . . .

Those who read or hear this Rāyavācakamu *will become wise and clever and gain the power of discrimination. Becoming blessed with both material and spiritual wealth, they will live in happiness for as long as the sun and moon endure. Offered to Lord Rama. Victory to Lord Rama! This concludes the* Rāyavācakamu.

A·B·B·R·E·V·I·A·T·I·O·N·S

ARADH

Annual Report of the Archaeological Department of Hyderabad. Hyderabad: H.E.H. the Nizam's Government.

ARE

Annual Report on Epigraphy. Madras: Government Press.

ARMAD 1932

Annual Report of the Mysore Archaeological Department for the Year 1932. Bangalore: Government Press, 1935.

Artha Śāstra

Kautilya's Artha Sastra. Translated by R. Shamasastry. Mysore: Wesleyan Mission Press, 1923.

Baddenītulu

Baddinītulu (Nītisāramuktāvaḷi): Rāja, Sēvaka, Lōkanītulu. Edited by Celikāni Laccārāvu. Pithapuram, A.P., India: Śrī Vidvajjana Manōranjanī Mudrākṣaraśāla, 1917.

CITD 2

A Corpus of Inscriptions in the Telingana Districts of H.E.H. the Nizam's Dominions. Pt. 2. Edited by P. Sreenivasachar. Hyderabad Archaeological Series, no. 13. Hyderabad, 1940.

EC

Epigraphia Carnatica. Edited by B. Lewis Rice et al. 16 vols. Bangalore, Mangalore, and Mysore: Government Press, 1889–1955.

EI

Epigraphia Indica. Calcutta and New Delhi: Archaeological Survey of India, 1892–.

FSVH

Further Sources of Vijayanagara History. Edited by K. A. Nilakanta Sastri, and N. Venkataramanayya. 3 vols. Madras University Historical Series, no. 18. Madras: University of Madras, 1946.

IAP Warangal

Inscriptions of Andhra Pradesh: Warangal District. Edited by N. Venkataramanayya. Andhra Pradesh State Department of Archaeology and Museums, Epigraphical Series, no. 6. Hyderabad: Government of Andhra Pradesh, 1974.

Kavikarṇarasāyanamu

Kavikarṇarasāyanamu. By Sankusāla Nṛsiṃhakavi. Edited by Mācarla Rāmakṛṣṇakavi. Hyderabad: Andhra Pradesh Sahitya Akademi, 1967.

Mānava Dharma Śāstra

The Laws of Manu. Translated by George Bühler. Sacred Books of the East Series, no. 25. Oxford: Clarendon Press, 1886.

Mayamata

Mayamata: Traité Sanskrit d'Architecture. Edited and translated by Bruno Dagens. 2 vols. Publications de l'Institut Français d'Indologie, no. 40. Pondicherry: Institut Français d'Indologie, 1970–1976.

Nītiśāstramuktāvaḷi

Bhadra-bhūpāla-praṇītambagu Nītiśāstramuktāvaḷi. Edited by M. Ramakrishnakavi. Tanuku, A.P., India: Śrī Narēndranātha Sāhityamaṇḍ.ali.

OED

The Compact Edition of the Oxford English Dictionary. 2 vols. Oxford: Oxford University Press, 1979.

Raghunāthābhyudayamu

Raghunāthanāyakābhyudayamu (dwipada kāvya) and Raghunāthābhyudayamu (yakshagāna) by Vijayarāghava Nāyaka. Edited with an introduction and notes by N. Venkataramanayya and M. Somasekhara Sarma. Tanjore Saraswathi Mahal Series, no. 32. Tanjore: T.M.S.S.M. Library, 1951.

Śabdakalpadrumaḥ

Śabdakalpadrumaḥ. By Raja Radhakantadeva. 5 vols. Chowkamba Sanskrit Series, no. 93. Varanasi: Chowkhamba Sanskrit Series Office, 1961.

Śabdaratnākaramu

Śabdaratnākaramu: A Dictionary of the Telugu Language. Compiled by B. Sītārāmāchāryulu, with an appendix by N. Venkata Rao. Madras: Madras School Book and Literature Society, 1969.

SII

South Indian Inscriptions. Madras: Government Press, 1890–.

Śukranītisāra

The Śukranīti. Translated by Benoy Kumar Sarkar. 1914. Reprint. New Delhi: Oriental Books Reprint Corp., 1975.

Sulakṣaṇasāramu

Sulakṣaṇasāramu [*chaṃdaśśāstramu*], *Liṃgamaguṃṭa Timmakavi viracitamu*. Edited by Rāvūri Dorasāmiśarma and Bulusu Vēṃkaṭaramaṇayya. Kurnool, A.P., India: Balasaraswathi Book Depot, 1983.

SVH

Sources of Vijayanagara History. Edited by S. Krishnaswami Ayyangar, and compiled by S. Rangasvami Sarasvati. Madras University Historical Series, no. 1. Madras: University of Madras, 1919.

A·P·P·E·N·D·I·X A

Rāyavācakamu Fragments Translated or Paraphrased in *Sources of Vijayanagara History (SVH)* and *Further Sources of Vijayanagara History (FSVH)*

Page (and Line) Numbers in the Present Translation	*Excerpt Number and Title*
75	. . .
77–79 (36)	*FSVH* 96, "Vīra Narasimha"
79 (36)–86	. . .
87–88 (22)	*FSVH* 109, "The Coronation of Kṛṣṇadēvarāya"
88 (22)–90 (12)	*FSVH* 137, "On Principles of Government"
90 (13)–94 (27)	. . .
94 (28)–95 (10)	*FSVH* 137, "On Principles of Government"
95 (11)–96 (15)	. . .
96 (15)–96 (21)	*FSVH* 137, "On Principles of Government"
96 (22)–107 (22)	*FSVH* 138, "Administrative Measures of Kṛṣṇadēvarāya"
107 (23)–108	*FSVH* 131(b), "Saluva Timmarasa"
109–112 (21)	*FSVH* 129(b), "Krishnaraya and the Muhammadans: The Affairs of Bijapur"
112 (21)–114 (26)	*FSVH* 129(g), "Krishnaraya and the Muhammadans" (there is no section title)
114 (27)–115 (21)	*FSVH* 129(c), "Krishnaraya and the Muhammadans: Precautionary Measures at Ahmadnagara and Golkonda"
115 (22)–116 (18)	*FSVH* 129(d), "Krishnaraya and the Muhammadans: Punishments and Rewards in the Mussalman Kingdoms"
116 (19)–119 (31)	*FSVH* 129(e), "Krishnaraya and the Muhammadans: Preparations of War in the Mussalman Kingdoms"

119 (32)–121 (15)	*FSVH* 129(f), "Krishnaraya and the Muhammadans: Meeting of the Ministerial Council"
121 (15)–122 (13)	*FSVH* 129(h), "Krishnaraya and the Muhammadans: The Summoning of the Amara-Nayakas"
122 (14)–122 (21)	*FSVH* 129(a), "Krishnaraya and the Muhammadans: The Origins of the Muhammadan Kingdoms of the Deccan" (summary)
122 (22)–123 (21)	. . .
123 (22)–124	*FSVH* 129(a), "Krishnaraya and the Muhammadans: The Origins of the Muhammadan Kingdoms of the Deccan" (summary)
125 (1–11)	*FSVH* 118, "About the Kingdom of Orissa" (summary)
125 (11)–127 (4)	. . .
127 (5–16)	*FSVH* 118, "About the Kingdom of Orissa" (summary)
127 (16)–128 (22)	. . .
128 (23)–129 (35)	*FSVH* 118, "About the Kingdom of Orissa" (summary)
129 (36)–133 (9)	. . .
133 (10)–134 (10)	*FSVH* 120, "Gymnasia at the Capital of the Gajapati"
134 (11–16)	. . .
134 (16)–135 (11)	*FSVH* 119, "Timmarasayya on the Character of the Gajapati" (summary)
135 (11)–136 (12)	. . .
136 (13)–160 (4)	*SVH* 38, "Rāyavāchakamu—Account of Krishna Raya's Campaigns" (close paraphrase)
160 (5–29)	. . .

A·P·P·E·N·D·I·X B

The *Vidyāraṇya-kṛti* on the Founding of Vijayanagara

The following excerpt is translated from the Sanskrit *Vidyāraṇya-kālajñāna* manuscript (no. A-47) preserved in the collection of the Oriental Research Institute of the University of Mysore. The manuscript is a modern copy on paper; it is not known at what date or from what original this copy was made. The manuscript actually consists of a number of distinct but related works, the bulk of which are Sanskrit *Kālajñānas* or "prophecies" concerning the history of the Vijayanagara empire. These include the *Vidyāraṇya-kṛti, Vidyāraṇya-śaka, Vidyāraṇya-kālajñāna, Śivaskanda-saṃvāda, Vidyāraṇya-kośa* (together with a commentary, the *Vidyāraṇya-kośa-vyākhyā*), *Śivanandi-saṃvāda, Dattātreya-saṃhitā, Pitāmaha-saṃhitā,* and *Ānegondi-śāsana*. In addition to these Sanskrit works, the manuscript also contains a series of prophecies in Kannada prose, called *purātana-vacanagaḷu* and ascribed to various Virashaiva saints. The various works appear to have been redacted by different authors during the period from about 1580 to 1600 (*ARMAD 1932*, 1935, p. 101).

The section known as *Vidyāraṇya-kṛti* (not actually so named in the text) runs from page 1 to page 29 of the manuscript. The following translation omits only the lengthy section in which Vyasa instructs Vidyaranya in the Tantric lore regarding the *śrī-cakra* or *śrī-purī* (pp. 4–19 of the manuscript). Ellipses indicates a lacuna or corrupt passage in the text.

Salutations to Lord Ganesha! May [the composition of] Vidyaranya Kalajnana be auspicious! May there be no obstacles!

I forever praise the great Vedavyasa of spotless fame, the son of Parashara, the ultimate person who is the sole source of all Vedas, a bearer of knowledge, bestower of clear mindedness, who may be known through the Veda and Vedanta, who is forever peaceful, by whom passion has been extinguished, the pure and wise one!

I praise Vidyatirtha, who is Shiva himself, whose breath is the Vedas, who produced the entire universe from the Vedas!

I, Shri Vidyaranya, will tell in brief what happened to me at an earlier time, while I was in the Vindhya mountains. May all people listen attentively to my story!

One day I addressed my guru and master, "O Lord among Gods, teacher who rules my life! I have decided to go to Kashi in order to resolve my doubts about the commentaries on the four Vedas. Please show me your grace, my lord! There are sages who live there. . . ."

One morning in the Vindhyas, I came across Shringin of the Prishni gotra. He had the form of a Brahmarakshasa, his body surrounded by. . . . With his emaciated body, he was frightening to behold . . . having become . . . there in the forest. "Sir," I asked him, "how is it that you have become so emaciated? Why do you wander here?"

"Listen to me and I will tell you the reason, O ascetic," he said. "Long ago in the Treta age, Rama, whose heart is virtue itself, gave me a donation known as the Tulapurusha. I had not first performed the proper penance to receive that donation, and thus do I now suffer here in the forest, having been turned into a Rakshasa. Please give me some food and water and assuage the sufferings of one who is hungry, thirsty, and homeless."

"But, O twice born," I replied to him, "I am a mendicant, and mendicants are incapable of giving gifts of food."

Shringin of the Prishni gotra said, "I will tell you of a way to obtain all powers. Lord Vyasa will appear in a form that everyone would want to avoid and go to worship Vishveshvara in Kashi. Once he has done that, he will start for the Badari forest. Recognize his true form, O ascetic, and quickly grab his lotus feet. The four Vedas will be following after him in the form of dogs. He will say to you, 'O mendicant, someone has told you my true identity, and thus you have recognized me.' You must reply, 'I know because Shringin told me; please show me your grace!' and then that master will become favorably disposed toward you."

When he had finished speaking, I replied with respect, "I shall do exactly as you say. Please take me to meet Vyasa."

And the man said, "I will take you to him."

He led me to the sacred ground that extends to a distance of five *krośas* around Kashi. I left that trembling man and entered the sacred zone. After I had purified myself by bathing in the Ganga, I went to the doorway of the god's temple, eager to behold Lord Vishvanatha. Just then, a vile-looking man appeared; dogs were following at his feet. As soon as I saw him, there was no doubt in my mind. "This is he," I thought. "It is Lord Badarayana Vyasa himself, there is no doubt about it." Immediately and joyously, I fell at his lotus feet.

When I had done this, the great sage Vyasa spoke to me. "I am but a despicable hunter who takes pleasure in wine and meat. O ascetic, let go of my feet, and go wherever you will. Get up and go away, and be sure to bathe in the Ganga to regain your purity!"

But I did not give up. "My lord, my lord, O great god that you are!" I cried. "O holy one, supreme lord! I am but a dumb fool! Protect me! O most excellent of ascetics, ocean of compassion!"

That ocean of compassion heard my plea, and his heart filled with kindness. The great sage spoke. "Someone has told you; that must be how you know my true form. Tell me, O mendicant—did you recognize me by yourself, or was it with someone else's help? Could it have been Shringin who informed you?"

"Master! It was Shringin who told me; that is how I recognized you. Please show me your grace, my lord!" So saying, I repeatedly prostrated myself before Vyasa, my eyes filling with tears of joy as I took refuge at his feet.

Vyasa spoke to me kindly, "Come to the Badari forest this afternoon, and bring Shringin along with you. I will grant you every blessing, as is your desire."

When Vyasa had spoken, I left the sacred zone of Kashi and returned to my own *āśrama*. I told Shringin everything that had happened; when he heard my amazing story, he was overjoyed. He held on to me with both his arms, and thus we went together to the Badari forest, where the divine being Vyasa appeared before our very eyes. I prostrated myself before that treasury of ascetic virtue. Then, wishing to favor me as though I were his own child, the sage bestowed omniscience on me as a lasting gift, together with the three powers—including the ability to become as small as an atom—and the power of knowing past, present, and future.

Vyasa declared, "The *śrutis, smṛtis, purāṇas,* and *itihāsas;* innumerable *artha-śāstras* and *kāma-śāstras;* and the works on the principles of religion, such as the sixty-four *saṃhitās* composed by the sages and teaching the secret lore expounded by Shiva—through my grace, all this shall become clear to you. And you must do something to relieve Shringin's hunger, thirst, and homelessness. Long ago, his ancestors the Prishnis—who were seers rich in austerities and possessed of the knowledge of past, present, and future—made a throne and presented it to a king. In the same way should you now build a throne and cause Shringin to be honored with food. Out of affection for you, I shall tell you what is said in the *Yāmaḷa* and other Tantras. . . .

When he had finished speaking, that excellent sage disappeared before our very eyes. Shringin, who had heard all that the sage had said, asked me, "So what am I to do now?"

"You come along with me. I will tell you everything, O man of good vows."

Soon, Shringin and I arrived at Kishkindha, where we beheld Virupaksha on the bank of the Tungabhadra River. We duly performed *pūja* for him, and, as we stood there, that god who was none other than Shiva spoke to us:

"The city named Vijaya, which was counted among the eight *pīṭhas,* once measured two *yojanas* in extent. At its center shone the mountain called Matanga, granting all desires. With the passage of time, the city has fallen into ruins. Now I enjoin you to study all the Tantras carefully, and to rebuild this city to its former glory, and to see to it that food offerings will be made for me once more."

After hearing this, I went and stayed in a cave on Matanga mountain. While I was staying there, two people—named Sayana and Mayana—came to me and asked to be blessed with progeny. I told them, "It is not your fortune to bear progeny."

My words made them worried and distressed. "Then please enable us to attain the blessings of those who have sons by taking the large sums we have earned and expending them on religious charities," they said. I took pity on them and had them compose the works known as the *Sāyaṇīya* and *Māyaṇīya* as well as various other works regarding the Shastras. Looking on them as my own disciples, I enabled them to do all this.

Some time later, two princes of the Kuru lineage, who had served as guards in the treasury of the [Kakatiya] king Virarudra [i.e., Prataparudra], came to Shilapuri after being defeated by the Yavanas and entered the service of Ramanatha [of the dynasty of Kampilaraya], working in the king's treasury. Broad chested and strong armed, they were themselves endowed with the qualities of rulers. One day they crossed the Krishna River in a raft and went to fight with the [Hoysala] king Ballala, who defeated them. They came to me and related their story, and then they worshiped me and took refuge with me. On my advice, they went and attacked Ballala again, and this time they were victorious. Thus did they win a kingdom and establish themselves in the city named Hastikona [i.e., Anegondi].

Some time later, the two kings decided to go hunting, so they crossed over to the south side of the Tungabhadra River. After walking around for a while in a woody grove, they spotted a small rabbit. They released a pair of dogs to catch the rabbit. When the kings' hunters caught up with the dogs, they arrived just in time to witness the rabbit turn and attack the dogs. The dogs fled, and the rabbit disappeared into thin air. The hunters were surprised to see this amazing sight, so they returned and reported the whole incident to the king. Out of curiosity, the two kings asked me about this great wonder, and, when I had heard what they said, I went together with them to inspect the wood where it had happened. I examined the spot with care and then told them that the place was destined to be the site of a royal capital.

Then, in the cyclic year Dhatu, on the seventh day of the bright fortnight of the month of Vaishakha, at an auspicious time when the constellation of Magha was in the ascendant, when [1]258 years of the Śaka era had expired, after placating Bhairava who dwells on the battleground by performing countless thousands of human sacrifices, I laid out a beautiful city in the form of a man. It had nine major gateways and a number of subsidiary gateways.[1] . . . I carefully studied the *vāstu-śāstras* of Maya and other authors, who say that "if a city has nine roads running to the east and nine running to the north, if it has gates and minor gates, if it has paved roads and blind alleys, as well as the palace of a king, it is of the type called 'Jayanga.' "[2] As for the definition of the type of city called "Vijaya": "A city that has ten roads running to the east and ten roads running to the north, that has a royal palace, that has many alleys disposed in a useful way, and that has many paved roads, such a city is called 'Vijaya' by the sages."[3] . . . After considering all this, I built the city in accordance with the *śāstras*.[4]

The city will eventually be ruined on account of a "tortoise rupture" [*kūrma-bheda*], after a period of 360 years by divine reckoning. After 360 years, the city will fall into destruction because of a rupture in one of its weak spots [*marma-bheda*], there can be no doubt about it.

---

1. *upadvāra-saṃkhyābhidhā-purā*. Sense uncertain. I am also unable to make sense of the following verse, indicated by the ellipsis: *anuloma-vilomākhyām sampuṭa-dvitayena ca parāvṛtti-krameṇaiva mahā-śilpi-prakārataḥ*.

2. Quoted from *Mayamata* 10.67b–68.

3. *Mayamata* 10.69–70a.

4. At the point of the ellipses, there are three additional corrupt *vāstu-śāstra* verses (the first nearly identical with *Mayamata* 7.42½), the exact senses of which are uncertain. They appear to deal with layout and features of the city's *vāstu-puruṣa-maṇḍala*.

N·O·T·E·S T·O P·A·R·T O·N·E

The *Rāyavacākamu:* A Source of Vijayanagara History?

1. The term *historical literature* (*cāritraka-vāṅmayamu,* a neologism) covers a number of distinct genres in both prose and verse, devoted to such varied topics as dynastic history *(caritramu),* royal biography *(abhyudaya-kāvyamu),* family history *(vaṃśāvaḷi),* and local and temple histories *(kaifiyat).* In addition to these genres, all of which are represented by written texts, there is the related oral genre of local epic *(katha),* several traditions of which still live orally even today in parts of Andhra Pradesh. The major examples of these oral epics have passed into popular written versions as well, and there is evidence to suggest that even in the sixteenth century there was interplay between oral and written historical genres; the early genre of *caritramu,* e.g., clearly bears the influence of oral *katha* tradition.

Cāritraka-vāṅmayamu has been treated in a general survey by Arunakumari (1978) and in passing by Kulasekhara Rao (1974, pp. 490–530), both in Telugu; there are as yet, however, no general studies of this literature available in English. Translations are likewise limited in number, but mention may be made of one example of temple *kaifiyat* that has recently been published together with an English translation (*Srisailam Temple Kaifiyat;* Sitapati 1981–1982) and of the important study and translation of one of the major oral *kathas (Palnāṭi-vīrula-katha;* Roghair 1982; for a discussion of the ideological dimensions of such epics, see Narayana Rao 1986). The third volume of Nilakanta Sastri and Venkataramanayya (1946) provides translations of brief excerpts from a broad range of Telugu historical works relating to the history of Vijayanagara, including the *Rāyavācakamu* (see app. A). Stimulating interpretations of three examples of Tamil historiography—representing three separate genres, including one *(vamcāvaḷi)* that is cognate with the Telugu *vaṃśāvaḷi* genre—have been offered by Dirks (1982, 1987).

2. For general accounts of the history of Vijayanagara, see Nilakanta Sastri (1976), Sewell (1962), and Rama Sharma (1978). (Sewell [1962] is of value primarily for its translations of the sixteenth-century Portuguese accounts of Paes and Nuniz.) Stein (1989) is a masterly synthesis that moves beyond political history to offer a stimulating interpretation of changes in the social and economic orders that characterized the period. Among the numerous more specialized works, Dallapiccola and Zingel-Avé Lallement (1985) is par-

ticularly noteworthy, containing articles from the 1983 interdisciplinary symposium on Vijayanagara and an exhaustive bibliography of Vijayanagara studies.

3. For details regarding the text's modern editions, see Ramachandra Rao (1982, pp. xl–xliii).

4. For a review of nineteenth- and twentieth-century Indian historiography as it relates to Vijayanagara, see Stein (1989, pp. 2–12).

5. The fragments published in these volumes are accompanied by translations or closely paraphrased synopses; for a list indicating the relation between these fragments and the present translation, see app. A.

6. The work is not a poem, either in the sense of a verse composition (the text is in prose) or in the sense of a work of belletristic literature (the work is outside the mainstream tradition of "high" or courtly literature). And, while the text is in fact fictively cast as an eyewitness account of Krishnadevaraya's doings, it does not even pretend to be a personal diary or record by the king. The text is not even a work of Krishnadevaraya's period, but rather dates to the early Nayaka period some eighty or ninety years later.

7. The list would include the "indigenous" Dravidian and Indo-European languages of South India (Kannada, Malayalam, Tamil, Telugu, and Sanskrit) as well as the languages of the major intrusive or colonial polities (Persian and Urdu, Portuguese, and Marathi) and several languages in which foreign travelers and traders have left important accounts (Arabic, Chinese, Italian, and Russian).

8. The *Rāyavācakamu* is by no means the only important Telugu text that has been misunderstood on the basis of translated excerpts. A more drastic case is provided by Krishnadevaraya's *Āmuktamālyada,* a work of courtly poetry taking as its theme the lives of the Alvar saints Periyalvar and his daughter Andal. The text has apparently come to be mistaken for a political treatise by some historians; e.g., it has recently been described as a "book of political maxims" (Palat 1987, p. 40) or as a "didactic poem" (Stein 1989, pp. 51, 93). The work is in fact one of the finest examples of the Telugu *prabandham* style of descriptive court poetry, in which plot, character, and theme are all ultimately subordinated to aesthetic effect. The work has never been made available in a complete English translation. The source of the misconception is the often-cited article by A. Rangasvami Sarasvati "Political Maxims of the Emperor-Poet, Krishnadeva Raya" (1926), which includes a translation of an eighty-verse passage in which one of the poem's characters (the Vaishnava *ācārya* Yamuna) recites *nīti* verses on proper political conduct for the edification of the Pandya crown prince.

9. Referred to variously as Vishvanatha, Vishvappa, or Vissappa.

10. Contemporary Telugu folk tradition does in fact distinguish between narratives of events that "really happened" *(nijaṃgā jarigina katha)* and those that are considered to be made-up "fabrications" told for amusement *(kaṭṭu katha),* yet it is readily apparent that the overlap between this distinc-

tion and our own history-myth dichotomy is very slight. The category *kaṭṭu katha* would in fact appear to coincide more with our idea of fiction, while history and myth would be subsumed equally under the label *nijaṃgā jarigina katha*. Thus, Narayana Rao reports that Telugu folk epics are, by definition, seen as "really having happened" by the communities that own them (see Narayana Rao 1986, pp. 131–134)—notwithstanding the fact that they contain many elements that from a modern perspective would be recognized as "mythical." But, since this distinction is not drawn indigenously, we can only conclude that such texts—whether contemporary folk epics or earlier historiographic works like the present one—were perceived as organic entities, not as accidental patchworks made up of elements with the opposing cultural values suggested by the terms *history* and *myth*.

11. According to the text's own chronology.

12. The destruction of Vijayanagara would ultimately lead to the development of a new political order, characterized, in Dirks' words, by an "encroachment of the 'periphery' over the 'center' . . . reversing . . . the medieval balance between dynamic centers and encompassed peripheries" (1987, p. 27).

13. The usual Telugu spelling of this word is *vācikamu;* it is used alike in Telugu, Sanskrit, and Kannada in the sense of "news, tidings, intelligence." The form *vācakamu* that occurs in the title of the work is unusual and is more frequently used in the sense of "a word used denotatively" (*vācyārthamunu telipeḍu śabdamu; Śabdaratnākaramu*, p. 702). Ramachandra Rao (1982, p. xlv, n. 1) suggests that the author has used the spelling *vācakamu* since it more closely approximates the spoken pronunciation of the word *vācikamu*.

14. That is, not in our text's sense as a diplomatic representative. The term does figure frequently in medieval inscriptions, but it generally designates the manager of a temple. See, e.g., Dutt (1967, p. 318), under both *sthānapati* and *sthānāpati*. According to Sircar (1966, p. 323), the term does occur in the sense of "a civil agent kept by the Nāyakas at the imperial court at Vijayanagara," but his reference appears defective, and I am unable to trace any epigraphic source of such a usage.

15. An example of a Telugu historiographic work that follows these conventions is Kāse Sarvappa's *Siddhēśvara Caritramu* (1960).

16. It should be noted that the author is sometimes characterized as a *sthānāpati* in the service of Kashi Vishvanatha Nayanayya (whose identity is discussed below). For example, Ramachandra Rao states that "the author of the *Rāyavācakamu* informs us of his position as 'the *sthānāpati* of the great and prosperous ruler Kashi Vishvanatha Nayanayya,' although he does not tell us what his name is" (1982, p. ii). Clearly, however, this conclusion rests on nothing more than the unquestioned assumption that the "personality" of the narrator must be an accurate reflection of the author's actual identity. It is true that the "omniscient narrator" characteristic of traditional narrative is customarily held to be "objective" and is seen as identical with the

author simply by virtue of the fact that he does not become a part of the content of his own discourse. In the words of Scholes and Kellogg, "Since there is no ironic distance between the author and the teller of a traditional story, we are not in the habit of distinguishing between them" (1966, p. 37). But this is hardly the case with the present text, in which such "ironic distance" is forcefully established by means of the two passages framing the "report" in which the narrator represents himself as a *sthānāpati*. Consequently, the narrator in this text is moved out of the "objective" realm and thrust directly into the fabric of the narrative, where he obtains a status comparable to that of any other character represented therein. The fact that he serves the author in a more direct fashion as the primary means of advancing the narration is still no ground for conflating his identity with that of the author.

17. In the present case, I mean to distinguish between successive historical phases of the same, South Indian, society: that of Krishnadevaraya's Vijayanagara—the subject of the text—and that of Nayaka Madurai, of which the text is a cultural product, as argued here.

18. The first is the Telugu *Kavikarṇarasāyanam* of Sankusala Nrisimhakavi, a work believed to date at the earliest to 1540, eleven years at the very least after the reign of Krishnadevaraya; the verse beginning "With an impetuous thirst for conquest" is taken from this work. The second work in question is the Telugu *Sabhāpati Vacanamu,* believed to be no earlier than the middle of the sixteenth century; the borrowing from this work is extensive, constituting nearly the entire section in which Krishnadevaraya is instructed by his ministers (from the verse at line 13 of p. 89 through line 27 of p. 94).

19. I have not been able to make positive identifications of three of the eighteen sites visited. The sites are enumerated in the order of a travel itinerary, however, so even the unidentified sites may be broadly localized (see map 2). It should also be mentioned that the site where Krishnadevaraya worships Vandishvara may be in the Madurai country or it may represent a third stop between Kalinga and Madurai. This does appear to represent a single site or site cluster, which I have not been able to identify.

20. A comparable strategy may be seen in the nearly contemporary chronicles of the northern Thai kingdom of Lanna, which have the Buddha miraculously fly a thousand miles from Banaras to northern Thailand, in order to sanctify the region with his footsteps and generate a sacred geography that establishes Lanna as both a cosmological and a political center (Swearer 1987, pp. 107–111).

21. See, e.g., nn. 2 and 3, chap. 2, and n. 16, chap. 4, of the translation as well as the index of proper names.

22. See maps 1–3. Only places and physical features that are mentioned in the text are plotted on these maps.

23. The text's account of Krishnadevaraya's military campaigns against the Muslim kingdoms of the Deccan, the Gajapati of Orissa, and the rebellious

feudatory Gangaraya of Ummattur, e.g., agree in broad detail with what is known about these campaigns from the testimony of epigraphic records and historical writings in Persian and Portuguese; moreover, most of the aspects of the *Rāyavācakamu*'s account that are at variance with the other sources—e.g., the relative chronology of the three campaigns—are readily understood in the light of the author's deeper purpose of making the overall course of Krishnadevaraya's campaigns more closely approximate the paradigmatic clockwise progression of an imperial "conquest of the quarters" *(dig-vijaya)*. (See the discussion in the notes to chaps. 6 and 7, passim.) For an example of the text's awareness of courtly practice, see the discussion of the distinction in the *Rāyavācakamu* between the active and the reserve treasuries (*cinna-* and *pedda-bhaṃḍāraṃ*, lit., "small" and "large" treasuries) and its agreement with the Portuguese account of the visitor Paes (n. 5, chap. 3). Not only does the author of the *Rāyavācakamu* manifest a deep interest in the minutiae of courtly life at Krishnadevaraya's Vijayanagara, but he is also keenly attentive to the differences in courtly ritual and cultural practice that obtain at the foreign capitals of the Muslim "Turks" in the northern Deccan and of the Hindu Gajapati in Orissa.

24. This should not be taken to imply that historiographic writing itself was always located within a courtly setting. To the contrary, there were other, noncourtly traditions of historiography in Telugu, such as the village-level tradition of the *kaifiyat* or local history and the temple-based tradition of the *māhātmyamu* or sacred history. Both types of works often contain detailed and accurate historical information, but information inevitably of a sort that is more restricted in geographic scope and pertains directly to the locality, offering a striking contrast to the more cosmopolitan awareness that is evident in the *Rāyavācakamu*.

25. See, e.g., pp. 100ff. (and the accompanying notes) on Allalanatha's report on the state of the treasury.

26. Thus, the author reveals an awareness not only of the contemporary chiefs and generals active in South India but even of important political figures far to the north, such as Raja Man Singh, the famous Rajput general who served the Mughals under Akbar (also mentioned in the text). Although distant, the Mughals would presumably have become the subject of increasing interest in South Indian courtly circles in the closing years of the sixteenth century. We may recall that Akbar was campaigning in the northern Deccan in the 1590s and that in 1600 he succeeded in capturing the Ahmadnagar fort. In the same year, he sent an embassy to the Vijayanagara court at Chandragiri, which was received with suspicion by Venkatapati II (Hayavadana Rao 1930, p. 2191).

27. The Rayalaseema districts of Southern Andhra Pradesh, which had been the core area of Vijayanagara's last dynasty, were by this time under the control of the Muslim kingdom of Golconda.

28. For a concise overview of the history of this period, see Stein (1989,

pp. 120–139); more detailed studies include Sathianathaier (1956), Sathyanatha Aiyar (1924), Vriddhagirisan (1942), Hayavadana Rao (1948), and Swaminathan (1957).

29. For a translation and interpretation of this episode as it occurs in a Tamil chronicle of Madurai dating from the second half of the eighteenth century and preserved in the Mackenzie collection, see Dirks (1987, pp. 96–106). Similar versions of the story of the founding of Madurai occur in Telugu historiographic texts as well, such as *Balijavaṃśapurāṇaṃ*, *Karṇāṭa-Kōṭikam Rājula Kaifiyat,* and *Taṃjāvūri Āṃdhra Rājula Caritramu* (excerpts given in *FSVH,* vols. 2–3, nos. 151, 152; and *SVH,* no. 98).

30. For detailed accounts of the period comprising the battle of Rakshasa-Tangadi and its aftermath, see *FSVH,* 1:263–309; and Hayavadana Rao (1930, pp. 2059–2170).

31. The Nayakas' earlier relationship of subordination to Vijayanagara was never completely forgotten, but, by the mid-seventeenth century, references to Vijayanagara had become increasingly perfunctory and formulaic, so that during the reign of Tirumala Nayaka (1623–1659), e.g., the only mention of Vijayanagara in Nayaka inscriptions is in the context of regnal dating (Dirks 1987, p. 46).

32. Harihara (r. 1336–1357), the first king of Vijayanagara's first or Sangama dynasty.

33. This is an unpublished manuscript (no. A-47 of the Oriental Research Institute of the University of Mysore) that contains the most important collection of Vidyaranya material known. For a discussion of this manuscript and brief summaries of the various narratives it contains, see *ARMAD 1932* (1935, pp. 100–123); for a recent review of the "Vidyaranya problem" and a stimulating reappraisal of the Vidyaranya legend in the broadest cultural terms, see Kulke (1985).

34. In fact, the sage does teach Vidyaranya in the *Rāyavācakamu,* but nothing more than "the secrets of several mantras."

35. The text is available in editions by K. Lakshmiranjanam (1969) and C. V. Ramachandra Rao (1984).

36. The text concludes by noting, "The great king Madhava Varman obtained the goddess Padmakshi's favor and thus gained undisputed control of the realm; his successors built Ekashilanagara [i.e., Warangal] and ruled with great prowess for one thousand years, up through the reign of Shrimat Prataparudra" (Ramachandra Rao 1984, p. 71; translation mine).

37. The motif of the test is found in this text, but the reward here is the granting of yogic powers and the mastery of religious and ritual texts.

38. *ARMAD 1932* (1935, p. 110). The motif also occurs in connection with the founding of the capital of the Bahmanis at Bidar and the founding of the fort of the Nayakas of Tarikere (Heras 1929, p. 9); yet another example may be found in a slightly different context in the description of Pancai in the Ballad of Kattapomman (Dirks 1987, p. 64).

39. For the full story of the conflict between Vali and Sugriva, see Shastri (1957–1959, 2:185–234).

40. For the implications of the text concerning the status of Vijayanagara as a cosmic city, see n. 29, chap. 1, of the translation.

41. For a discussion of Aravidu inscriptions in which Penugonda and Chandragiri are referred to as *Vijayanagara,* see Heras (1927, pp. 266, 312–313) and Hayavadana Rao (1930, pp. 2135–2136, 2181–2182).

42. The Telugu term *turaka* is a borrowing from the Sanskrit *turaka,* in turn most likely derived directly or indirectly from the Turkic *Türk,* the national name for the Central Asian Turks. The ultimate Turkic origin of the name is still a matter of dispute among Turkologists (see Kwanten 1979, p. 29), and the relation of the Sanskrit *turaka* with the similar but earlier term *turuṣka* is also unclear. Some have suggested a connection between *turuṣka* and *tuṣāra/tuḥkhāra,* a term used as early as the *Atharva-veda* to refer to a northwest Indian or Central Asian people (cf. the Greek *tokharoi*) and later applied regularly to the Central Asian Kushans (Rosenfield 1967, p. 8). In any case, the term *turaka* is used consistently by medieval Telugu authors to refer to Islamic peoples, regardless of their actual ethnic identity as Turks, Persians, Afghans, etc. The term sometimes carries a pejorative sense as well (suggestive of a vicious, cruel barbarian), not unlike the English usage of *Turk* through the nineteenth century to denote "a cruel, rigourous, or tyrannical man; anyone behaving as a barbarian or a savage" (*OED,* p. 3435, meaning 4).

43. For a concise formulation of the anticommunalist critique, see Thapar, Mukhia, and Chandra (1969).

44. The term is derived from the Sanskrit *kartṛ*. The cognate Bengali term *kartā* was used as a synonym for Allah by the eighteenth-century Muslim Bengali poet ʻAli Raja (Richard M. Eaton, personal communication); similarly, *karta* is the word most commonly used for Allah in Tamil Muslim texts (David Shulman, personal communication).

45. Two separate reports are presented, one about Bijapur and another joint report about Ahmadnagar and Golconda, but they are similar in general tenor and so can be considered together here.

46. Although there is nothing quite as gruesome as this in the report from Bijapur, the discussion following the report suggests that much the same thing goes on there. In characterizing the ruler of Bijapur's way of dealing with his advisers, Krishnadevaraya's ministers Ayyamarasu and Kondamarasu point out that, "if these advisers ever disagree among themselves, their lord threatens their lives. . . . Naturally, the advisers . . . are always anxious to put aside their differences and reach a consensus."

47. See, e.g., the episode of the Gajapati's ambush by some enemy lords in chap. 5, which really serves no other purpose than to establish this point.

48. For a discussion of the method of *daṇḍa* within the context of traditional Indian political theory, see Zimmer (1951, pp. 118–123).

49. According to D. C. Sircar (1965, pp. 338–339), *Ashvapati, Gajapati,* and *Narapati* are first found in the sense of royal titles in the inscriptions of the Kalachuri king of northern India, Karna (r. 1041–1071), who adopted the epithet *Aśvapati-Gajapati-Narapati-rāja-traya-adhipati;* the same epithet was later adopted (in its Kannada translation, *Aśvapati-Gajapati-Narapati-mū-vara-rāyara-gaṇḍa*) by the Vijayanagara kings. Sircar believes that the expression refers to the king adopting it as "lord of the threefold sovereignty, i.e. of the three wings of sovereignty, viz. the cavalry, elephant force, and infantry." He goes on to explain that "some of the medieval Indian kings considered themselves sufficiently strong in all the three wings of sovereignty and claimed the comprehensive title referred to above, while their neighbours were inclined to apply to them any one of the three epithets with reference to the wing in which they were regarded as especially strong. This is how the latest rulers of the Imperial Ganga dynasty of Orissa and their Suryavamsi successors gradually became famous as Gajapati" (1965, p. 339). In a note to this statement, Sircar cites Mahalingam to the effect that the Vijayanagara kings were "specially known as *Aśvapati* because of the strength of their cavalry"; according to the present text, however, the Vijayanagara kings are known as *Narapati,* while it is the kings of Delhi who are known as *Ashvapati.*

The *Rāyavācakamu*'s division of the world into three kingdoms ruled by an Ashvapati, Gajapati, and Narapati would appear to be a medieval transformation of the ancient South Indian conception of the "three crowned kings" (Tamil *mutiyutai mū vēntar* [see Stein 1978, pp. 117–118]), expanded and reinterpreted in the light of the Sanskritic royal ideology expressed in these North Indian royal titles.

50. The text is in fact far from unequivocal with regard to the identity of the Ashvapati and his capital, offering, in effect, a composite representation that combines attributes of both the then-reigning Mughals and the earlier Delhi sultanate. In one important passage (pp. 116–117), it is the "king of Agra" *(aghapuraṃ-vāru)* who is clearly identified as the incumbent of the Lion-Throne of the Ashvapati. Another passage, however, suggests that it is the "sultan of Delhi" *(ḍhilli-suradhāṇi)* who is the Ashvapati (pp. 122–123). This identification is made within the context of 'Ain-ul-Mulk's account of the battle between the Delhi sultan and Kakatiya Prataparudra (r. 1289–1323) some two hundred years earlier and thus would suggest that the author sees the difference between the Delhi sultanate and the Mughal empire as representing nothing more than a dynastic change within an otherwise continuous "Ashvapati" polity. The only anachronism is introduced when ambassadors of both the sultan of Delhi and the lord of Agra are said to be present at the Gajapati court (p. 127).

51. The text specifies Bidar (Telugu *Beḍadakōṭa*), which is actually located to the west of Golconda, and thus places the Gajapati's boundary too far to the west. Either the author intended another town of the same name—

which, however, I am unable to identify—or this is one of several instances where his geographic knowledge is faulty.

52. In actuality, this tract would extend quite some distance further to the east; Golconda is to the east of Bidar (see n. 51 above).

53. The designation "kingdoms of the Three Clans" is itself strongly suggestive of the mutual strife and divisiveness that characterizes the Turks since the word *tega* is used in the sense not merely of "clan" but also of "division" and "faction."

54. The "water pot" *(giṇḍi)* is a small spouted vessel, cognate in both name and form with the Southeast Asian *kendi* (for an eighteenth-century Indian example from Kerala, see Welch [1985, no. 8]). According to Nilakanta Sastri and Venkataramanayya, the *giṇḍi* "formed one of the articles of royal insignia in the Hindu kingdoms. It was customary for a person to stand before the king on ceremonial occasions carrying in his hands a golden *giṇḍi* containing water with which the king rinsed his mouth when he was inclined to do so. It is not known whether this practice also obtained at the Mussalman courts" (1946, 3:118).

55. I am grateful to Cynthia Talbot for helping me clarify my thinking on this important point.

56. For translations of Sanskrit versions, see O'Flaherty (1975, pp. 125–137) and Dimmitt and van Buitenen (1978, pp. 189–198); for a retelling and analysis of another (and much fuller) late medieval Southern version of this myth, see Shulman (1985, pp. 100–110).

57. See, e.g., pp. 89 (the king in general an *aṃśa* of Vishnu), 118 (Krishnadevaraya an *aṃśa* of Vishnu), 122–123 (Kakatiya Prataparudra an *aṃśa* of Shiva, "sultan of Delhi" an *aṃśa* of Vishnu), and 147 (Krishnadevaraya an *aṃśa* of Vishnu).

58. On the role of *mythoi* and similar paradigms in the structuring of historical narrative, see Finley (1965), Egan (1978), and Lowenthal (1986, pp. 214–217).

59. Here, the other triadic paradigm of the Three Lion-Thrones reinforces that of the Tripura myth in the matter of identifying three *dharmic* protagonists.

60. Inscriptions and literature from before this period do on occasion reveal a tentative awareness of Islam, but I have been unable to discover anything in earlier literature or epigraphy that approximates the sustained, detailed polemic articulated in the present text. A few random examples: an inscription of A.D. 1267 from Pangal (Nalgonda District, Andhra Pradesh) describes the Yadava prince Sharngapani-deva as "the great Boar [incarnation of Vishnu] in raising the earth from the calamity caused by the Turks" (*turuḥkōpaplava-mēdinī-samuddharaṇa-mahā-varāha; CITD* 2, no. 34, lines 65–66); an inscription dated A.D. 1357 from Pillalamarri (Nalgonda District, Andhra Pradesh) records the reconsecration of a local temple "since its deity, Erakeśvara-dēvara, had been damaged by the Sultan 'Alā al-Dīn

[Khilji] during the troubles in the place at that time" (*tat-kāla-dēśa-viḍvarālanu Alāvadīnu-suratāṇi cētanu Erakēśvara-dēvara upahati ayitēni; CITD* 2, no. 40, lines 6–8); the imprecation of an inscription dated A.D. 1516 from Nelakondapalli (Krishna District, Andhra Pradesh) specifies different sanctions against "Hindu" and "Turk" violators of the gift: "If Hindus violate this gift, they shall incur the sin that comes from slaying cows and brahmans in Banaras; if Turks violate it, they shall incur the sin that comes from eating pork" (*yī dharmmānaku iṃddulu tappirā Vāraṇāśilōnu gō-brāhmaṇa-hatya cēśina pāpānaṃbōvu-vāru* [//] *Turukalu=dappirā paṃdi diṃnna dōṣāna=bōvuvāru; ARADH* for 1933–1934, p. 38); the *Prapannāmṛtam* of Anantarya describes the advance of the "Yavanas" (Muslims) toward Shrirangam and compares the Yavana leader to the demonic Kamsa of *Bhāgavata-purāṇa* fame: "Just like Kamsa of old, the brahman-killing Yavana laid waste to all the lands belonging to gods and brahmans" (*deva-brāhmaṇa-saṃbandhān yavano brahmaghātukaḥ / deśān vidhvaṃsayāmāsa sarvān kaṃso yathā purā;* Krishnaswami Ayyangar 1919, p. 36).

61. For the concept of "open" and "closed" cultures, see Lotman and Piatigorsky (1978, p. 236).

A Note on the Translation

1. For a discussion of the text's language and style, see Ramachandra Rao (1982, pp. xxiii–xl).

N·O·T·E·S T·O P·A·R·T T·W·O

Introduction

1. *Shri Kashi Vishvanatha Nayanayya:* Shri Kashi Vishvanatha Nayanayya, the fictive recipient of the *sthānāpati*'s report, may be a representation of the author's patron. If this is the case, he must be identified with Vissappa, who, together with his brother Krishnappa II, was co-regent of Madurai during the period 1595–1602 (see the introduction).

1. The Founding of Vijayanagara

1. *Viranrisimharaya:* Viranrisimharaya, the elder brother and immediate predecessor of Krishnadevaraya; his reign was from 1505 to 1509.

2. Some of the works mentioned are specific literary works, while others appear to represent generic types. In some cases, it is not clear whether a specific work or a generic class is intended. *Songs of the Pandavas (Pāṃḍava-gītalu),* e.g., might refer to a type of song about the Pandavas (the heroes of the *Mahābhārata* epic), or it might refer to the specific Sanskrit work known as *Pāṇḍu-gīta* or *Prapanna-gīta,* a hymn *(stotra)* on the greatness of Vishnu (Gonda 1977, p. 276). Many of the works, such as the epics *Bhārata* and *Rāmāyaṇa* and the *Bhāgavata-purāṇa,* are Sanskrit works for which there are also medieval Telugu translations—in these cases, either the Sanskrit or the Telugu versions might be intended.

According to Venkata Rao (1960, p. 316), *Garlands of Names of the Worshipful One (Ārādhyula-nāmāvaḷulu)* is another name for the *Sahasra-gaṇa-mālika* of Mallikarjuna Panditaradhya, which survives in both Telugu and Kannada versions. *Songs of Spiritual Praise (Adhyātma-saṃkīrtanalu)* is the title of one of the collections of devotional songs by Tallapaka Annamacaryulu (1408–1503), the well-known temple poet and musician from Tirupati; the songs are in Telugu and are addressed to Venkateshvara, the god of Tirupati. The *story of the liberation of the elephant king,* the *story of the descent of the Ganga,* the *praise of the rivers,* the *Mucukunda-stuti,* the *Akrūra-stuti,* and the *Bhīṣma-stuti* are all devotional verses of praise *(stuti)* associated with characters from epic and *purāṇa* literature. The *Bhārata-sāvitri* is a group of four verses found at the end of the *Mahābhārata* (18.5.204–208) that embody the moral of the story (Rice 1934, p. 84). *Sañjaya's Nīti, Vidura's Nīti, Cāṇūra's Nīti,* and *Baddena's Nīti* are all examples of *nīti* texts dealing with politics and the conduct of kings. The first two of these texts cannot be positively identified. *Cāṇūra's Nīti* is probably identical with *Cāṇūkya's Nīti* mentioned later in the text (see n. 3, chap. 3), which would appear to refer to either Kautilya's *Artha-śāstra* or some later Telugu adaptation of it. *Baddena's Nīti* is one of the best-known Telugu *nīti* texts, *Badde-nīti,* dating to the twelfth or thirteenth century. The text actually reads *Padya-nīti* (lit., "the verse *nīti*"), but Venkata Rao (1960, p. 317) has suggested that this title is actually a corrupt variant of the title *Badde-nīti.*

3. *after he had first looked at himself in a mirror . . . and gained the auspicious sight of a group of excellent brahmans:* These are auspicious acts, performed in the morning to ensure that the day will be favorable.

4. *the 108 Vishnu Temples . . . the Seventy-two Temples of Shiva:* These are ideological networks through which the more important temples of the period were conceptually linked together. The 108 Vishnu Temples (lit., the "108 Tirupatis") are a network of the Shrivaishnava sect, with Tirupati in Southern Andhra Pradesh as the central node (Hardy 1978, p. 125). The precise sectarian affiliation of the Seventy-two Temples of Shiva *(ḍebbhai-remḍu dēvasthaḷālu)* is uncertain; that they are broadly Saivite is clear from the subsequent lines.

5. *Dharmasanam Dharmayya, the minister of religious gifts:* Strictly speaking, *Dharmasanam* is not part of the minister's name but rather the title of his position, which may be loosely translated as "minister of religious gifts." The pattern of alliteration between the first syllable of the title of the position and that of the incumbent's proper name is found in a number of other instances in the text (cf. pp. 87 and 127 and n. 6, chap. 5), making it clear that the figures in question must not be taken as actual historical individuals.

6. *the six* śāstras: Although this term is usually used to designate the fundamental writings of the "six *darśanas*" or orthodox philosophical schools of Hinduism (Nyaya, Vaisesika, Samkhya, Yoga, Purva-Mimamsa, and Vedanta), it is defined somewhat differently elsewhere in the present text (see p. 92 and n. 38, chap. 2).

7. *the five sacrifices:* These are (1) reciting and teaching the Veda, (2) worshiping the ancestors, (3) worshiping the gods, (4) worshiping all created beings, and (5) offering hospitality to guests.

8. The different types of forts are described and classified in works such as the *Mānava Dharma Śāstra* (7.70–75), Kautilya's *Artha Śāstra* (2.3), and the *Śukranītisāra* (4.4), the classifications often varying considerably in detail. The present fourfold classification *(giri-durga, vana-durga, jala-durga,* and *sthala-durga)* is met with frequently in the medieval period and appears to be derived from Kautilya's classification (*Artha Śāstra* 2.3.51) into the four types: hill fort *(parvata-durga),* forest fort *(vana-durga),* water-protected fort

(audaka-durga), and desert fort *(dhānvana-durga).* In another context (7.10.294), Kautilya refers to another type of fort that is not protected by any special geographic feature but is just situated on an open plain; this is called *sthala-durga.* In the popular medieval scheme, the *sthala-durga* has replaced Kautilya's desert fort.

9. *come back and inform them once the gods had been seated on their chariots:* Nothing further is mentioned about this festival throughout the rest of the text. This is one of several cases in which the narrative lapses.

10. *met with them in a private audience . . . came back into the full court and summoned all the members of the assembly:* In this and other passages, the text distinguishes between two different types of royal audience: the *niṃḍu-koluvu* or "full court," in which the king meets publicly with all the members of his court (identified either as the *sakala sāmājikulu,* "all the courtiers," or as the *ḍebbhai-reṃḍu viniyōgamulavāru,* "the Seventy-two Officers"; see n. 12 below), and the *ēkāṃtapu-koluvu* or "private audience," in which the king meets privately with a small number of ministers and military commanders. The terms *pedda-koluvu* and *pērōlagambu,* both meaning "Great Court," are used as synonyms for *niṃḍu-koluvu.* The place where the *niṃḍu-koluvu* convenes is identified in the text as the *hajāramu,* "audience hall," or, in many passages, as the *niṃḍu-koluvu, pedda-koluvu,* or simply *koluvu.* Several passages in the text suggest that this area was conceived of as spatially distinct from "the palace" *(nagaru).*

11. *Sons and Sons-in-Law of the palace:* The phrase *nagari alluṃḍlu komāḷḷu* literally means "sons-in-law and sons of the palace." Nilakanta Sastri and Venkataramanayya note, "The terms sons and sons-in-law must not be understood literally. They represent two classes of the royal servants who were admitted into the respective classes when the Rāya desired to honour them" (1949, 3:79). The institution appears to be cognate with that of the *kumāra-varkkam* at the Nayaka kingdom of Madurai (Dirks 1987, p. 50).

12. *and the rest of the Seventy-two Officers:* This term *(ḍebbhai-reṃḍu viniyōgālavāru,* or equivalents such as *bāhattara-niyōgamulu)* is commonly met with in literary and epigraphic sources from medieval Andhra, where the "Seventy-two Offices" appear as a stereotyped feature of both political and temple administrations. For a complete list of the "Seventy-two Officers" (in the political context), see Dutt (1967, pp. xlv–xlvii). The number seventy-two clearly must have held some auspicious or other significance: compare the Seventy-two Temples of Shiva discussed in n. 4 above and also the tradition preserved in Tamil of Vishvanatha Nayaka having built a new fort at Madurai with seventy-two bastions to be guarded by seventy-two commanders (see Dirks 1987, pp. 49–50, citing Taylor 1835).

13. *Vidyaranya Shripada:* This is the great brahman scholar Madhavacharya (d. 1386), who is better known by the name *Vidyaranya* (lit., "forest of wisdom"), which he adopted after becoming a renunciant ascetic *(saṃnyāsi).* He belonged to the Bharadvaja-gotra and was the son of Mayana and Shri-

mati; his gurus were Vidyatirtha, Bharatitirtha, and Shrikantha. From 1374 until his death, he was the pontiff *(jagadguru)* of the Shankara-matha at Shringeri. He was the author of many Sanskrit works on Advaita philosophy, *dharma-śāstra,* and other topics; together with his brother Sayana, author of the best-known commentary on the four Vedas (the *Veda-bhāṣya*), he appears to have been one of the major architects of a new system of South Indian "orthodoxy," consciously conceived in reaction to the advance of Islam in the fourteenth century (Kulke 1985, pp. 127–132, 135).

14. Sayings of Vidyāraṇya *and the work called* Vijñānēśvaram: I have been unable to identify either of these works—referred to in the text as *Vidyāraṇyula-vacanālu* and *Vijñānēśvaram anu vacanālu*—among the known corpus of texts dealing with the mythology of Vidyaranya and his founding of the city of Vijayanagara. The most important collection of this material is the so-called Vidyāraṇya-Kālajñāna Series, an unpublished manuscript preserved in the library of the Oriental Research Institute of the University of Mysore (no. A-47). This manuscript contains the following related works: *Vidyāraṇya-kṛti, Vidyāraṇya-śaka, Vidyāraṇya-kālajñāna, Śivaskanda-samvāda, Vidyāraṇya-kośa* (together with a commentary, the *Vidyāraṇya-kośa-vyākhyā), Śivanandi-samvāda, Dattātreya-samhitā, Pitāmaha-samhitā,* and *Ānegondi-śāsana.* For a discussion of the manuscript and brief summaries of these various narratives, see *ARMAD 1932* (1935, pp. 100–123). The *Vidyāraṇya-kṛti* relates another version of the story of the city's founding, which differs from the account in the *Rāyavācakamu* in important respects (see the introduction); this account has been translated in app. B below.

15. The story of Vidyaranya and the founding of Vijayanagara: The implications of this episode for the primacy of the city of Vijayanagara as a cultural and political icon in the sixteenth century have been discussed in the introduction in the section "The 'City of Victory' as Talisman of Authority". The *Rāyavācakamu* follows a popular tradition in casting Vidyaranya as an intimate adviser of the earliest Sangama kings and giving him a direct role in the foundation of the city of Vijayanagara, although there is no genuine, contemporary evidence to link the historical Madhavacharya (see n. 13 above) with any of Vijayanagara's earliest rulers. The Madhava who appears in a number of authentic fourteenth-century epigraphs as a *mantrin* or adviser of the early Sangamas has proved to be a different individual from Madhava-Vidyaranya; see Kulke (1985, p. 128) for his identity and Lorenzen (1972, pp. 161–164) for his Kalamukha sectarian affiliation. The tradition of Vidyaranya's role in the founding of Vijayanagara does not appear until the sixteenth century, when it rapidly attains currency in a broad variety of different sources, ranging from literary works like the present text to forged epigraphs spuriously dated back to the fourteenth century. The tradition appears to have been fabricated and promulgated under the auspices of the Shringeri-matha during the pontificate of Ramachandra Bharati (1508–1560), in an attempt to counter a shifting trend in

royal patronage as the Tuluva rulers Krishnadevaraya and Achyutaraya began to favor the Vaishnava temple at Tirupati over the Shaivite establishment of the Shringeri pontiffs (Heras 1929, pp. 11–35; Kulke 1985, pp. 122–123). Kulke's important 1985 article offers a comprehensive treatment of the Vidyaranya problem and the entire range of related historiographic issues.

16. *circumambulation of the earth:* The *bhū-pradakṣaṇamu* is an ideal type of pilgrimage in the Hindu tradition, in which the devotee visits the major pilgrimage centers in the course of a clockwise circumambulation of the earth (i.e., India). The classic description is found in the third book of the *Mahābhārata* (see van Buitenen 1975, pp. 366–514; and Bhardwaj 1973, chaps. 2, 3). If the sites and regions visited by Vidyaranya are plotted on a map (see map 3), however, it becomes clear that his journey is not clockwise but roughly counterclockwise. From Mukambika (on the southwestern coast) he goes northeast to the Varata country in Maharashtra, then continues further in the same direction until he reaches Kashi. From that point he proceeds further east to Gaya, turns west to Prayag, and then heads in a northwesterly direction to Kashmir, at which point he turns south again, passing through Ujjain and Kolhapur before finally reaching the banks of the Tungabhadra. Counterclockwise circumambulation *(apasavyam)* has an important place in the rituals of some "Tantric" sects (such as the Pashupatas; Collins 1982, p. 608), in which many ritual actions are reversed. There are several other motifs with possible "Tantric" significance in the Vidyaranya episode: the reverse image in which Vyasa appears (see n. 24 below); Vidyaranya's visit to Kashmir, where he is initiated into the Lakshmi cult and the *Cintāmaṇi-mantra;* and his visit to two major centers of goddess worship (Ujjain and Kolhapur) on his return southward.

17. *Shingiri Bhatlu:* This is the "Shringin" of the *Vidyāraṇya-kṛti* (cf. the introduction and app. B). The name *Shingiri Bhatlu* may be understood as "the Brahman of Shringeri," Shringeri being the home of the Shankarite Advaita-matha with which the historical Vidyaranya was associated (see Kulke 1985). It is worth noting in this connection that today there is a small shrine behind the matha at Shringeri dedicated to Shringin (*ARMAD 1932*, 1935, p. 105).

18. *appointed me officiant for the King-in-the-Balance Donation:* According to the *Vidyāraṇya-kṛti* (app. B), Shringin is not the officiating priest for the *tulā-puruṣa-dāna* ritual but rather the recipient of the gold that is donated.

19. *Vedavyasa:* This sage's name means literally "Compiler of the Vedas." Tradition remembers him as the "author" of the epic *Mahābhārata* (in which he also figures as an important character) and as the compiler or editor of the Vedas and *purāṇas,* two of the most important classes of Hindu scripture. As author/editor of the major religious texts of Hinduism, he comes to be seen as the very embodiment of orthodoxy.

20. *the goddess Annapurna, the wide-eyed goddess Vishalakshi, and the lord of the universe himself, Vishvanatha:* Annapurna is the goddess of food.

Vishvanatha (lit., "the lord of the universe") is a specific form of Shiva who resides in Kashi; Vishalakshi (lit., "the wide-eyed goddess") is his consort.

21. *Pampa River:* Tungabhadra River.

22. *a king named Harihara:* This is the first king of Vijayanagara's first or Sangama dynasty.

23. *brahman-caste demon: brahma-rākṣasa.* Like human beings, demons too are believed to be socially organized into castes. Vidyaranya concludes—mistakenly—that Shingiri Bhatlu must be a demon in order to explain his uncanny knowledge of things; given that he is a demon, he must be a brahman-caste demon on account of his appearance and way of living. In the *Vidyāraṇya-kṛti,* Shringin actually is a *brahma-rākṣasa* (see app. B).

24. Vyasa's Appearance in the Form of a Low-Caste Person: Like Vidyaranya's counterclockwise "circumambulation of the earth," Vyasa's appearance is another example of the reversal motif (see n. 16 above). As a venerable sage and paradigm of orthodoxy, Vyasa would not be expected to drink, yet he carries a yoke with wine pots over his shoulder *(kāvaḍikuṃḍalatō madhuvuṃnnu bhujāna vuṃcukoni);* he would not be expected to wear leather products, yet he wears a leather cap *(tōlu-kuḷḷāyi)* and tasseled sandals *(billa ceppulu)* that are apparently made of leather; and, while he is usually pictured as being accompanied by the four Vedas, here he appears instead with four dogs—the lowliest and most despicable of creatures in traditional India—who follow at his sides "like the four Vedas" *(vubhaya-pārśvamulu catur-vēda-samānamulaina nālugu śunakamulu gūḍi).* In short, he appears in the "vile form" *(nikṛṣṭamayina rūpamu)* and speaks in the manner of a low-caste person *(hīnakulācārapu-māṭalugā).* But, thanks to his determined steadfastness, Vidyaranya is able to recognize in this negative image its opposite, "true form," representing the orthodoxy that will reign in his new capital.

An analogous motif is found in the hagiographic tradition of the various *Śaṅkara-vijayas,* in which the low-caste pariah whom Shankara meets in Kashi and orders out of his path turns out to be none other than Shiva himself and whose four dogs turn out to be the Vedas. See, e.g., the beginning of the third *taraṅga* of the *Ācārya-vijaya* of Shriparameshvara Kavikanthirava (Antarkar 1968, pp. 35–36).

25. *in order to make Shingiri Bhatlu happy, they must every day feed one thousand brahmans:* Shingiri Bhatlu's peculiar obsession with food seen here and again on p. 83 below is never really accounted for in the *Rāyavācakamu,* but, in the *Vidyāraṇya-kṛti* (app. B), it is explained that Shringin is cursed with a state of perpetual hunger as a result of his having received the King-in-the-Balance Donation from Rama without having first performed the requisite penance. There, Vidyaranya's purpose in founding the city is simply to provide a means of satiating the hungry ascetic's appetite.

26. *Then he sent Vidyaranya off:* Shingiri Bhatlu apparently sends Vidyaranya off to Kashmir so that he can receive the further religious and spiritual

training that he will need in order to found his city. In the account of the *Vidyāraṇya-kṛti*, Vyasa takes both Vidyaranya and Shringin to Badari (Badrinatha, in the Uttar Pradesh Himalaya, not quite as far north as Kashmir), where Vidyaranya is tutored in numerous religious texts. From this point on, there is no further mention of Shingiri Bhatlu in the *Rāyavācakamu*.

27. *It is a general rule . . . increase of sons and grandsons: bhūlōkamamdu evvani pērayinā yennāḷḷu velayatā vunnadō annāḷḷunnu prajalaku svargādi-bhōgamulunnu aiśvarya-pradamunnu putra-pautrādi-vṛddhinni kaligi vuṃḍunu.* In order to make this passage intelligible, I follow V. Narayana Rao (personal communication) in emending the text's *prajalaku* to *tanaku*.

28. *Now proceed on your way without turning back and looking at me:* That Lakshmi says this to Vidyaranya might suggest that something further is going to happen later on in the episode, but he is apparently faithful in following her advice. That the goddess of fortune follows only as long as one does not turn around to look at her is a popular motif in Indian folklore, but Vidyaranya's eventual undoing is caused by other means. Again, there seems to be a parallel with the Shankara hagiographic tradition, according to which the goddess of learning, Sharada, promises to come with Shankara as long as he does not look back to see if she is following. When he happens to do so while crossing the Tungabhadra River at the site of the present Shringeri, the goddess's feet stick to the ground, and she is unable to move further. For this reason, Shankara chooses Shringeri as the site for one of his *maṭhas*, the *Śaradā-pīṭha*, "seat of the goddess of learning" (Mahadevan 1968, pp. 53–54).

29. MATANGA HILL AND THE PLAN OF VIJAYANAGARA: The *Rāyavācakamu* affords abundant evidence suggesting that sixteenth-century Vijayanagara was understood as a "cosmic" city and that Matanga hill—the ancient site of the mythical sage Matanga's hermitage and the location where Vidyaranya has witnessed the omen of the hare and the hound—was conceived as the city's symbolic center. When on the basis of the omen Vidyaranya decides that he must build his city "in this place," he is standing on the peak of Matanga hill, and "this place" must thus be understood as referring to the lower-lying, flatter land surrounding the elevated central point of Matanga. Further confirmation of this interpretation is provided in even more graphically explicit terms in the *Vidyāraṇya-kṛti* extract translated in app. B, according to which the god Virupaksha reveals to Vidyaranya that the first City of Victory had measured two *yojanas* in extent and that, "at its center shone the mountain called Matanga, granting all desires" *(Mataṃga iti tanmadhyē rājatē sarva-kāmadaḥ)*.

Matanga hill *(Matanga-parvata)* is in fact a prominent feature of the Vijayanagara site, referred to in numerous Vijayanagara- and pre-Vijayanagara-period epigraphs at the site (including one dating as early as 1199; see *SII*, vol. 4, no. 260), and still referred to with this name by the local populace. Although not occupying the geographic center of the site—it is located toward the western side of the northern half of the site designated the city's "sacred center" (Vijayanagara map series, square NM; see Fritz and Michell 1985, figs. 56, 68)—it clearly dominates the city as its highest natural feature. Moreover, many important buildings and gateways throughout the site are subordinated to this mountain through visual alignment, such as the Ramachandra temple, which forms the primary node of the city's "royal center" (Fritz 1985, p. 267 and fig. 6), as well as numerous other structures, for which the evidence is discussed in as yet unpublished articles by Fritz and Malville (n.d.), Malville and Fritz (n.d.), and Wagoner (n.d.). It appears that these alignments were made to establish a network of axes channeling the power of the sage's curse out into the surroundings and thus to envelop the entire city with the mountain's protective power.

30. *the three kingdoms:* In this text, the kingdom of the Ashvapati ("Lord of Horses") is identified as the empire of the Mughals in their capital at Agra (or, in several other contexts, as the Delhi sultanate), the kingdom of the Gajapati ("Lord of Elephants") as the Gajapati kingdom of Orissa and coastal Andhra, and the kingdom of the Narapati ("Lord of Men") as the Vijayanagara kingdom (see the introduction).

31. The Ritual Foundation of the City: Two distinct rituals are described together here, the setting up of the gnomon *(śaṃku-sthāpana)* and the establishment of the *vāstupuruṣa (vāstupuruṣa-pratiṣṭha)*. The auspicious moment described as falling on "the bright full moon day in the month of Chaitra" is the time set for the establishment of the *vāstupuruṣa*, whereas in the next sentence the text seems to imply that the setting up of the gnomon occurs during the night of the preceeding new moon day two weeks earlier —even though the narration gives no indication of two weeks having elapsed between these ceremonies.

The use of the gnomon—a wooden shadow-casting pole like the stylus of a sundial—is quite different from that described in Sanskrit texts on architecture, such as the *Mayamata* (sixth *adhyāya*). There, the gnomon or *śaṅku* is set up at the center of the site at sunrise, and a circle is drawn around this central point. The two points where the shadow of the gnomon's tip crosses this circle during the course of the day are connected to establish the east-west axis, and the north-south axis is derived secondarily from this through the application of basic geometric principles. In the present passage, however, there are two important ritual reversals (see nn. 16 and 24 above on the reversal motif)—the ceremony is carried out not by day but by night, and it is the north-south axis that is laid out first. The exact procedure is unclear, but it seems that the *śaṅku* is used here more as a marking peg (cf. the *khāta-śaṅku* of *Mayamata* 6.16–17) than as a gnomon proper and that the axis is marked by sighting between the pole star Dhruva and a well-known constellation in the southern sky, Trishanku (i.e., the Southern Cross). The ritual precedence of the north-south axis described here may have some relation with the actual plan of the city, which is in fact clearly organized around such an axis (see Fritz 1985).

The implantation seems to be analogous to the textually prescribed rite of *garbha-vinyāsa* or implantation of the foundation deposit (see *Mayamata* 9.101–128, 12.1–114). While the *garbha* of this rite is a box containing various magical substances (ranging from lotus roots and other vegetable matter to precious gems), it is here replaced by the *vāstupuruṣa,* an effigy of the spirit of the site made from gold. In both cases, however, the proper performance of the rite is accorded the greatest importance. The *Mayamata* states that "a foundation deposit complete with all the prescribed elements will be the source of success; an incomplete foundation or the lack of a deposit will cause all sorts of calamities. For this reason one should perform the deposit properly and with all possible care" (12.2–3a). This attitude corresponds with the *Rāyavācakamu*'s insistence that the stability of the city depends on the foundation of the *vāstupuruṣa* being carried out at precisely the right moment.

32. *the nine gates: nava-dvāramulu.* Other texts—such as the *Vidyāraṇya-kṛti* (see app. B)—also describe the city as possessing nine gates. The significance of such statements would appear to be more symbolic than archaeological since it is clear that the city of Vijayanagara possessed far more than nine gates, even if one counts only the major gateways referred to in contemporary inscriptions as *hebbāgilu, bāgilu,* and *aguse* (thirteen such gates are documented in Patil [1991]; see also Nagaraja Rao and Patil [1985]). By insisting on the existence of nine gates, such texts suggest a homologous equivalence between city and man, who also possesses nine "gates" or apertures of the body: the eyes, ears, nostrils, mouth, sexual opening, and anus. The influence of this symbolic paradigm may be seen as well in Federici's observation (c. 1570) that the "royal palace" still standing within the recently abandoned city possessed "nine gates" (Kerr 1824, p. 160); whether this statement is based on his own accurate observation or on the interpretive testimony of local people is immaterial.

33. *an auspicious moment—favorable by both astrological and other factors:* The day of the full moon is always an auspicious time for performing rituals. Additionally, this full moon day is the first day of the month of Chaitra (March–April) and hence of the year according to the traditional Indian calendar. Significantly, the annual festival of the marriage of Virupaksha and Pampa—the patron deities of Vijayanagara—is celebrated on this date in Hampi today (Shapiro, n.d.).

34. *the cyclic year named Prabhava:* The traditional calendrical system includes a cycle of sixty named years. In Ś. (Śaka) 1127, however, the cyclical year would have been not Prabhava but Krodhana; the nearest Prabhava would have fallen in Ś. 1129. The author has perhaps stated Prabhava since it is the first year of the sixty-year Jupiter cycle and hence serves as an auspicious beginning.

35. *the 1127th year of the Shalivahana-Shaka era:* If 1127 is taken as an error for 1129, the date would work out to A.D. 15 March 1207. But, as Ramachandra Rao points out (1982, pp. vii–viii), Ś. 1127 (i.e., A.D. 1205) does seem to be the date actually intended by the author—who at any rate specifies this date twice, once in words and then in numerals—given Vyasa's pronouncement that the city will endure for 360 years. Working back 360 years from the date of the Rakshasa-Tangadi battle and the destruction of Vijayanagara in Ś. 1487 (A.D. 1565), the date of the foundation would indeed fall in Ś. 1127 or A.D. 1205. In any case, this date is more than a century earlier than the traditional date for the city's foundation, A.D. 1336.

It should also be noted that this traditional date is no longer accepted by most contemporary scholars. On the one hand, it is now evident that an incipient urban center of some sort was present in the area of the site long before 1336; on the other hand, however, it is recognized that this location was not adopted as a capital by the new Sangama house until the reign of Bukka I in the 1350s. For a detailed and important discussion of the issues surrounding the city's foundation and its early history as it relates to the rise of the Vijayanagara state, see Filliozat (1973).

36. *ceremonially sprinkling water three times:* Here and in the following sentence, the word *tripuraṣiṃci* is of doubtful meaning. It may possibly be irregularly derived from the Sanskrit *tri-*, "three," and *pṛṣ*, "to sprinkle."

37. *with sixteen* maṇuvus *of gold:* The *maṇuvu* is a unit of weight (the "maund") that at the beginning of this century was equal to about twenty-five pounds. Its value during the time of this text is uncertain. Appadorai (1936, p. 784) gives seventy-five pounds as the value of the maund, but without specifying at what time and place.

2. The Coronation and Education of Krishnaraya

1. *After hearing the story of the city's foundation . . . he may begin to rule the kingdom:* There are two short lacunae at this point in the text, but the sense of the passage seems to be as translated.

2. The Ministers of Krishnadevaraya: The ministers mentioned here are actually called *daḷanāyakulu* or "commanders"; I have differentiated them as "ministers" since numerous other passages in the text clearly present them as functioning in that specialized capacity. At the same time, however, it is well known that brahman "ministers" under Krishnadevaraya often bore military responsibilities as well, as a number of subsequent passages in the present text also testify. In this connection, it is also worth pointing out that the suffix *-arasu,* occurring in the names of the first five ministers mentioned, is a Telugu loan word from Kannada meaning "lord, king."

Three of the six ministers mentioned here are readily identified as historical individuals who served Krishnadevaraya.

The foremost is of course Appaji (lit., "honored father") or Saluva Timmarasu (also Timmayya, Timmarasayya), here uncharacteristically mentioned last. He was Krishnadevaraya's most trusted adviser throughout most of his reign. He was a brahman of the Kaundinya gotra, the son of Racaya and the grandson of Vemaya (*EI,* 6:234). He was appointed governor of the Kondavidu-*sīma* following its capture, in recognition of his role in the siege of the fort there (*EI,* 6:111ff.). According to the chronicle of Nuniz, he was greatly respected by Krishnadevaraya until about 1524, when he fell from favor owing to the suspicion that he had been responsible for the murder of Krishnadevaraya's young son Tirumaladeva; the king had him blinded and imprisoned (Sewell 1962, pp. 340–342). See Krishna Sastri (1912, p. 183) and Hayavadana Rao (1930, pp. 1790–1794).

Kondamarasu, also known as Kondamarasayya, Kondapparasayya, Kondama Nayaka, or Kondama Nayudu, was another of Krishnadevaraya's well-known advisers. He was a brahman of the Bharadvaja gotra, the son of Timmarasayya and Singayamma. He is often styled *Rayasam Kondamarasayya,* suggesting that he began his career as a *rāyasam* or clerk. He was charged with the command of Udayagiri after its capture (see Hayavadana Rao 1930, pp. 1795–1796).

Ayyamarasu is probably to be identified with Ayyapparasu (also Ayyapparasayya), who was Kondamarasu's son. According to Nuniz, who calls him *Ajaboisa,* he succeeded Saluva Timmarasayya as Krishnadevaraya's chief adviser after his fall from favor. An epigraph of his dated to 1527 is known (see Hayavadana Rao 1930, pp. 1795–1797).

3. The Commanders and other Officials of Krishnadevaraya: In contrast to the case of the later list of Amaranayakas summoned by Krishnadevaraya (p. 121), where the great majority of names given are those of historical individuals (see n. 16, chap. 4), only a few of the names of the commanders *(daḷanāyakas)* and other officials mentioned here are readily identifiable.

Arviti Bukkaraju was a prominent general under Saluva Narasimha (r. 1486–1491) and is counted among the progenitors of Vijayanagara's fourth dynasty, the Aravidu. He appears in Aravidu genealogies as the great-grandfather of Aliya Rama Raya and is credited with the accomplishment of "firmly establishing" Saluva Narasimha's kingdom (see Hayavadana Rao 1930, p. 2114).

Saluva Makaraju, also mentioned in the list of Amaranayakas, was a rebellious Vijayanagara chief who fought on the side of Gobburi Jaggaraya against the legitimate Aravidu rulers Shriranga II (1614) and Ramadevaraya (1618–1630) during the civil war of 1614–1629 (see also *FSVH,* 1:326–333; and *FSVH,* vols. 2–3, no. 208).

Some chiefs are identified only by the names of their families' respective bases of power (e.g., "the chief of Budahalli"); all these represent chiefly families who held varying degrees of influence in the sixteenth century. The chiefs of Nandyal (see Hayavadana Rao 1930, p. 2108) and the Velama chiefs of Velugodu (identified by the family name Velugoti; see Venkataramanayya [1939]) were especially prominent in the political intrigues and wars of the latter half of the sixteenth century.

4. The name of one or more commanders is lost through a lacuna following *Dalavayi Lingarasu*. The text then reads: *Sāḷuvanārā . . . kāḍu*.

5. Lacunae following *the chief of Avuku* and following *the chief of Velugodu*.

6. *the master of a thousand things at once: sahasrāvadhānulu*. Exact sense uncertain.

7. *the eighteen royal instruments:* The group of five royal instruments *(pañca-mahā-śabda)*—consisting of horn *(śṛṅga)*, tabor *(tammaḷa)*, conch shell *(śaṅkha)*, kettle drum *(bhēri)*, and gong *(jayaghaṇṭa)*—is frequently mentioned in epigraphic records as a mark of royalty (Dutt 1967, p. xxii). I am unaware, however, of any other occurrence of a grouping of eighteen such instruments.

8. *draped him with a yellow shawl:* The yellow shawl *(pītāṃbaraṃ)* is a characteristic attribute of the god Krishna and is perhaps used in this context to suggest the homologization between the newly anointed king Krishnaraya and his divine eponym.

9. *the* Shorter Rāmāyaṇa: *saṃkṣēpa-rāmāyaṇamu*. The seventy-nine-verse synopsis of the story of Rama, found at the beginning of the Ramayana epic (*Bāla-kāṇḍa, sarga* 1; see Goldman 1984, pp. 121–126). In Sanskrit, this epitome is more commonly known as *Saṃkṣipta Rāmāyaṇa*.

10. *my brothers Achyutaraya and Chandramauli:* Achyutaraya succeeded to the throne after Krishnadevaraya's death and reigned from 1529 to 1542. The identity of Chandramauli is uncertain—he may be the same as Sadashiva (r. 1542–1576), who, however, was Krishnadevaraya's nephew, not his brother.

11. Lacuna after *skillfulness*.

12. *Narāṇāṃ ca narādhipam:* Quotation taken from Bhagavad-Gita, 10.27, in the context of Krishna's revelation to Arjuna that he may be found as the best being in each category. The full verse reads: *Uccaiḥśravasam aśvānāṃ viddhi mām amṛtodbhavaṃ / airāvataṃ gajendrāṇāṃ narāṇāṃ ca narādhipam //* "Uccaiḥśravas [Indra's steed] of horses, / Sprung from the nectar [churned out of ocean], know me to be; / Of princely elephants, Airāvata [Indra's elephant], / And of men, the king" (Edgerton 1972, p. 103).

13. The Ministers Instruct Krishnadevaraya in the Matter of Ruling the Kingdom: The entire passage following, from p. 89, line 13, to p. 94, line 27, is taken from another literary work, the anonymous *Sabhāpati Vacanamu*, which may be dated to the middle of the sixteenth century (Kulasekhara Rao 1974, p. 433). The work is in prose and is devoted to a discussion of how a king (*sabhāpati*, lit., "Lord of the Assembly") should act—thus its title. The work is cast as an index of numerically defined categories (e.g., the three universal qualities, the four goals of life, the five elements, and so on). Although the principle is not followed very strictly, the general arrangement is such that the work starts with categories of sevens, jumps

back to threes, and then continues on in an ascending progression through fours, fives, sixes, eights, nines, tens, and sixteens. (There is considerable jumbling among the eights, nines, and tens.) This principle of arrangement is of considerable antiquity in India and is found at least as early as the Pali *Anguttara Nikāya,* in which the *suttas* are grouped in sections *(nipāta)* titled by numbers from one to eleven and arranged in ascending numerical order. "Every section contains Suttas dealing with subjects which are in some way or other connected with the number of the corresponding section. The first Sutta in the Eka-Nipāta, for instance, deals with the *one,* which more than anything else darkens the mind of man, that is, woman. The section of five begins with Suttas which deal with the *pañca sekhabalāni,* etc." (Geiger 1956, p. 18). In the medieval period, the principle was often adopted in the arrangement of topics discussed in the philosophical-ritual compendiums of Agamic Saivism.

14. *With the radiance of youth and precious gems:* According to Venkata Rao (1960, p. 317), this verse is taken from the *Nīti* of Baddena, but I am unable to locate it in either of the printed versions that I have consulted *(Baddinītulu; Nītiśāstramuktāvaḷi).*

15. *the seven-limbed state:* These are Kautilya's seven elements of sovereignty (see *Artha Śāstra* 6.1).

16. *the seven techniques for dealing with an enemy:* These are the four principal *upāyas* or "political expedients"—*sāma, bheda, dāna,* and *daṇḍa*—plus the three additional means of *māyā, upekṣā,* and *(mahā-)indrajāla.* For a detailed discussion, see Zimmer (1951, pp. 118–123).

17. *seven royal vices:* Kautilya (*Artha Śāstra* 8.3.328–330) discusses four royal vices, which are—in ascending order of seriousness—hunting, gambling, women, and drinking. The origin of the remaining three vices is unknown to me.

18. *the "sevenfold progeny":* The concept of *sapta-saṃtānambulu* is quite popular in medieval Andhra, where it is met with in both epigraphic and literary sources. The idea is that, in addition to a son, there are six other things worthy of consideration as "progeny" since they ensure the patron's fame and spiritual well-being in the afterlife. There are sometimes discrepancies in specific identities between one list and the next.

19. *the sevenfold assembly: sabhā-saptāṃga.* Note that the seventh is not mentioned. I am unaware of other sources describing this grouping.

20. *the seven constituents of the body: sapta-dhātuvulu* (Sanskrit *dhātu*). Instead of *rasa,* which is the "vital humor" of the standard classification (see *Śabdakalpadruma,* 2:790), the text has the apparently analogous term *dhātu.*

21. *the seven worthy gifts:* This is a slight variation on the listing given on p. 89.

22. *dealing, respectively, with logic, wisdom, and the principles of war:* There is, in fact, a small lacuna between *logic* and *the principles of war,* but the context suggests *wisdom* or some equivalent.

23. *running nimbly on his feet:* Small lacuna in text here: *pada . . . lāghava.*

24. *the three powers coming from material resources, good counsel, and personal bravery:* These are the three powers *(śakti)* of the *Artha Śāstra* (9.1.339), respectively, *prabhava-śakti, mantra-śakti,* and *utsāha-śakti.* Kautilya ranks them in order of ascending importance: *utsāha, prabhava,* and, finally, *mantra.*

25. *the threefold* sandhya *worship:* A thrice-daily worship consisting of the ritual sipping of water *(ācamana)* and recitation of certain prayers is enjoined on all twice-born castes. These rites are carried out at the three junctures *(sandhyā)* of the day: morning, noon, and evening (Sridhara Babu 1975, p. 81).

26. *the three universal qualities of clarity, activity, and inertia:* These are the three *guṇas* of Samkhya philosophy: *sattva, rajas,* and *tamas.*

27. *the three types of heroes:* The division *uttama, madhyama,* and *adhama* is common in many later *Alamkāra-śāstra* works. For textual references, see De (1976, 2:269).

28. *maintain an army composed of the four divisions:* The fourfold army *(caturaṃga-bala)* remains an ideal concept in later medieval political thought, even though chariot divisions were no longer used. In some contexts in the present text, the term *caturaṃga-bala* is used to connote "a complete army," i.e., one that includes the three divisions of elephants, horses, and foot soldiers.

29. *the four psychological constituents:* mind *(manas),* intellect *(buddhi),* ego *(ahaṃkāra),* and consciousness *(cittam).*

30. *the different types of erotic heroes:* The significance of the first three terms is unknown to me; definitions of the three types of male confidants may be found in the *Kāma Sūtra* of Vatsyayana (see Burton 1964, p. 79).

31. *the four different types of women:* The classification of the four types of women is expounded in medieval works on erotics such as the *Ratirahasya.* For definitions, see Comfort (1965, pp. 103–106).

32. *alienation of friends, gaining friends, war and peace, loss of gains, and rashness: mitra-bheda, suhṛl-lābha, saṃdhi-vigraha, labdha-nāśana,* and *asaṃprēkṣva.* These refer to the subjects dealt with in the five books of the Sanskrit *Pañcatantra,* the celebrated collection of animal fables.

33. *seats of the five vital airs:* The *Yoga-bhāṣya* of Vyasa describes these as follows: "Life which shows itself as the operations of *prāṇa* (vital breath) and others, is the manifestation of all the powers of sensation and action. Its action is five-fold. The *prāṇa* moves through the mouth and the nose, and manifests itself within the chest. The *samāna* manifests itself up to the navel. It is so called because it carries equally *(sama)* [to all parts of the body, the juice of food, etc.]. Manifesting down to the soles of the feet [all over] is the *apāna,* so called because it carries away *(apa).* Manifesting up to the head is the *udāna,* so called because it carries upward *(ut).* The *vyāna* is so called because it pervades the whole body in every direction. Of these, the *prāṇa* is the chief" (Radhakrishnan and Moore 1957, pp. 475–476).

34. *know the five great classes of musical sounds: ūduṭa mīṭuṭa vrēyuṭa raccupaikaṃ ālāpaṃbulanu paṃca-mahā-vādyaṃbulan eriṃgi.* The exact senses of *raccupaikaṃ,* which I have rendered as "produced by bowing," and *ālāpaṃbu,* rendered "produced . . . by the human voice," are unclear.

35. *know the five types of food: bhakṣya-bhōjya-lēhya-cōṣya-pānīyaṃbulanu paṃca-vidha āhāraṃbulan eriṃgi.*

36. *the six activities of a king:* These are the *rāja-ṣāḍ-guṇyam,* which form the subject matter of the *Artha Śāstra* 7. They are briefly defined as follows: "Of these, agreement with pledges is peace [*saṃdhi*]; offensive operation is war [*vigraha*]; indifference is neutrality [*āsana*]; making preparations is marching [*yāna*]; seeking the protection of another is alliance [*saṃśraya*]; and making peace with one and waging war with another is termed a double policy [*dvaidhībhāva*]. These are the six forms" (*Artha Śāstra* 7.1.6–12).

37. *the six philosophical schools:* The names of two of the schools are lost through a lacuna. Although the term *ṣaḍ-darśana* generally refers to the six *orthodox* schools (Nyaya, Vaisheshika, Samkhya, Yoga, Mimamsa, and Vedanta), the schools here identified are all considered unorthodox or heretical.

38. *the six* śāstras: This list appears redundant since both Bhatta and Prabhakara are subschools of Purva-Mimamsa and Vedanta and Uttara-Mimamsa are identical.

39. *the eight matters of warriors:* Another item—*rāge*—is mentioned after "handling the reins," but its sense is uncertain.

40. *show skill in manifesting the sentiments:* These are the eight *rasas* of classical Indian aesthetic theory: *śṛṅgāra, vīra, karuṇa, adbhuta, hāsya, bhayānaka, bhībatsa,* and *raudra.*

41. *the nine treasures of the God of Wealth:* According to the Sanskrit lexicographical tradition, Kubera, the god of wealth, is the lord of nine personified treasures or *nidhis.* Our text's enumeration is actually at variance with the standard lists in that it gives "Kunda" instead of "Nanda" and "Vara" instead of "Kharva." The first six of these "treasures" are associated with the life-giving waters of abundance (*padma* is lotus, *mahāpadma* is great lotus, *śaṅkha* is conch, *makara* is crocodile, *kacchapa* is tortoise, and *mukunda* is red lotus); the last three are of uncertain origin (*nanda* is happy, *nīla* is dark blue or black, and *kharva* is imperfect, mutilated, dwarfish).

42. *the eight syllabic groupings used in poetic meters:* These *gaṇas* are defined in terms of light (∪) and heavy (—) syllables as follows: *sa-gaṇa:* ∪ ∪ —; *na-gaṇa:* ∪ ∪ ∪; *ya-gaṇa:* ∪ — —; *ma-gaṇa:* — — —; *bha-gaṇa:* — ∪ ∪; *ra-gaṇa:* — ∪ —; *ta-gaṇa:* — — ∪; and *ja-gaṇa:* ∪ — ∪ (*Sulakṣaṇasāramu* 11–17).

43. *the twenty types of rhyming or* yati: Telugu verse is subject not only to metrical rules but also to the requirements of *yati* or "rhyming." As Narayana Rao has aptly characterized it, *yati* requires "that a specific syllable in the body of the line must chime (through an identical or related consonant and vowel) with the initial syllable of the line" (Heifetz and Narayana Rao

1987, p. 167). The twenty different types of *yati* here named apply to the different letters and combinations of letters possible in Telugu. Definitions for most of them can be found in *Sulakṣaṇasāramu* 92–165.

44. *cakkaṭi:* emend from *takkaṭi.*

45. *the eighteen types of description:* Use of the *aṣṭādaśa-varṇanamulu* or "eighteen [stereotyped] descriptions" becomes one of the symbolic hallmarks of later Telugu poetry of the *prabandham* genre, underlining the modal shift that distinguishes this essentially descriptive genre from the more narrative *purāṇamu* works that preceded it (Narayana Rao 1978, p. 55). Peddana's *Manucaritramu,* composed under Krishnadevaraya's patronage, is generally recognized as the first, full-fledged *prabandham*-type work.

46. *verses that are in proper meter and abound in smooth descriptions:* The phrase that follows this—*vākyaṃ daśa pītābhāvavaibhavaṃbulan eriṃgi*—is of uncertain significance and has been left untranslated.

47. *know the secrets of the ten stages of love:* The text reads: *cūcuṭa ciṃtiṃcuṭa vagacuṭa ussuranuṭa koniyāḍuṭa siggun eruṃgaka yuṃḍuṭa annaṃbarōcakam aguṭa jvaramu vaccuṭa nāluka toṭrupaḍuṭa jīvaṃ tolagajūcuṭa aniyeḍu daśāvasthala marmamulan eriṃgi.*

48. *the sixteen stages of death:* Only fifteen stages are enumerated; *vunna cōṭa kelasuṭa,* translated provisionally as "forgetting where one is," is of uncertain sense. The text reads: *vaṇakuṭa, noppivaccuṭa, garigarika viḍucuṭa, kalahiyaguṭa, ciṃtanoṃḍuṭa, dainyamunoṃḍuṭa, duḥkhiyaguṭa, vōrpula pogaluṭa, vunna cōṭa kelasuṭa, ātma maracuṭa, nirāhāriyaguṭa, krāguṭa, maunaṃbu dālcuṭa, arajīvaṃ tolaguṭa, paṃcatvamanaṃb arigina ṣōḍaśāvasthala bhēdaṃbul eriṃgi.*

49. *To acquire wealth:* Verse quoted from the Telugu *Nīti* of Baddena (ca. twelfth to thirteenth century). See *Baddinītulu* 1.4 or *Nītiśāstramuktāvaḷi* 3.

50. THE STORY OF KING PARIKSHIT AND THE DHARMA COW: Parikshit was the sole member of the Pandava lineage to survive the great cataclysm of the Bharata war (the subject of the *Mahābhārata* epic), which marks the dividing line between the Dvapara and the Kali ages. He is thus the first king of the present age. For the theme of the progressive decline of *dharma* from the Krita to the Kali age, see the excerpts from the *Kūrma-* and *Viṣṇupurāṇas* translated in Dimmitt and van Buitenen (1978, pp. 38–41).

51. *King Yudhishthira:* Yudhishthira, leader of the Pandavas. As elder brother of Arjuna—the grandfather of Parikshit—he is Parikshit's great uncle and dynastic predecessor. He is such a model of kingly virtue that he is regarded as an emanation *(aṃśa)* of the god Dharma himself (*Mahābhārata* 1.[7]61.84; van Buitenen 1973, p. 154).

52. *Up to this point, Ishvara Nayaka, Narasa-Nayaka, and Viranrisimharaya have ruled the kingdom:* These three, Krishnadevaraya's predecessors in the Tuluva dynasty, are, respectively, his grandfather, father, and elder brother. Ishvara Nayaka was a prominent military commander who served Saluva Narasimha during the last decades of the Sangama dynasty; he was not, however, a "ruler of the kingdom" in any real sense. His son Narasa Nayaka

served from 1491 to 1503 as regent for Saluva Narasimha's son, who had acceded to the Vijayanagara throne as the second and last king of the Saluva dynasty. Narasa Nayaka's son Viranrisimharaya ruled from 1505 to 1509 and is usually considered to have been the first legitimate king of the new Tuluva dynasty.

3. Krishnaraya and Timmarasu

1. *a certain street in one ward of the city: yī pāḷyāṇa yiṭuvaṃṭi vīdhini.* Venkataramanayya (1935, p. 266) suggests that the city was divided into a number of *pāḷyams* (variant form *pāḷem*) or wards for the purpose of patrolling by the *talāris* or inspectors. He refers to a *kaḍita* record dated A.D. 1604, describing the seventy-seven *pāḷems* into which the Aravidu king Venkata II divided his capital of Chandragiri, claiming as his precedent the division of the city of Vijayanagara effected by Venkata's ancestor Krishnadevaraya.

2. *Padyaniti Chandrayya: Padyaniti* is an ephithet and not part of Chandrayya's proper name; the sense is "Chandrayya, the master of *Padyanīti.*" The literal meaning of *Padyanīti* is "verse *nīti,*" but Venkata Rao (1960, p. 317) has suggested that the word is actually a corrupt variant of the title of one of the well-known Telugu *nīti* texts, *Badde-nīti* (the *Nīti* of Baddena, ca. twelfth to thirteenth century). The verse recited by Chandrayya's son is in fact quoted from this text.

3. *works on royal conduct such as* Sañjaya's Nīti, Vidura's Nīti, Cāṇukya's Nīti, *and* Bhartṛhari's Collection of One Hundred Verses on Nīti: With the exception of *Bhartṛhari's Collection of One Hundred Verses on Nīti*—the Sanskrit *Bhartṛhari-nīti-śatakam* (translated in Miller 1967, pp. 8–59)—these various *nīti* texts cannot be positively identified. *Cāṇukya* is a variant form of Chanakya Kautilya, the author of the *Artha Śāstra,* so *Cāṇukya's Nīti* may refer either to this Sanskrit text or to some later Telugu adaptation of it.

4. *If his army is greater / than the forces of his feudatories:* Verse quoted from the Telugu *Nīti* of Baddena (ca. twelfth to thirteenth century). See *Baddenītulu* 1.20 or *Nītiśāstramuktāvaḷi* 11.

5. *the amount of deposited treasure: sthāpiṃciyuṃcina nikṣepamulu.* The term literally means "buried treasures that have been established and kept." A passage in Paes suggests the possible significance of this term: "And now I wish you to know that the previous kings of this place for many years past have held it a custom to maintain a treasury, which treasury, after the death of each, is kept locked and sealed in such a way that it cannot be seen by any one, nor opened, nor do the kings who succeed to the kingdom open them or know what is in them. They are not opened except when the kings have great need, and thus the kingdom has great supplies to meet its needs" (Sewell 1962, p. 271).

6. *Allalanatha, who was keeper of the small treasury:* "Small treasury," *cinnabhaṃḍāraṃ.* Venkataramanayya (1935, pp. 107–109) is of the opinion that the

term *cinna-bhaṃḍāraṃ* refers to the "active" treasury of the reigning king, in contrast to an implied *pedda-bhaṃḍāraṃ* or "big treasury" (not actually so named in the sources), which would have housed the "deposited treasure" (see n. 5 above) of the earlier monarchs.

7. ALLALANATHA'S REPORT ON THE STATE OF THE TREASURY: This interesting passage is, unfortunately, one of the most convoluted and confusing sections of the text. The value of the passage lies, not in the specific values of the figures reported, but rather in the economic and political relations implied by the structure and form of the report. This report—together with three related passages that help clarify its significance (pp. 105–106, 107, and 121–122)—would in fact appear to constitute the most detailed, indigenous textual evidence for the nature of the "*nāyaka* system" in sixteenth-century South India. Since the very existence of such a system of ordered, semifeudal relations based on military service tenures *(amaraṃ)* has recently been called into question (see Stein 1980, pp. 396–397 and chap. 7 passim), the proper interpretation of this passage takes on an added importance.

The primary obstacles to understanding the passage spring from a number of textual difficulties, including a lack of agreement between certain figures that are clearly intended to tally, the presence of several obvious lacunae that have not been marked by the text's editor, and an extremely convoluted syntax (the five sentences from *In this kingdom* . . . to . . . *sufficient for the maintenance of the 24,000 horses, 1,200 elephants, and 200,000 foot soldiers with which they serve you,* e.g., represent what in the original is a single, tortuously involved sentence). But, through careful comparison of this section with the related passages signaled above, it is possible not only to resolve the complexities of the syntax but also to make emendations clarifying the problems of the lacunae and nonagreement of the figures. The emendations that I have made are given in the individual annotations that follow.

The key to understanding the passage is the proper recognition of the king's motivation in requesting the treasurer's report. His concern is not with fiscal matters per se, but only insofar as they relate to the strength and composition of his army. This interest is revealed by the king's reaction to the *nīti* verse read to him in the episode immediately preceding this section and by the continued focus of attention on military matters in the remaining portion of the present chapter. The king wishes to determine only, in the words of the *nīti* verse, whether "*his* army is greater than the forces of his feudatories"; accordingly, he specifically requests the treasurer to supply figures "for the palace's salaried forces, including elephants, horses, and their attendants" *(nagari-kaijītaṃ-yēnuga gurraṃ-parijanālakunnu vivaramugā lekkha vrāsi tecci caduvam ani)*. It is when the king realizes that Allalanatha has not reported "so much as a single elephant, horse, or attendant in the direct employ of the palace" but only figures for the troops supplied by "his feudatories," the Amaranayakas, that Krishnadevaraya becomes so concerned and devotes his attention to reforming the army together with his minister Appaji.

This entire discourse is predicated on a fundamental distinction that is drawn between two different types of troops in the king's service. The text refers to these as *nagari-kaijītaṃ* or simply *kaijītaṃ* forces, which I have translated as "the palace's salaried forces" or "the standing, salaried army," and *amaraṃ* or *amaranāyakaṃ* forces, which are supplied to the king by the *nāyakas* who maintain them and pay their salaries. The *kaijītaṃ* forces are paid and provided for directly from the palace treasury, as is made clear by the description of the elaborate arrangements that are made for the provision of the 12,000 new *kaijītaṃ* horses and 500 new *kaijītaṃ* elephants that Appaji acquires for the king.

Regarding the arrangements of the *amaraṃ* forces, the following details can be gleaned from our text's narrative. First, each *nāyaka* was required to provide a specific number of troops (elephants, horses, and foot soldiers) for the king; the exact figures for these levies were recorded in the palace register (p. 101; *Rāyalavāru karaṇālatōnu amaranāyakānaku nagari-kavile-kāvali-prakārānaku yēnugu-gurraṃ-baṃṭu-bayadalaku vivaramugā lekha vrāsi temmani ānaticcina*). Second, the palace assigned "estates" *(śīmalu)* for the *nāyakas* to rule on behalf of the king *(rājyamunnu yēlukoni kolustāvunnāru)*; the income thus derived was deemed sufficient to defray the expenses of maintaining the required *amaraṃ* forces (p. 101; *amaranāyakaṃ-gurrālu* [**yiruvaināluguvēlunnu*] *ēnugalunnu paṃdreṃḍuvēlunnu, kālbalamulu reṃḍulakṣalunnu, iṃduku rōjulakunnu āyakaṃ, ādavani, ceyyēṭidurgaṃ . . . modalaina vanadurgamulu dēśamulu gala rājyamunnu yēlukoni kolustāvunnāru*). Third, there was a direct correlation between the size of the *śīma* assigned and the number of troops that a *nāyaka* was required to provide, as is evident from the statement that, "although the Amaranayakas have occupied these estates in accordance with our figures, they have nonetheless failed to provide the correct number of elephants, horses, and foot soldiers" (p. 101; *lekkhakramāniki śīmalu koni yēnugu, gurramulu, baṃṭubayadalu, ā baddhatiki kolavaka vunnāru*). The text seems to imply that the size of any given *śīma* assignment was a function of the number of troops required of the *nāyaka*, the cost of maintaining them (calculated from the standard rates outlined on p. 101), and the productive yield of the land. Fourth, it is implied that a *nāyaka's* tenurial rights to his *śīma* are conditional, depending on his regular and satisfactory provision of the specified number of *amaraṃ* troops. Thus, if his levy falls below the required number and he is unable to make cash payments equal in value to the service he has failed to provide, he is liable to have his *śīma* confiscated. Thus, when the Nayakas beg to be forgiven for failing to discharge their duties, they suggest that, if the king will forgive their transgression *(tamamīdi nēraṃ tappipōtē)* this once and allow them to continue running their estates as usual *(śīmala yeppaṭivalenē naḍipitēnu)*, they will offer the elephants and horses that they currently own to the palace in lieu of the cash that they have been asked to pay and then acquire some more animals for themselves later.

8. *When Vidyaranya founded this city, the amount of treasure that he buried:* In the first paragraph of his report, Allalanatha seems to be reporting the contents of the supposed *pedda-bhaṃḍāraṃ,* while the second paragraph would appear to pertain to the *cinna-bhaṃḍāraṃ* (see n. 6 above).

9. *land grants for the maintenance of gods and brahmans, grants of rent-free lands, and grants for the support of monasteries:* These are various forms of eleemosynary tenures and stand in contrast to service tenures: *dēvādāyaṃ* (grants for gods, i.e., to temples, for the performance of worship), *brahmādāyaṃ* (grants for brahmans), *sarvamānyaṃ* (grants of tax-free lands), and *maṭhaparam* (grants for the support of *maṭhas* or monastic institutions) (Venkataramanayya 1935, pp. 183–184).

10. *the rate:* The text clearly and repeatedly states that the rate is *daily (rōju)* for horses and elephants, while for foot soldiers it first states that the rate is "two *gheṭṭi varāhas monthly* per soldier" *(baṃṭu okkhaṃṭiki* nelaku *ghaṭṭi reṃḍēśivarālalekka)* but then goes on to calculate that this comes to "a total of 400,000 *gheṭṭis daily* for 200,000 soldiers" *(reṃḍulakṣala baṃṭlaku* rōju *nālugu lakṣalunnu)*. At a later point in the text (p. 105), the total maintenance cost for the 24,000 horses, 1,200 elephants, and 200,000 *amaraṃ* horses is said to be "48 million per year—calculated from a monthly rate of 4 million" *(nela vokhaṃṭiki nalabhai lakṣalu vaṃtuna saṃvatsarāniki nālugukōṭluyenabhailakṣalaku)*. Since the total of the "daily" costs mentioned in the present passage does in fact come to 4 million (horses: 2,400,000; elephants: 1,200,000; foot soldiers: 400,000), I conclude that the multiple occurrences of *daily (rōju)* are in error for *monthly (nelaku)*. I have emended the text accordingly. Note that Nilakanta Sastri and Venkataramanayya (1946, 3:145n) also comment on the unreasonableness of the figures if taken as a daily maintenance cost but go on to suggest that they must represent an annual cost.

11. gheṭṭis: A *gheṭṭi* (alternate form *ghaṭṭi*) is a coin of uncertain value. According to Dutt (1967, p. 102), who cites its occurrence in an inscription at Vijayanagara dated 1561, it is a gold coin equal to a *varāha*. According to Nilakanta Sastri and Venkataramanayya (1946, 3:145), *gheṭṭi* is "a *ghaṭṭi varāha* equivalent to Rs. 4/-." The wording of the present text later in this paragraph would seem to confirm this interpretation.

12. *around the military commanders' forts at Nandyal, Shrirangapatnam, Ummattur, Vallamkota, Madurai, Palyamkota, and Dindikal:* Emend to: *naṃdyāla, śrīraṃgapaṭṇaṃ, vummattūru,* *~~*daḷanāyakula kōṭlā*~~*vallaṃkōṭa, madhura, pāḷyaṃkōṭa, diṃḍikallu modalaina* [**daḷanāyakula kōṭlunnu*].

13. *for the maintenance of the 24,000 horses, 1,200 elephants:* Emend to: *gurrālu* [**yiruvaināluguvēlunnu*] *ēnugalunnu paṃḍreṃḍu* *~~*vēlunnu*~~ [**vaṃdalunnu*].

14. *Although the Amaranayakas have occupied these estates in accordance with our figures, they have nonetheless failed to provide the correct number of elephants,*

horses, and foot soldiers: Emend to: *lekkhakramāniki śīmalu koni yēnugu, gurramulu, baṃṭubayadalu, ā baddhatiki *~~kolucuka~~* [**kolavaka*] *vunnāru.*

15. *the ministers would disapprove:* The next sentence in the text is unclear and has been omitted in this translation. The sentence reads: *kābaṭṭi vākiṭi pinna-peddalu tamarayye telusukoni oka kāryaṃ naḍipistē appuḍu tamaku svataṃtramugā naḍucunu anucu.* Nilakanta Sastri and Venkataramanayya offer the following translation: "Therefore, when the wise men of our court, having understood (what is good to the state) perform any work, we should be considered to have acted independently" (1946, 3:147).

16. *several leagues:* The text specifies a distance of two *āmaḍas,* which would work out to about sixteen miles.

17. *you can pluck a mere piece of grass and turn it into Mount Meru:* This statement calls to mind the Telugu proverb *tṛṇamu mēruva, mēruva tṛṇamu,* lit., "To make Mount Meru out of a piece of grass, to make a piece of grass out of Mount Meru." According to Carr, the purport of this proverb is that "the slightest favour done to a good man is gratefully acknowledged, but a bad man forgets the greatest benefits" (1868, no. 1105). In the present context, however, the implied, sarcastic meaning *(vyaṃgyōktulugā)* seems to be more along the lines of "to make mountains out of molehills, and molehills out of mountains." Perhaps Rayalu is sarcastically implying that Appaji has overreacted to his having left the city while at the same time not taking seriously enough Rayalu's concern over the lack of *kaijītaṃ* forces.

18. *I myself am nothing more than a worthless piece of grass . . . only the lord who is surrounded by great servants . . . will gain fame and renown:* In this speech, Appaji shows his wit by ignoring Rayalu's veiled criticism and acknowledging the superficial compliment. He then goes on to proclaim—in terms that further develop the theme set by Rayalu—that he himself is nothing but a worthless piece of grass *(tṛṇa-mātram).* But then he strikes back with an extended double entendre, appealing to the metaphor of the sapphire *(iṃdranīlam),* popularly known as *tṛṇa-grāhi* or "grass attracter" in recognition of the fact that a high-quality sapphire—when rubbed—attracts pieces of grass (by static electricity). If a sapphire fails to do this, "thinking" that it is only grass, then "it is not a fine sapphire and will have little value." It is thus the grass that proves the greatness of the sapphire, just as it is the great servants surrounding the king who prove their lord's greatness.

19. *120 elephant units:* An elephant unit *(yēnuga ghaṭṭam* or *ghaṭṭi)* consists of ten elephants.

20. *Appaji said to them:* The text states *rāyalavāru,* but the context demands that this be emended to *sāḷuva timmarasayya.*

21. *they agreed on 200* varāhas *per horse:* Emend to: *gurrāla krayaṃ gurraṃ vakkhaṃṭiki *~~yēnūru~~* [**yinnūru*] *varāla vaṃtuna.*

22. *Sad the king / who thinks women can be wives:* Verse quoted from the Telugu *Nīti* of Baddena (ca. twelfth to thirteenth century). See *Baddenītulu* 1.6 or *Nītiśāstramuktāvaḷi* 6.

4. Reports of the Turks

1. *palace gate: nagari-vākili.*

2. *in the audience hall before the hall of justice: dādi-mahalu muṃdugā muṃdara-divāṇaṃlō.*

3. *the Gajapati king Bahubalendra:* Bahubalendra Mukunda Gajapati, ruler of the Gajapati kingdom of Orissa from ca. 1560 to 1568, anachronistically cast as Krishnadevaraya's contemporary. The actual contemporary Gajapati ruler was Prataparudra Gajapati, r. 1497–1538.

4. *And among men, I am the Lord of Men:* See n. 12, chap. 2.

5. *Shankaranayadu of Ikkeri Basavapatnam and other such princes and to Boyi Ramappa:* The mentioning of these names in the present context—implying that they are local rulers enjoying a feudatory relationship with Bijapur—is problematic. In a later passage (p. 121), Boyi Ramappa is included in the group of Krishnadevaraya's most intimate subordinates, the "Eighteen Sons of the Eating Dish," and Shankaranayadu is here implied to be the lord of Ikkeri and Basavapatnam, two major fortified centers within the Malnad region in the heart of the Vijayanagara territory. Although the identity of the Shankaranayadu mentioned here is uncertain, his situation does bear a close resemblance to that of a chief of the same name who was a contemporary of Shriranga I (r. 1572–1585) and is mentioned by Ferishta (Briggs [1966, 3:85], where the name is spelled *Shunkur Naik*) as being in control of Karoor (i.e., Kadur, according to Hayavadana Rao [1930, p. 2144], about twenty miles southeast of Basavapatnam). According to Ferishta, he was the leader of several local chiefs in the area who left the service of Vijayanagara to become tributaries of Ali Adil Shah of Bijapur in 1575.

6. *the placing of cannons, mortars, and rockets . . . and horse trippers outside the fort to prevent any horses from entering:* Translation provisional. Several of the weapons are not definitely identifiable. The original reads: *phiraṃgi, javuru-jaṃgulu, guṃṭṭu-kōvulu, daṃtena-rāḷḷu, yettu-rāḷḷu, gaśikalu, puli-talalu, kōṭa velupaṭa gurrālu joccirākuṃḍā gurrapu-nilupu-rāḷḷu vēyiṃcēdinni.* According to Ramachandra Rao (1982, p. 87), *javuru-jaṃgi* is a type of cannon. According to Brown (1979, p. 371), *guṇṭa-kōvi* is "a firepot, a rocket in an iron tube on a pole; . . . a kind of cannon." *Daṃtena-rāḷḷu* are literally "rake stones"—perhaps a row of long, thin stones planted close together in the ground to prevent the passage of horses? *Ettu-rāḷḷu,* translated provisionally as "boulders," is of uncertain sense. *Puli-tala,* (lit., "tiger's head") is most likely a type of cannon with the muzzle cast in the form of a tiger's head; actual examples are known from Seringapatam in the late eighteenth century (illustrated in Welch 1985, no. 188).

7. *the people who live in the border tracts . . . have begun sending their own troops:* Translation provisional. In actuality, the identity of what is being sent—*ciṭi-pāṭi cikku cilvānamulu*—is not at all clear. The text reads: *sarudula*

uṃḍēvārlu yī vārta vini ciṭi-pāṭi cikku cilvānamulu vijayāpurānaku aṃputāvunnāru.

8. *they appoint only brahmans to serve the palace:* Literally, "they appoint only brahmans to serve the royal gateway" *(vākiṭi-pārupatyamaṃtā vārinē śēyamani).*

9. *Thus you can see that the Lords of the Three Clans are not their own masters:* The notion implicit in this passage is expressed more clearly in a verse from Baddena's *Nīti: svāyattuḍuttamuṃḍu pa / rāyattuṃḍainabhūtalādhipukaṃṭen / svāyattukaṃṭe mēlubha / yāyattuṃḍaṃḍru daśadiśābharaṇāṃkā.* To paraphrase this verse, a king who is "his own master" *(svāyattuṃḍu)* is better than one who is "subject to another" *(parāyattuṃḍu),* i.e., totally dependent on the advice of his ministers. But the best type of king, it is said, is one who is "subject to both" *(ubhayāyattuṃḍu),* in other words, has his own initiative while yet heeding the advice of ministers.

10. *Shiva himself will be the archer:* The text actually states *rathikuṃḍu* (lit., "charioteer").

11. muqims: Instead of *sthānāpati,* the standard Telugu word for ambassador, the text has *mukhāmulu,* derived from the Persian *muqim.*

12. *sixty-four years:* Note that there is a discrepancy here with the chronology implied in chap. 1, according to which Krishnadevaraya has sixty years to rule (see p. 86).

13. *what does he give to his standing army, to his cavalry troops: nilicina vārikēmi rauturāṇuvakēmi.* The precise sense of *nilicina vāru,* translated here as "standing army," is uncertain.

14. *Is it really courtesy:* Source of verse unknown.

15. *Sons of the Eating Dish from the Eighteen Districts: harivāṇaṃ komāḷḷayina padunenimidi kappaṇālavārunnu. Harivāṇam* or *arivāṇam* is a type of copper dish for eating. According to Nilakanta Sastri and Venkataramanayya, the "Sons of the Eating Dish" are a class of honored retainers—fictively adopted as the king's "sons" (see n. 11, chap. 1)—who enjoy the privilege of "partaking [of] the food left in the plate of the king . . . after he finishes his meal. . . . They appear to have been recruited exclusively from the province of Āraga which was sub-divided into 18 divisions known as *Kampaṇas*" (1946, 3: 133n). For the identities of the individuals named in this class, see n. 16 below.

16. KRISHNADEVARAYA SUMMONS THE AMARANAYAKAS: Many of the Amaranayakas named here are readily identifiable as Vijayanagara subordinates who were prominent at one time or another between the periods of Krishnadevaraya (1509–1529) and Venkatapati II (1586–1614). Several of them went on, in the period just after our text's composition, to become key figures in the civil wars sparked by the disputes over the successions of the Aravidu rulers Shriranga II (1614) and Ramadevaraya (1616–1630).

'Ain-ul-Mulk appears to have been a Muslim warrior who left Bijapur to take up service at Vijayanagara under Aliya Rama Raya. According to Venkataramanayya (*FSVH,* 1:259–260), he was closely associated with Jagadeva Rao (Rana Jagadeva of the present text; see below) in a series of campaigns undertaken by Rama Raya against Golconda. He is known from an inscription at Bevinahalli (dated 1551) to have petitioned the Vijayanagara king to sanction a gift of land to a brahmin (*EI,* vol. 14, no. 210; cited by Hayavadana Rao 1930, p. 2110); another inscription (dated 1562) shows him holding Dummesima as his *amaraṃ* estate (*EC,* vol. 7, Ci. 69; cited by Ramachandra Rao 1982, p. xiii).

Ankusha Rao may possibly be identifiable with Ankushendra, the younger brother of Rana Jagadeva (according to the dedication of Ponnatota Aubhala Kavi's *Vāmana-purāṇamu; FSVH,* vols. 2–3, no. 205), since the present text presents him together with Jagadeva and 'Ain-ul-Mulk as someone who has resided at Bijapur and is an authority on the Turks. The *Rāmarājana Bakhair* includes an Ankusha Rao in a list of Vijayanagara warriors slain in the battle of Rakṣasa-Tangaḍi (*FSVH,* 3:233), but it is not clear whether this is the same figure.

Rana Jagadeva or Immadi Jagadeva was a major political figure during the reign of Sadashivaraya and the early years of the Aravidu dynasty. In 1580, he built the fort at Chennapatnam, which thereafter served as his base. According to Venkataramanayya, he served first the Qutb Shahis of Golconda and then the Imad Shahis of Berar before migrating to Vijayanagara (*FSVH,* 1: 258; see also Ramachandra Rao 1982, p. x).

Pemmasani Ramalingama Nayadu belonged to the influential Pemmasani family that ruled the Gandikota-*sīma* during the second half of the sixteenth century and provided several prominent ministers, including Pemmasani Timma, who served Vijayanagara under the Aravidu dynasty (Heras 1927, p. 266). A *cāṭu* verse praising his nephew, Pemmasani Narasimha, refers to Ramalinga's having "caused the three Viziers to fall in prostration" (*muguru vajīrlanu mokka parace; FSVH,* vol. 2, no. 166), an apparent reference to the same incident that is recounted later in the present text (see pp. 138–139). It is not clear whether he served Krishnadevaraya or a later ruler.

Hande Malla Rao is an otherwise unidentified member of the Hande family, which controlled large parts of the Rayalaseema country and was influential, if not always loyal, during the period of the Aravidu dynasty (see *SVH,* nos. 56, 73; *FSVH,* vol. 1, chaps. 23–24 passim).

Saluva Nayadu, better known as Saluva Nayaka or Sellappa, was an Amaranayaka under Krishnadevaraya and Achyutaraya and appears to have been in control of the Chola and Pandya countries (*FSVH,* 1:240–241; Hayavadana Rao 1930, pp. 1797–1798).

Komara Timmappa is probably to be identified with Kumara Timma, also known as Yara Timma Nayadu; a member of the Velugoti family, he was the son of Gani Timma and was a prominent subordinate and supporter of Aliya Rama Raya (*FSVH,* vol. 3, no. 181a; Venkataramanayya 1939, pp. 48–50).

Kotakam Vishvanatha Nayadu, better known as Vishvanatha Nayaka (r. 1529–1564), is the younger contemporary and subordinate of Krishnadevaraya who is remembered as the founder of the Nayaka kingdom of Madurai (see Sathyanatha Aiyar 1924, pp. 48–67; *FSVH,* 1:239–241; *FSVH,* vols. 2–3, nos. 151–155).

Chevvappa Nayadu, also called Shevappa or Shivappa Nayaka (r. ca. 1550–1580), was a subordinate of Achyutaraya and was married to Murtyamba, the younger sister of Achyuta's queen Tirumalamba. He is remembered as the founder of the Nayaka kingdom of Tanjore (see *SVH,* nos. 91, 98; *FSVH,* vols. 2–3, no. 151).

Krishnappa Nayadu or *Krishnappa Nayaka* is a name shared by several members of the house that ruled the Nayaka kingdom of Gingee (also Chenji). Since the name is here mentioned in the context of the founders of the other Nayaka kingdoms, it should probably be taken as referring to Tubaki Krishnappa (ca. 1490–1520), the general of Krishnadevaraya who is considered the founder of the kingdom (see Stein 1989, p. 57; Michell 1991a, p. 143). It should be mentioned, however, that Ramachandra Rao (1982, p. xii) proposes a different identification, suggesting that he may be Krishnappa Nayaka, the son of Adapam Bayappa Nayaka and possessor of an *amaraṃ* estate in Hasan District in the 1560s.

Velugoti Yachama Nayadu was the leader of the Velugoti family during the period spanning the close of the sixteenth century and the civil war of the first quarter of the seventeenth. He was a constant supporter of the Aravidu throne, helping Venkatapati II in 1601 break the power of Linga, the recalcitrant Nayaka ruler of Vellore. After Venkata's death in 1614, Velugoti Yachama Nayadu become the leader of the loyalists who resisted the efforts of Gobburi Jaggaraya to break the Aravidu power (Venkataramanayya 1939, pp. 56–58; *FSVH,* 1:321–324, 326–336; Stein 1989, pp. 122–123).

Saluva Makaraju is to be identified with the Saluva Makaraja who fought on the side of Gobburi Jaggaraya against the legitimate Aravidu rulers Sriranga II (1614) and Ramadevaraya (1616–1630) during the civil war of 1614–1629 (Ramachandra Rao 1982, p. xi; *FSVH,* 1:326–333; and *FSVH,* vols. 2–3, no. 208).

Matla Anantaraju or Matla Ananta controlled Pulugula-nadu, Pottapi, and Siddhavatam in Cuddapah District during the reign of Venkatapati II, to whom he lent his powerful support during the invasions of Quli Qutb Shah of Golconda (ca. 1589) and several rebellions against Aravidu authority in Rayalaseema, Kolar, and the Tamil country during the 1590s (see *SVH,* no. 81; *FSVH,* 1:310–325; *FSVH,* vols. 2–3, nos. 215, 216a, 216b, 216c, 235; Hayavadana Rao 1930, pp. 2128, 2218–2219).

17. 'AIN-UL-MULK'S ACCOUNT OF THE HISTORY OF THE TURKISH KINGDOMS: This intriguing explanation of the Muslim presence in the Deccan begins with an allusion to the Khalji and Tughluq conquests in the early fourteenth century ("a fifteen years' war between the sultan of Delhi . . .

and Prataparudra, king of Warangal"), then moves directly to the early sixteenth century with the foundation of the kingdoms of Ahmadnagar, Bijapur, and Golconda, completely ignoring the two-hundred-year reign of the Bahmani sultanate to which the latter kingdoms succeeded.

18. *Prataparudra, king of Warangal:* Prataparudra (r. 1289–1323) was the last king of the Kakatiya dynasty, which dominated the Telangana region of the eastern Deccan from the mid-twelfth through the early fourteenth centuries. For the campaigns of the Delhi sultanate against Warangal, see Yazdani (1982, 2:643–657).

The episode about the sultan's mother and her vision of Prataparudra and the sultan as Shiva and Vishnu is in perfect accordance with the text's doctrine of the Three Lion-Thrones existing as emanations *(aṃśas)* of the gods Shiva, Vishnu, and Brahma; in this episode, the Delhi sultan is explicitly identified as the Ashvapati, while the Kakatiyas are implied by Telugu tradition to be the forerunners of the Vijayanagara kings and thus may have been seen as the earlier occupants of the Narapati throne. A slightly different version of the story about Prataparudra and the sultan's mother is found in the Telugu *Pratāparudracaritramu;* according to this earlier text (early sixteenth century), the sultan and Prataparudra were sleeping side by side on a magnificent bed when the sultan's mother went to see them: "She beheld in them a great radiance consisting of the forms of Vishnu and Shiva themselves. Brilliant light came out of their bodies and, merging together, rose up into the sky" (Ramachandra Rao 1984, pp. 66–67; translation mine).

19. *a fellow named Barid of Bidar:* The founders of the sultanates of Bijapur, Ahmadnagar, and Golconda in actuality started their careers as officers of the last significant Bahmani sultan, Mahmud Shah; but the present text casts them instead as servants of "Barid of Bidar," identifiable as Mahmud Shah's chief minister Qasim Barid and himself the eponymous founder of the Barid Shahi sultanate of Bidar. Qasim Barid appears to have been the de facto ruler during Mahmud Shah's reign, and, moreover, he retained Bidar, the seat of Bahmani authority, as the capital of his own dynasty; accordingly, the identity of the Bahmanis and the Barid Shahis appears to have been merged together on the level of popular memory represented by this story.

20. *go wash your hair and prepare for the march:* "Washing of the hair" (with oil) is one of the rituals performed in preparation for battle. The warrior's hair was believed to be a repository of heroic power; it was traditionally grown long and tied in a knot or bun on top of the head known as *vīra-jaḍa.*

5. Account of the Gajapati Kingdom

1. *Shripurushottamam:* Puri, the temple city of the god Jagannatha in Orissa. The text variously uses the names *(Śrī)Puruṣōttamaṃ* (lit., "place of [Shri]Purushottama," after another name of Jagannatha meaning "the

supreme person") and *Jagannātham* (lit., "place of Jagannatha") to refer to this site.

It should be noted that there are inconsistencies in the author's treatment of the historical geography of the Gajapati kingdom, apparently due to the conflation of details pertaining to several distinct periods into one anachronistic and topographically impossible condensation. Thus, although at the beginning of their report the spies explicitly state that the Gajapati king was "staying in the presence of Lord Jagannatha" at Shripurushottamam or Puri, they refer later in their report to the Gajapati's daily expedition to the Godavari River, a manifest impossibility given the fact that, even at its closest point, the Godavari is more than three hundred miles southwest of Puri.

The ritual center of Puri and the nearby capital city of Cuttack were indeed the centers of Gajapati power during the reign of Prataparudra (r. 1497–1538), Krishnadevaraya's actual contemporary; but immediately after the reign of Mukunda Gajapati (r. 1557–1568), who is named in the text as Krishnadevaraya's contemporary, Cuttack and Puri were occupied by the Afghan Kalapahar, and Puri became the seat of a Muslim governor. From 1568 until about 1590, the image of Jagannatha was hidden in the inaccessible mountains somewhere in southern Orissa, and the weakened associates and would-be successors of Mukunda Gajapati attempted to consolidate their positions at strongholds in Kalinga or even at places farther south, such as Rajahmandry in the Godavari delta. Meanwhile, in 1571, Golconda annexed most of Kalinga and southern Orissa up to Shrikakulam, and then, in 1590, Akbar's general Man Singh defeated the Afghans and declared Puri and its environs as Mughal crown lands. In the same year, the Khurda king Ramachandra renewed the Jagannatha cult at Puri and, with Akbar's approval, presented his dynasty as the legitimate successor to that of the Gajapatis (Kulke 1986, pp. 322–329).

The spies' statement that the Gajapati is staying in the presence of Jagannatha at Puri suggests, perhaps, an accurate memory of the situation during the period of Krishnadevaraya and Prataparudra, further bolstered by a knowledge of the recent renewal of Puri and of the Khurda Rajas' "restoration" of the Gajapati imperium. At the same time, certain other details—the Gajapati's daily trip to bathe in the Godavari, his being threatened by Mughal cavalry, and the fact that Jagannatha is in this context presented as a portable deity who is transported around in a "*pūja* box"—together suggest a memory of the geopolitical situation obtaining immediately after the fall of Mukunda Gajapati, when the bases of Gajapati power had shifted to Rajahmundry and other locations near the Godavari, when the Mughal forces under Man Singh were pressing in on Orissa, and when Jagannatha was still living incognito in the hills of south Orissa and Kalinga.

Still later in the text, when Krishnadevaraya descends from the passes of the Eastern Ghats to Potnur-Simhadri, some two hundred miles southwest of Puri, he finds the Gajapati waiting for him there in a palace *(nagaru)* in his capital *(modaṭi-sthaḷaṃ,* lit., "primary base"). While an engagement between Krishnadevaraya and the Gajapati's forces at Potnur-Simhadri is clearly attested in epigraphic and other contemporary sources, none of these sources refer to Potnur as the Gajapati's capital; on the contrary, several works clearly imply that, after his victory at Potnur, Krishnadevaraya or his army advanced on as far as Cuttack, the actual site of the Gajapati capital in Prataparudra's day (see, e.g., *SVH,* nos. 40, 41). The *Rāyavācakamu*'s identification of Potnur-Simhadri as the Gajapati capital *(modaṭi-sthaḷaṃ)* and thus the terminus of Krishnadevaraya's Kalinga campaign would appear to present another instance where knowledge of the recent geopolitical situation in Orissa and coastal Andhra has colored the author's representation of events from earlier in the sixteenth century.

2. *Whichever way you look . . . a city rich and glorious:* Source of verse unidentified.

3. *They distribute the lord's* prasād *there . . . the pollution that would ordinarily come from mixing with people of other classes:* This is a loose translation, but I believe that it reflects the sense that seems to be implied in the original phrase, which is somewhat vague: *svāmi yokka prasādaṃ mīru vāranaka svāmi dēvaḷamulō sṛṣṭi-dōṣaṃ dṛṣṭi-dōṣaṃ varnnāśrama-dharmā-nīta śuci aśuci kali-yuga-vaikuṃṭhamai.*

4. *the Sixteen Patras:* The Gajapati's *pātras,* also known as *pātra-sāmantas* or *mahāpātras,* represent a class of feudatory ministers who are the Orissan equivalent of Vijayanagara's Amaranayakas. Credit for instituting the so-called Mahapatra system is usually given to the Ganga ruler of Orissa, Bhanudeva I (r. 1263–1278), who appointed sixteen *pātra-sāmantas* to strengthen his rule over a kingdom that was being buffeted by the Muslim invasions of the latter half of the thirteenth century. The *pātras* eventually gained enough power that they could influence the royal succession; it was their discontent with the last Ganga, Bhanudeva IV (r. 1409–1434), that led to their support of Kapilendra's accession and the establishment of the Gajapati dynasty (Panda 1985, pp. 89–90).

5. *the inner chambers: Inner chambers* translates *puramu-gṛhamu,* which I have taken in the sense of *antaḥpuramu.*

6. *the* sthānāpatis *of the other rulers: The other rulers* translates *para-dunēdārlu,* lit., "the other swordsmen." In the language of the original text, there is a consistent pattern of alliteration between the first syllable of the ambassador's name and the first syllable of the name of the kingdom or lord he represents (see also n. 5, chap. 1), making it clear that the figures must not be taken as actual historical individuals. In the translation, this pattern is obscured in several cases by my use of standardized, modern forms for the geographic names. A more literal translation would read: "Anantōji Pantulu of Aghapuram's Lord, Mādhavayya of Māna Śinggu, Cennagirayya of Cāndu's Lord, Karuṇākarayya of Kaṭakaṃ's Lord, Vōbaḷayya of Vōragallu's

Lord, Ḍhākōji Pantulu of the Ḍhilli Sultan, Bēkōji Pantulu of Beḍadakōṭa's Lord, Gōpāji Pantulu of Gōlakoṇḍa's Lord, Ayyaparāju of Ahamudānagaram, Vīramarāju of Vijayāpuram, Purandarayya of Purāṇapuram, and Bābōji Pantulu of Bāgānagaram."

7. *Man Singh:* Raja Man Singh, the famous Rajput general who served the Mughals under Akbar. His representation at the Gajapati's court is particularly appropriate since it was he who was responsible for ousting the Afghans from Puri and declaring the area as Mughal crown land in 1590 (see n. 1 above).

8. *the lord of Cuttack:* At first sight, it appears astonishing that the "lord of Cuttack" should be represented at the Gajapati's court since Cuttack was the capital of the Gajapatis throughout their reign. If, however, one keeps in mind the geopolitical situation in Orissa during the period 1568–1590 just before the composition of the *Rāyavācakamu* (see n. 1 above), the inclusion of the "lord of Cuttack" among the list of rulers represented at the Gajapati court is understandable and serves as further evidence that the author of our text considered the center of Gajapati power to be outside the Cuttack-Puri region.

9. *Ayyaparaju, representing the lord of Ahmadnagar:* Emended, following Nilakanta Sastri and Venkataramanayya (1946, 2:148), from *payyaparājunnu* to *ayyaparājunnu* to preserve the alliterative pattern (see n. 6 above).

10. *100 seers of eighteen-karat gold:* 100 seers is approximately 62 pounds; *eighteen karat* translates *padi-vanne,* lit., "ten touch." In the *vanne* scale, used in measuring the purity of gold with a touchstone, sixteen represents absolute purity or twenty-four karats; "ten touch" would actually work out to fifteen karats.

11. *While he ate, he was attended by maidservants . . . he would not munch on the same thing again:* This passage suggests the observance of some royal dietary tabu, the exact significance of which is unclear.

12. *he walked one hundred steps while someone recited the* Shorter Rāmāyaṇa: Note that Krishnadevaraya performs the same ritual after eating his coronation meal (see p. 88 and n. 9, chap. 2).

13. *came into the single-storied audience hall: vakha-aṃtastu-cāvaḷḷōniki vacci.* Interpretation of *vakha-aṃtastu-cāvaḍi* is problematic since *aṃtastu* has two distinct meanings—"story" and "a secret or secluded place"—and since *cāvaḍi* is used to refer to a variety of different types of chambers, porticoes, and pillared halls. The phrase could equally well be interpreted as "came into a secluded portico."

14. *daily expedition to bathe in the Godavari River:* See n. 1 above.

15. *The Patra coolly drew his "death blade": Death blade* translates *martyākhaṃḍaṃ.*

16. *damask steel "death blades": rummi matte-khaṃḍaṃ.* I have followed Ramachandra Rao's (1982, p. 91) suggestion that the text's *rummi* may be taken in the sense of *rūmī,* lit., "Roman," i.e., pertaining to western Asia.

The term would thus imply an imported sword of western Islamic manufacture, such as a weapon made of damask steel.

6. The Battle with the Turks

1. *the battle tent:* the term is *veli-guḍāramu,* lit., "outside tent." According to N. Venkataramanayya (1972, p. 47), this was the Hindu equivalent of the battle tent *(guḍāramu)* set up by the forces of the Muslim kings (for which, see n. 6 below). It was an important part of the symbolic inauguration of a battle campaign and accordingly had to be set up at an auspicious astrological moment. A passage in Paes' account of the Mahanavami festival at Vijayanagara would seem to refer to the same tent being set up at the conclusion of the festival (and at the beginning of the season for military campaigns): "When these days of festival are past, the king holds a review of all his forces, and the review is thus arranged. The King commands to pitch his tent of Mecca velvet a full league from the city, at a place already fixed for that purpose; and in this tent they place the idol in honour of which all these festivals are celebrated [Durga]. From this tent to the king's palace the captains arrange themselves with their troops and array, each one in his place according to his rank in the king's household. . . . In this way it went on till the king arrived at the place where the tent was that I have already mentioned, and he entered this and performed his usual ceremonies and prayers" (Sewell 1962, pp. 264, 268).

2. The Battle with the Turks: Venkataramanayya (1972, pp. 44–51) has convincingly argued that the description of this battle broadly fits the descriptions of a battle at Devni or Devli (Diwani in the Persian sources; exact location unidentified) that are given in Islamic historical sources *(Burhān-i-ma'āsir* and *Tārīkh-i-Sultān Muhammad Qulī Qutb Shāhī).* The battle is said to have occurred in 1509/1510 (see also *FSVH,* 1:189–193). Arunakumari's belief that this section describes the Raichur campaign of 1520 would thus appear to be mistaken (see Arunakumari 1978, p. 181).

According to the *Burhān-i-ma'āsir* and *Tārīkh-i-Sultān Muhammad Qulī Qutb Shāhī,* the Muslim forces had marched toward the Vijayanagara border in accordance with the policy of an annual *jihād* against the Hindu infidels inaugurated by the Bahmani ruler Mahmud Shah (r. 1482–1518). The force was made up of the armies of the chief Bahmani officers—including Ahmad Nizam Shah Bahri of Ahmadnagar, Yusuf Adil Khan of Bijapur, and Qutb-al-Mulk of Golconda, who were just then in the process of establishing their own independent sultanates—and was nominally led by Mahmud Shah Bahmani, by then only a figurehead under the control of the minister Qasim Barid (founder of the Barid Shahi sultanate of Bidar). Mahmud Shah was at the center of the attacking army, and the cavalry forces of his officers were ranged around him. When the force of Qutb-al-Mulk, positioned to his right, began to attack the southern flank of the Hindu army, Mahmud was thrown by his rearing horse and sustained serious injuries. He was rushed from the scene, and the Muslim forces retreated, leaving the Hindus victorious.

The *Rāyavācakamu* does not mention Mahmud Shah Bahmani (in fact, the author never recognizes the fact that the Bahmanis existed; see n. 17, chap. 4), but, as Venkataramanayya argues, the battle tent set up by the Turks at the center of their camp clearly corresponds to the position of the Bahmani king described in the Persian sources. An inscription of Krishnadevaraya's dated January 1510, of which two copies exist in the Virupaksha temple at Hampi (*SII,* 4:258–259), includes the epithet *paribhūta-suratrāṇa* ("by whom the sultan was disgraced") as one of the king's titles, apparently adopted after the defeat of Mahmud Shah's armies at Devli.

3. *until there is not a single man, cow, sheep, goat, or horse remaining:* The text includes a word of unknown meaning, *prāyalu,* between *cow* and *sheep.* From the context, it must be yet another type of animal.

4. *the Karnataka kingdom:* The Vijayanagara kingdom. The sense is of suppliers who are in the direct service of the crown, as opposed to independent contractors.

5. *First the army went to Ummattur-Shivasamudram and attacked Ganga Rao's city:* This campaign is attested to by other historical sources and can be dated to 1512, i.e., *after* the present campaign against the Turks (see Venkataramanayya 1972, pp. 21–32). The order seems to have been reversed, as Venkataramanayya suggests (1972, p. 45), so that the overall course of Krishnadevaraya's campaigns will more closely approximate the paradigmatic clockwise progression of a conquest of the quarters.

Ganga Rao or Gangaraya (r. 1511–1512) belonged to a prominent family of local chiefs who ruled the upper reaches of the Kaveri River from Ummattur. Shivasamudram, a "water fort" strategically built on an island in the Kaveri, was another major stronghold of these chiefs. The Ummattur chiefs had been feudatories of Vijayanagara under the Saluvas, but, with the uncertainties that followed the establishment of the Tuluva dynasty, they began to make a bid for independence. By the time of Krishnadevaraya's accession, these rebellious feudatories had extended their sway as far as Penugonda in Anantapur District, posing a serious threat to the integrity of the empire. Accordingly, Krishnadevaraya marched against these chiefs, first taking Penugonda, and then Ummattur, Shivasamudram, and Shrirangapatnam (another fort held by the Ummattur chiefs). An inscription dating to 22 September 1512 from Bukkapatnam near Penugonda (*SII,* 16:49) records an order issued by Krishnadevaraya reconfirming some religious land grants in the Penugonda province; the order was made after the king had gone to Shivasamudram "on state business" *(rāca-kāryānaku),* clearly an allusion to the Ummattur campaign.

6. *When he heard that the Turks had crossed the Krishna River and set up their battle tent within his own territory, Rayalu grew furious:* Venkataramanayya

explains that "the significance of setting up the tent is symbolic: it serves as an indication that the sultan who sets it up is prepared to stay there resolutely until such time as he attains victory and conquers his enemies" (1972, p. 47). This accounts both for the king's anger and for the specific plan of cutting the tent ropes that Pemmasani Ramalinga suggests below.

7. *Pemmasani Ramalingama Nayadu:* For this figure's historical identity, see n. 16, chap. 4.

8. *Mukku Timmayya:* Also known as Nandi-Timmayya, and respected as one of the greatest Telugu poets of Krishnadevaraya's day, he is the author of the *Parijātāpaharaṇamu,* a *prabandham*-style *mahākāvya* based on the theme of Krishna's theft of the Parijata tree from Indra's paradise as a favor for his wife Satyabhama. The work is dedicated to his patron, Krishnadevaraya (Hayavadana Rao 1930, p. 1912).

7. The Gajapati Campaign

1. Krishnadevaraya's Court Poets: The three poets mentioned were among the greatest Telugu poets of Krishnadevaraya's day. For Mukku Timmayya, see n. 8, chap. 6. Alasani Peddanna is by common consent the greatest Telugu poet of the period. He is the author of *Manucaritramu,* a *prabandham*-style *mahākāvya* based on the story of the second Manu, Svarochisha, as told in the *Mārkaṇḍeya-purāṇa.* This work is dedicated to his patron Krishnadevaraya, who evidently held him in high esteem. According to a *cāṭu* verse ascribed to him (*SVH,* no. 49[1]), he received various honors from the king, including the title "Grandfather to Telugu Poetry" *(Āṃdhra-kavitā-pitāmaha),* an anklet of honor called "hero among poets" *(kavi-gaṇḍa-peṃḍēraṃ),* and several grants of land, including the *agrahāram* village of Kokata in Rayalaseema (Hayavadana Rao 1930, pp. 1909–1912). Madanagari Mallayya, better known as Madayagari Mallana, is the author of *Rājaśēkharacaritramu,* a *prabandham*-style *mahākāvya* based on the romantic tale of a prince and his adventures. Mallana's patron was Nadendla Appana Mantri, a subordinate of Krishnadevaraya who ruled in the Rayalaseema districts of Andhra (Hayavadana Rao 1930, p. 1913).

2. The Gajapati Campaign: Although the *Rāyavācakamu* describes Krishnadevaraya's war against the Gajapati as a single campaign, following immediately on his victory over the Turks (datable to 1510; see n. 2, chap. 6), on the basis of the evidence afforded by contemporary inscriptions, literary dedications, Portuguese documents, and Persian historical texts Venkataramanayya (1972, pp. 61–94; see also *FSVH,* 1:200–211) has argued that the Gajapati campaign did not begin until 1513. Moreover, the evidence suggests that this campaign actually comprised several distinct expeditions and was not concluded until as late as 1518.

According to Venkataramanayya, the outlines of the entire campaign are as follows. (1) In Ś. 1434 (A.D. 1513), Krishnadevaraya marches with his army to Udayagiri and lays siege to the fort. During the course of the lengthy siege, Krishnadevaraya returns to the capital several times. Sometime before the month of Ashadha, Ś. 1436 (A.D. 1514), the fort is broken, and Krishnadevaraya captures Tirumala Kataraya, the uncle of Prataparudra Gajapati. On his way back to the capital, Krishnadevaraya stops at Tirupati with his two queens and makes gifts to Venkateshvara. (2) The king's army stays in the coastal districts under the command of Saluva Timmarasu and lays siege to the main forts of the Kondavidu area: Addanki, Vinukonda, Bellamkonda, Nagarjunakonda, Tangedu, and Ketavaram. Once these forts have fallen, the fort at Kondavidu itself is besieged and taken. The Gajapati king's son Virabhadraraya and eight important feudatories *(pātra-sāmanta)* of the Gajapati are taken captive and then released. Krishnadevaraya, who has rejoined his army at some point in this phase of the campaign, returns to Vijayanagara with Timmarasu and the army. The king and his two queens stop at Dharanikota (Amaravati) and Shriparvata (Shrishailam) to worship and make gifts to Amareshvara and Mallikarjuna, respectively (Ś. 1438, Shravana [A.D. 1515, July]). (3) After remaining in the capital for several days, the king sets out to resume his conquest of Kalinga. He stops first at Tirupati and Ahobalam, where he makes gifts to Venkateshvara and Narasimha, respectively; he then proceeds to Kondapalli, gateway to the Telangana region. After several months, he captures the fort at Kondapalli and also captures several more Gajapati feudatories. (4) He then proceeds on into Ṭelangana, taking the forts at Anantagiri, Undrakonda, Urlugonda, Aruvapalli, Jallipalli, Kandikonda, Kappaluvayi, Nallagonda, Khammamet, Kanakagiri, and Shankaragiri. (5) From Telangana, he crosses over into coastal Andhra and marches north to Simhadri-Potnuru, where he sets up a pillar of victory *(jaya-stambha)* and performs donative acts. (6) He returns to the capital while his army presses on into the heart of the Gajapati territory and takes the capital, Cuttack.

3. *With an impetuous thirst for conquest:* This verse is quoted (with slight variations) from Sankusala Nrisimhakavi's *Kavikarṇarasāyanamu* (2.64–65), a Telugu *kāvya* dating to the 1540s (Ramachandra Rao 1982, p. vii).

4. *He left the fort in Kampanna's charge:* Venkataramanayya (1972, p. 77, n. 7) suggests that it may be possible to identify this figure with Saluva Kamparaju, who was Krishnadevaraya's sword bearer.

5. *he decided to leave Kondayya there as officer-in-charge:* This Kondayya is probably the same as the minister Rayasam Kondamarasa, referred to as *Kondamarasu* in the text. Several inscriptions record grants of lands lying within the area of the Kondavidu country, made by Rayasam Kondamarasu, who was "sent by the great king Shri Krishnadeva" (*SII,* vol. 16, no. 54, lines 2–3; see also *SII,* vol. 16, no. 63; and *ARADH* 1933–1934, pp. 37–38). Here, his name has perhaps been simplified to Kondayya so as to suggest a different individual and thus allow Kondamarasu to continue on the campaign with Krishnadevaraya.

6. *Ahmadnagar:* This is the name of an outpost of the Gajapati kingdom and is not to be confused with the capital of the Muslim kingdom of the same name. The two names are spelled differently in the text: the Gajapati outpost is *Ahamudunagaraṃ;* the Muslim kingdom and its capital are both *Ahamudānagaraṃ.*

7. *Chitapu Khan:* Better known as Chittapa Khana or Shitab Khan. He was a Hindu chief who flourished ca. 1500–1518 and controlled the old Kakatiya capital of Warangal. It is generally assumed that he first rose to prominence by serving the Bahmanis, from whom he might have received a *jāgīr* and the title *Khān,* which he continued to employ. Whatever his origins, it is clear from an inscription preserved in the Warangal fort and dating to 1504, that he had by that time set up the standard of independence and was involved in a campaign to restore Warangal to its former glory and resurrect the memory of the Kakatiyas (*IAP Warangal,* no. 111). He appears to have allied himself with the Gajapatis during the period of Prataparudra's reign (1497–1539) (see Venkataramanayya 1974, pp. xxvii–xxviii).

8. *Potlur-Simhadri:* Simhadri or Simhachalam is a major Vaisnava center in Vishakhapatnam District dedicated to the composite deity Varaha-Narasimha; the nearby town of Potlur (more commonly Potnur) appears, on the basis of epigraphic evidence, to have been the provincial headquarters during the period of Ganga rule over the Kalinga region (Sundaram 1984, p. 70).

9. PEDDA GAJAPATI'S ANNEXATION OF VIJAYANAGARA TERRITORY: *Pedda Gajapati,* lit., "elder Gajapati" or "senior Gajapati," refers to an otherwise unnamed predecessor of the present king. It was Kapilendra (r. 1435–1466), the founder of the Suryavamshi Gajapati dynasty, who first succeeded in annexing large portions of Vijayanagara's territory along the northern Coromandel coast. During the last two years of his reign, he extended his sway as far south as the Kaveri delta (Panda 1985, p. 91). All the temples mentioned as having been ransacked by him are located either in the Tondai region around present-day Madras or in the Kaveri delta in the heart of the Chola country.

10. *the raid of old on Prince Uttara's cattle: Uttara-gō-grahaṇaṃ.* This story is related in the *Go-haraṇa-parvan* of the *Mahābhārata.* 4(47) (translated in van Buitenen 1978, pp. 63–119). Uttara was the young son of Virata, king of the Matsyas. The Kauravas went to raid the cattle of Virata, at whose court the Pandavas were staying incognito during the thirteenth and final year of their exile. Arjuna, disguised as the transvestite dance teacher Brihannada, serves as Uttara's charioteer when he rides out to repel the attacking Kauravas. When Uttara loses his nerve, Arjuna proclaims his true identity (the period of exile having just concluded) and himself takes up weapons to defeat the Kauravas.

11. *pillar of victory:* This pillar of victory is mentioned by other sixteenth-century authors, including the court poets Peddana and Lakshminarayana and the Portuguese chronicler Nuniz (*FSVH,* 1:209). An inscription dated

to 1517 states that it was the minister Kondamarasu who was actually responsible for establishing this pillar as well as another at Shrikurmam (*ARE* no. 76 of 1912, cited in Sundaram 1984, p. 70). No trace of the pillar remains at Potnur today (Īśvaradattu 1979, p. 227).

12. KRISHNADEVARAYA MARRIES THE GAJAPATI'S DAUGHTER: Although she is mentioned by the name of Jaganmohini only in the present text, a number of other sixteenth-century sources confirm that one of Krishnadevaraya's wives was a Gajapati princess. Paes' contemporary Portuguese account refers to the three principal wives of Krishnadevaraya, one of whom is "the daughter of the king of Orya [Orissa]" (Sewell 1962, p. 239), and the marriage is also referred to in the *Prabodha-candrodaya-vyākhya* of Nadindla Gopa-mantri, where she is identified simply as the "daughter of Prataparudra Gajapati" (*pratāparudrasya gajeśvarasya putrīṃ; SVH,* no. 45). Tradition ascribes authorship of five Sanskrit verses to her, giving her name as Tukka; in the verses, she bemoans her fate of being neglected by her husband (*SVH,* no. 44).

It may be noted that, in the text, while presenting his daughter the Gajapati recites a Telugu verse that refers to the dowry gifts that are appropiate for the father of the bride to present to the groom. The verse is fragmentary owing to lacunae and has not been translated: *hāṭaka-pēṭī śāṭī, ghōṭīśakaṭī madēbhakōṭīvīṭī / pēṭībhṛccēṭī . . . mayūrikalu . . . vēḍkan.*

13. *Our customs are crooked . . . could we ever hope to renounce our ugly ways:* I am unable to identify the source of this verse. It would appear to be quoted from some larger poetic context, in which a group of demons (*asuras* or *rākṣasas*) is surrendering to the god Vishnu or one of his incarnations.

14. KRISHNADEVARAYA SUPPRESSES A REVOLT AT GULBARGA: It has been suggested by Hayavadana Rao (1930, pp. 1852–1854) that this passage alludes to a campaign undertaken by Krishnadevaraya against Gulbarga, with the purpose of releasing a captive Bahmani ruler and restoring him to his position of nominal authority over a united Deccani kingdom, thus checking the power of his chief officers, who were then in the process of establishing Ahmadnagar, Bijapur, and Golconda as independent and more threatening kingdoms. Venkataramanayya also discusses the Gulbarga campaign, without, however, suggesting that the present episode is in any way connected to it (*FSVH,* 1:195–196). The two authorities arrive at somewhat divergent conclusions concerning the details of this campaign, including both its date and the identity of those involved on the Muslim side.

Whether or not the present passage can in any way be construed as an allusion to this campaign, it would appear more relevant to read it within the context of the preceding episode in which the Turks come to profess their submission to Krishnadevaraya. The fact that some of these same "barbarians" have turned in defiance almost immediately on Krishnadevaraya's departure gives added poignance to the last lines of the verse quoted earlier: "Who can hope to change his inborn nature? How, O King, could we ever hope to renounce our ugly ways?" The message is clear that Turks—even repentant ones—are simply not to be trusted.

15. Krishnaraya visits Tirupati and other pilgrimage centers in the South: All but three of the sites visited by Krishnadevaraya while returning to his capital can be readily identified, and, as will be seen from map 2, the great majority of them are located in the Madurai country in the deepest south of the Vijayanagara territory. It is this emphasis on sites in the Madurai country that has led me to suggest this region as the location of the text's production (see the introduction).

Tirupati (also Tirumalai, Venkatachalam) is the famous Vaishnava center in Southern Andhra; *Venkateshvara* is the name of the form of Vishnu worshiped there. *Alamelumanga (Alamēlumaṃgā)* is the Telugu spelling of *Alaimeḷmangai,* the Tamil equivalent of the Sanskrit *Padmāvatī* (lit., "Lotus Woman"), the name of the consort of Venkateshvara enshrined in her own temple at nearby Tiruchanur. The description of the "copper" image *(tāmbrāna-pratibimbamu)* of Krishnadevaraya and his two queens donated to the temple accords perfectly with the justly famous repoussé portrait triad (Figure 1), nearly life-size, which still stands today in a portico just inside the temple's eastern gopuram. The image and its situation are discussed briefly in Harle (1986, pp. 337, 340) and Michell (1989, p. 480).

Kalahasti is a major Shaiva temple center some twenty miles northeast of Tirupati; the unnamed "lord" worshiped there by Krishnadevaraya would have been Shri-Kalahastishvara, the local form of Shiva. This deity was heavily patronized by the rulers of Vijayanagara's Tuluva dynasty and was the subject of two important Telugu literary works of the period by the temple poet Dhurjati (see Heifetz and Narayana Rao 1987).

Vandishvaram, the next site visited, has not proved identifiable. The wording of the text seems to imply that "the three places that had been worshiped by the Tripuras" are at a single site or site cluster and that it is the location of a deity known as "Vandishvara." (This appears to be the interpretation adopted both by Rangaswami Saraswati [*SVH,* no. 117] and by Hayavadana Rao [1930, p. 1881], who were also unable to identify this site.) This site may be in the Madurai country, or it may represent a third stop between Kalinga and Madurai.

Alagargudi is better known by its Tamil name *Alagarkoil* and is located some twelve miles northeast of Madurai. It takes its name from the temple of Alagarswami (lit., "the beautiful lord"), a local form of Vishnu who, since the days of Tirumala Nayaka (r. 1623–1659), has been ritually and mythically cast as the brother of the goddess Minakshi of Madurai during the annual Chittirai festival (Baliga 1960, pp. 406–408; Hudson 1977, 1982).

In addition to being the seat of the Nayaka rulers of the Madurai kingdom, Madurai is the site of the temple of the local goddess Minakshi and her consort Chokkanathaswami (lit., "the beautiful lord"; he is better known by the synonymous Sanskrit name *Sundareshvara*), the localized form of Shiva (Baliga 1960, pp. 394–403; Reynolds 1987).

Shrivilliputtur, located in Ramnathapuram District forty-seven miles southwest of Madurai, is famous in Vaishnava tradition as the birthplace of the female saint Andal. The deities worshiped here by Krishnadevaraya appear to correspond to those presently enshrined in the Nachchiyar-koil, one of the town's two major temples (Ramaswami 1972, pp. 967–969). *Sampengi Mannaruswami* clearly refers to the deity Rajamannar, a popular Tamil form of Krishna in his guise as the cowherd king Rajagopala (see Champakalakshmi 1981, pp. 142–143); *Cudukoduttunachyaru* represents a Telugu spelling *(Cūḍukoḍutunāccyāru)* of the Tamil epithet applied to the divinized Andal, *Śūḍi-kkoḍutta-nācciyār,* i.e., "she who gave garlands that had been worn," in reference to the popular hagiographic story that provides the basis of Krishnadevaraya's Telugu *prabandham, Āmuktamālyadā* (see Champakalakshmi 1981, pp. 219–222).

Karuvanallur is another site that I am unable to identify.

Shankaranarayanagudi, better known under its Tamil name *Shankaranarayana-koil,* is the headquarters of a taluk of the same name in Tirunelveli District. The town takes its name from the principal temple at the site, dedicated to the deity Shankaranarayana-swami, a form of Shiva ("Shankara," represented by a linga occupying the principal shrine), to which Vishnu has been subordinated as an aspect through the inclusion of an image of Narayana in a smaller, adjacent shrine. *Gometi* refers to the deity's consort, locally known as Gomati-amman. The "sacred pool of the snakes called Nagatirtha" is probably a bathing tank built to commemorate the serpents Shanka and Padma, whose quarrel over the relative greatness of Shiva and Vishnu led to the deity's manifestation in its present form to demonstrate their unity (Pate 1917, pp. 412–414); I have not been able to determine if such a tank presently exists at the site.

Tenkashi (lit., "Southern Kashi") is the headquarters of a taluk of the same name in Tirunelveli District. According to an inscription, the site's temple of the god Vishvanatha (the form of Shiva worshiped in Kasi or Banaras) was built in the fifteenth century by a local Pandya king to provide a new home for the god since his original abode in Vadakashi ("North Kashi") was going to ruin (Pate 1917, p. 467).

Trikutachalam, a pilgrimage site in the hills a few miles southwest of Tenkashi, is locally known by the shortened form *Kuttalam.* A series of magnificent waterfalls there cascades into a pool, the "Celestial Ganga pool," whose waters are noted for their ability to wash away one's accumulated sins (Pate 1917, pp. 459–460). The "Painted Hall" at which Krishnadevaraya worships after bathing is a nearby temple, known as *Chitra Sabhai* [lit., "painted hall"] and dedicated to Shiva in his form of Nataraja, king of dance. The temple's name reflects the fact that its walls are decorated throughout with paintings (Pate 1917, p. 461).

Agastyaparvatam is the name of the highest peak (6,125 feet) in the range of the Western Ghats running through Ambasamudram Taluk of the Tirunelveli District. It is named after the great brahman sage and Dravidian cultural hero Agastya, who is believed still to dwell on its peak, presiding over the fortunes of the Tamraparni River, which he created (Pate 1917, p. 4). The "Kalyanatirtham pool" lies at the base of another magnificent waterfall, known as *Papavinashanam* ("destroyer of sins"), where the Tamraparni cascades out of the lower reaches of Agastyaparvatam. The temple dedicated to Agastya, "Agasteshvara," for which Krishnadevaraya is credited with building a gopuram gateway, is located near the foot of these falls (Pate 1917, pp. 362–363).

Gajendramoksham (lit., "[place of the] liberation of the elephant king") is another site that I am unable to identify.

Shalivatapuram (Sanskrit, lit., "town surrounded by paddy") is another name for Tirunelveli (Tamil, lit., "sacred paddy hedge"), headquarters of the district of the same name. "Venuvaneshvara," lit., "Lord of the Bamboo Forest," is the name of the form of Shiva that presides over the temple there (Pate 1917, pp. 488–493).

Totadri-matham (also known as *Vanumamalai-matham*) is the headquarters of the Tenkalai-Srivaishnava sect; it is located in Nanguneri (headquarters of the taluk of the same name) some twenty miles south of Shalivatapuram (Pate 1917, p. 400).

Kurungudi, better known as Tirukkurungudi, is the site of a Shrivaishnava temple on the Nambiyar River some eight or nine miles southwest of the Totadri-matham in Nanguneri. The "five Nambis" would appear to be the five forms in which Vishnu is worshiped there: that of the Vamana or dwarf incarnation, that of the Vishvarupa assumed by Vamana in reclaiming the worlds, a seated form, a reclining form, and a standing form located at a separate temple nearby in the hills, the Malai Nambi Koil (Pate 1917, pp. 403–404).

Kanyakumari is the famous pilgrimage center at the southern tip of India (Cape Comorin), dedicated to Kanyakumari, the Virgin Goddess who slew the demon Bana there. According to local tradition, she waits on the shore preserving her virginity until the next dissolution of the cosmos, when Shiva will come from nearby Suchindram and abandon his celibacy to marry her (Shulman 1980, pp. 144–148).

Shrikanduru is identical with Tiruchendur, a coastal town and headquarters of a taluk of the same name in Tirunelveli District. It is located some fifty miles northeast of Kanyakumari. Local tradition credits the founding of the town to the war god Subrahmanyaswami, who is enshrined with his consorts Valli and Devayana in a temple on the shore, cut from a sandstone escarpment (Pate 1917, pp. 505–506).

The Nine Tirupatis are a group of nine temples in the vicinity of Alvar-Tirunagari (Tiruchendur Taluk, Tirunelveli District) that are ritually linked to the temple of Adinathaswami at that site. During the Vaikasi festival, which honors the great Vaishnava saint Nammalvar, who was born there, their deities are brought to greet the image of the Alvar and join him in the temple-cart procession (Pate 1917, pp. 497–499).

Setu (lit., "bridge") is another name for the major pilgrimage site of Rameshvaram (Ramanathapuram Taluk and District), located on an island lying between the Indian mainland and Sri Lanka. It is believed to be the place from which Rama built the bridge and crossed over to Lanka to battle with Ravana and rescue Sita. After slaying Ravana and returning with Sita, Rama was advised by the sages to establish a linga of Shiva and worship it in order to absolve himself from the sin incurred by slaying Ravana, a brahman. *Kashivishveshvara* is the name of the linga brought for the purpose from Mount Kailasa by the monkey Hanuman; *Ramalingaswami* is the name of the linga made for the same purpose by Sita on Hanuman's failure to return in time for the auspicious moment that had been set for the linga's consecration. Although Sita's linga is thus the primary deity of the Rameshvaram temple, Rama appeased the disappointed Hanuman by consecrating his linga in an adjacent shrine to the north and granting that it should be worshiped before Sita's by anyone visiting the temple. This point of ritual etiquette is observed by Krishnadevaraya just as it is by contemporary pilgrims to the site. Setumadhavaswami is a local form of Vishnu whose shrine is also encompassed within the walls of the temple complex. The goddess Parvatavardhana is the consort of Ramalingaswami; her image is housed in a separate shrine to the south of his. The site contains numerous sacred pools *(tīrtham)* for ritual bathing—as many as sixty-four, according to the local *sthalapurāṇa*. But the Koti-*tīrtham* is the most important; after bathing in it, one should leave Rameshvaram, as Krishnadevaraya appropriately does (see Ramaswami 1972, pp. 945–951).

Dhanushkoti, lit., "bow tip," is a sacred site lying at the southeastern end of the Rameshvaram island and takes its name from its position and the fact that the island's shape resembles that of a bow. It is some fifteen miles by sea from the site of the Rameshvaram temple; although now connected by train, pilgrims even today often prefer to approach it by boat from Rameshvaram. Its particular sanctity comes from the fact that it marks the spot of juncture between two "oceans" *(sāgara-saṃgamam):* the Indian Ocean and the Bay of Bengal (Ramaswami 1972, pp. 874–877, 945–946).

Gokarna (Shimoga District, Karnataka) is an important pilgrimage center along the western coast and is sacred to Shiva.

Shrirangapatnam (Mandya District, Karnataka) is a Vaishnava pilgrimage center near Mysore. The temple of "Adi Ranganayaka" (also known as Shri Ranganathaswami) is located within the island fort at the site.

16. Parijātāpaharaṇamu *and* Manucaritramu: These two Telugu *prabandhams* are the masterpieces of Mukku Timmayya and Alasani Peddana, respectively (see n. 8, chap. 6, and n. 1, chap. 7).

W·O·R·K·S C·I·T·E·D

Ahmad, Aziz.
1964. *Islamic Culture in the Indian Environment*. Oxford: Clarendon Press.

Antarkar, W. R., ed.
1968. "*Ācāryavijayaḥ* a/s *Ācāryavijayākhyānam* by Śrīparamēśvara Kavikaṇṭhīrava" (in Sanskrit). *Journal of the University of Bombay: Arts-Humanities and Social Sciences* n.s. 37:1–69.

Appadorai, A.
1936. *Economic Conditions in Southern India (1000–1500 AD)*. Madras University Historical Series, no. 12. Madras: University of Madras.

Apte, Vaman Shivram.
1965. *The Practical Sanskrit English Dictionary*. Rev. and enlarged ed. Delhi: Motilal Banarsidass.

Arunakumari, Bala.
1978. *Āndhravāṅmayamuna Cāritraka Kāvyamulu* (in Telugu). Waltair: Andhra University Press.

Baliga, B. S.
1960. *Madras District Gazetteers: Madurai*. Gazetteer of India. Madras: Government of Madras.

Bhardwaj, Surinder Mohan.
1973. *Hindu Places of Pilgrimage in India*. Berkeley: University of California Press.

Briggs, John, trans.
1966. *History of the Rise of the Mahomedan Power in India till the Year A.D. 1612, Translated from the Original Persian of Mahomed Kasim Ferishta*. 1829. Reprint. Calcutta: Editions Indian.

Brown, Charles Philip.
1979. *Dictionary Telugu-English: Nighaṃṭu Telugu Iṃglīṣ*. 2d ed., rev. M. Venkataratnam, W. H. Campbell, and Rao Bahadur K. Veeresalingam. 1905. Reprint. New Delhi: Asian Educational Service.

Burton, Sir Richard F., trans.
1964. *The Kama Sutra of Vatsyayana*. 1883. Reprint. New York: E. P. Dutton.

Canary, Robert H., and Henry Kozicki, eds.
1978. *The Writing of History: Literary Form and Historical Understanding.* Madison: University of Wisconsin Press.

Carr, M. W.
1868. *Āṃdhra Lōkōkti Caṃdrika: A Collection of Telugu Proverbs, Translated, Illustrated, and Explained; Together with Some Sanscrit Proverbs Printed in the Devanāgarī and Telugu Characters.* Madras and London: Christian Knowledge Society Press and Trübner & Co.

Champakalakshmi, R.
1981. *Vaiṣṇava Iconography in the Tamil Country.* New Delhi: Orient Longman.

Cohn, Bernard S.
1968. "Ethnohistory." *International Encyclopedia of the Social Sciences,* 6: 440–448. New York: Macmillan/Free Press.
1981. "Anthropology and History in the 1980s: Toward a Rapprochement." *Journal of Interdisciplinary History* 12 (2): 227–252.

Collins, Charles D.
1982. "Elephanta and the Ritual of the Lakulīśa-Pāśupatas." *Journal of the American Oriental Society* 102 (4): 605–617.

Comfort, Alex.
1965. *The Koka Shastra: Being the Ratirahasya of Kokkoka and Other Medieval Indian Writings on Love.* New York: Stein & Day.

Dallapiccola, Anna Libera, and Stephanie Zingel-Avé Lallement, eds.
1985. *Vijayanagara—City and Empire: New Currents of Research.* 2 vols. Beiträge zur Südasienforschung, Südasien-Institut, Universität Heidelberg, vol. 100. Stuttgart: Steiner Verlag Wiesbaden Gmbh.

De, Sushil Kumar.
1976. *History of Sanskrit Poetics.* 2 vols. Reprint. Calcutta: Firma KLM Private Ltd.

Dimmitt, Cornelia, and J. A. B. van Buitenen.
1978. *Classical Hindu Mythology: A Reader in the Sanskrit Puranas.* Philadelphia: Temple University Press.

Dirks, Nicholas B.
1982. "The Pasts of a Palaiyakarar: The Ethnohistory of a South Indian Little King." *Journal of Asian Studies* 41 (3): 655–683.
1987. *The Hollow Crown: Ethnohistory of an Indian Kingdom.* Cambridge: Cambridge University Press.

Dow, Alexander.
1973. *The History of Hindostan; from the Earliest Account of Time to the Death of Akbar.* 1768–1772. 3 vols. Reprint. New Delhi: Today and Tomorrow Publishers.

Dutt, K. Iswara.
1967. *Inscriptional Glossary of Andhra Pradesh.* Hyderabad: Andhra Pradesh Sahitya Akademi.

Edgerton, Franklin, trans.
1972. *The Bhagavad Gita*. Cambridge, Mass.: Harvard University Press.

Egan, Kieran.
1978. "Thucydides, Tragedian." In *The Writing of History: Literary Form and Historical Understanding*, ed. Robert H. Canary and Henry Kozicki, pp. 63–92. Madison: University of Wisconsin Press.

Eliade, Mircea.
1959. *Cosmos and History*. New York: Harper & Row.

Filliozat, Vasundhara.
1973. *L'épigraphie de Vijayanagar du début à Ś 1377*. Paris: École Française d'Extrême Orient.

Finley, M. I.
1965. "Myth, Memory, and History." *History and Theory* 4 (3): 281–302.

Fritz, John M.
1985. "Was Vijayanagara a 'Cosmic City'?" In *Vijayanagara—City and Empire: New Currents of Research*, ed. Anna Libera Dallapiccola and Stephanie Zingel-Avé Lallement, 1:257–273. Stuttgart: Steiner Verlag Wiesbaden Gmbh.
1986. "Vijayanagara: Authority and Meaning of a South Indian Imperial Capital." *American Anthropologist* 88 (1): 44–55.

Fritz, John M., and John McKim Malville.
n.d. "Recent Archaeo-Astronomical Research at Vijayanagara." Paper presented at the eleventh international conference of the Association of South Asian Archaeologists in Western Europe, Berlin, 1–5 July 1991.

Fritz, John M., and George Michell.
1985. "Map Series on Cultural Remains of Vijayanagara." In *Vijayanagara: Progress of Research, 1983–84*, pp. 164 and figs. 55–87. Vijayanagara Research Centre Series, no. 2. Mysore: Directorate of Archaeology and Museums.

Fritz, John M., George Michell, and M. S. Nagaraja Rao.
1984. *Where Kings and Gods Meet: The Royal Centre at Vijayanagara, India*. Tucson: University of Arizona Press.

Geiger, Wilhelm.
1956. *Pāli Literature and Language*. Translated by Batakrishna Ghosh. Calcutta: University of Calcutta.

Goldman, Robert P., trans.
1984. *The Rāmāyaṇa of Vālmīki: An Epic of Ancient India*. Vol. 1, *Bālakāṇḍa*. Princeton, N.J.: Princeton University Press.

Gonda, Jan.
1977. *Medieval Religious Literature in Sanskrit*. Wiesbaden: Otto Harrassowitz.

Hardy, Friedhelm.
1978. "Ideology and Cultural Contexts of the Srivaisnava Temple." In

Indian Temples: An Analytical Reconsideration, ed. Burton Stein. New Delhi: Vikas.

Harle, J. C.

1986. *The Art and Architecture of the Indian Subcontinent*. Pelican History of Art. Harmondsworth: Penguin Books.

Hayavadana Rao, C.

1930. *Mysore Gazetteer, Compiled for Government*. Vol. 2 *Historical*. Pt. 3, *Medieval: From the Foundation of the Vijayanagara Kingdom to the Destruction of Vijayanagara by Tipū Sultān in 1776*. Bangalore: Government Press.

1948. *History of Mysore (1399–1799 A.D.)*. 2 vols. Bangalore: Government Press.

Heifetz, Hank, and Velcheru Narayana Rao.

1987. *For the Lord of the Animals—Poems from the Telugu: The* Kāḷahastīśvara Śatakamu *of Dhūrjaṭi*. Berkeley and Los Angeles: University of California Press.

Heras, Henry.

1927. *The Aravidu Dynasty of Vijayanagara*. Madras: B. G. Paul & Co.

1929. *Beginnings of Vijayanagara History*. Studies in Indian History of the Indian Historical Research Institute, St. Xavier's College, Bombay, no. 4. Bombay: Indian Historical Research Institute.

Hudson, D. Dennis.

1977. "Śiva, Mīṇākṣi, Viṣṇu—Reflections on a Popular Myth in Madura." *Indian Economic and Social History Review* 14 (1): 107–118.

1982. "Two Citra Festivals in Madurai." In *Religious Festivals in South India and Sri Lanka*, ed. Guy R. Welbon and Glenn E. Yocum, pp. 101–156. New Delhi: Manohar.

Īśvaradattu, Kuṃdūri.

1979. *Prācīnāṃdhra Cāritraka Bhūgōḷamu*. 1963. Reprint. Hyderabad: Āṃdhra Pradēś Sāhitya Akāḍami.

Kāse, Sarvappa.

1960. *Śrī Siddhēśvara Caritramu* [*Kākatīyarājula Caritra—Pratāpa Caritra*]. Edited by K. Lakshmiranjanam. Hyderabad: Āṃdhra Racayitala Saṅghamu.

Kerr, Robert.

1824. *A General History and Collection of Voyages and Travels*. Vol. 8. Edinburgh.

Krishna Sastri, H.

1912. "The Second Vijayanagara Dynasty: Its Viceroys and Ministers." In *Archaeological Survey of India: Annual Report, 1908–9*, pp. 164–201. Calcutta.

Krishnaswami Ayyangar, S., ed.

1919. *Sources of Vijayanagara History*. Compiled by S. Rangaswami Sarasvati. Madras University Historical Series, no. 1. Madras: University of Madras.

Kulasekhara Rao, M.
1974. *Āndhra Vacana Vāṅmayamu* (in Telugu). Hyderabad.
Kulke, Hermann.
1985. "Maharajas, Mahants, and Historians: Reflections on the Historiography of Early Vijayanagara and Sringeri." In *Vijayanagara—City and Empire: New Currents of Research*, ed. Anna Libera Dallapiccola and Stephanie Zingel-Avé Lallement, 1:120–143. Stuttgart: Steiner Verlag Wiesbaden Gmbh.
1986. "The Struggle between the Rājās of Khurda and the Muslim Sūbahdārs of Cuttack for Dominance of the Jagannātha Temple." In *The Cult of Jagannath and the Regional Tradition of Orissa*, ed. Anncharlott Eschmann, Hermann Kulke, and Gaya Charan Tripathi, pp. 322–357. Delhi: Manohar.
Kwanten, Luc.
1979. *Imperial Nomads: A History of Central Asia, 500–1500*. Philadelphia: University of Pennsylvania Press.
Lakshmiranjanam, K., ed.
1969. *Ēkāṃbranāthuḍu: Pratāparudracaritramu*. Tanuku, A.P., India: Sri Narendranatha Sahityamandali.
Long, J. Bruce.
1975. "Life out of Death: A Structural Analysis of the Myth of the Churning of the Ocean of Milk." In *Hinduism: New Essays in the History of Religion*, ed. Bardwell Smith. Leiden: E. J. Brill.
Lorenzen, David N.
1972. *The Kāpālikas and Kālāmukhas: Two Lost Śaivite Sects*. Australian National University, Centre of Oriental Studies, Oriental Monograph Series, vol. 12. New Delhi: Thomson Press.
Lotman, Yu. M., and A. M. Piatigorsky.
1978. "Text and Function." *New Literary History* 9 (2): 233–245.
Lowenthal, David.
1986. *The Past Is a Foreign Country*. Cambridge: Cambridge University Press.
Mahadevan, T. M. P.
1968. *Sankaracharya*. National Biography Series. New Delhi: National Book Trust.
Malville, J. McKim, and John M. Fritz.
n.d. "Mapping the Sacred Geometry of Vijayanagara." Paper presented at the conference "Mapping Invisible Worlds," Saint David's University College, Lampeter, Wales, 2–4 September 1992.
Michell, George.
1981. "Man in Nature—Town Planning: The Site." In *Splendours of the Vijayanagara Empire: Hampi*, ed. George Michell and Vasundhara Filliozat, pp. 45–50. Bombay: Marg Publications.
1985a. "Architectural Traditions at Vijayanagara, II: Islamic Styles." In

Vijayanagara—City and Empire: New Currents of Research, ed. Anna Libera Dallapiccola and Stephanie Zingel-Avé Lallement, 1:282–286. Stuttgart: Steiner Verlag Wiesbaden Gmbh.

1985b. "Architecture of the Muslim Quarters at Vijayanagara." In *Vijayanagara: Progress of Research, 1983–84,* ed. M. S. Nagaraja Rao, pp. 101–118. Mysore: Directorate of Archaeology and Museums.

1989. *The Penguin Guide to the Monuments of India.* Vol. 1, *Buddhist, Jain, Hindu.* New York: Viking Penguin.

1991a. "Courtly Architecture at Gingee under the Nayakas." *South Asian Studies* 7:143–160.

1991b. *The Vijayanagara Courtly Style: Incorporation and Synthesis in the Royal Architecture of Southern India, 15th–17th Centuries.* Delhi: Manohar.

Miller, Barbara Stoler, trans.

1967. *Bhartṛhari: Poems.* New York: Columbia University Press.

Nagaraja Rao, M. S., ed.

1985. *Vijayanagara: Progress of Research, 1983–84.* Vijayanagara Research Centre Series, no. 2. Mysore: Directorate of Archaeology and Museums.

Nagaraja Rao, M. S., and C. S. Patil.

1985. "Epigraphical References to City Gates and Watch Towers of Vijayanagara." In *Vijayanagara: Progress of Research, 1983–84,* pp. 96–100. Vijayanagara Research Centre Series, no. 2. Mysore: Directorate of Archaeology and Museums.

Narayana Rao, Velcheru.

1978. *Telugulō Kavitā Viplavāla Svarūpaṃ* (in Telugu). Vijayawada: Viśālāndhra Pracūraṇālayam.

1986. "Epics and Ideologies: Six Telugu Folk Epics." In *Another Harmony: New Essays on the Folklore of India,* ed. Stuart H. Blackburn and A. K. Ramanujan. Berkeley: University of California Press.

Nilakanta Sastri, K. A.

1976. *A History of South India from Prehistoric Times to the Fall of Vijayanagara.* 4th ed. Madras: Oxford University Press.

Nilakanta Sastri, K. A., and N. Venkataramanayya, eds.

1946. *Further Sources of Vijayanagara History.* 3 vols. Madras University Historical Series, no. 18. Madras: University of Madras.

O'Flaherty, Wendy D.

1975. *Hindu Myths: A Sourcebook Translated from the Sanskrit.* Harmondsworth: Penguin Books.

Palat, Ravi Arvind.

1987. "Structures of Class Control in Late Medieval South Asia: Construction of an Interstate System (circa 1300–1600)." Paper presented at the thirty-ninth annual meeting of the Association for Asian Studies, Boston.

Panda, Shishir Kumar.

1985. "The Krishna-Godavari Delta: A Bone of Contention between the Gajapatis of Orissa and the Rāyas of Vijayanagara." In *Vijayanagara—City and Empire: New Currents of Research*, ed. Anna Libera Dallapiccola and Stephanie Zingel-Avé Lallement, 1:88–96. Stuttgart: Steiner Verlag Wiesbaden Gmbh.

Pate, H. R.

1917. *Madras District Gazetteers: Tinnevelly.* Madras: Government Press.

Patil, Channabasappa S.

1991. "Further Epigraphical References to City Gates and Watch Towers of Vijayanagara." In *Vijayanagara: Progress of Research, 1984–87*, pp. 191–194. Vijayanagara Research Centre Series, no. 6. Mysore: Directorate of Archaeology and Museums.

Pillay, K. K.

1953. *The Suchindram Temple.* Madras.

Radhakrishnan, Sarvepalli, and Charles A. Moore.

1957. *A Sourcebook in Indian Philosophy.* Princeton, N.J.: Princeton University Press.

Rama Rao, M.

1971. *Krishnadeva Raya.* New Delhi.

Ramachandraiya, Oruganti.

1953. *Studies on Kṛṣṇadēvarāya of Vijayanagara.* Waltair: Andhra University Press.

Ramachandra Rao, C. V., ed.

1982. *Rāyavācakamu* (in Telugu). Hyderabad: Andhra Pradesh Sahitya Akademi.

1984. *Ēkāmranāthuni Pratāparudracaritramu* (in Telugu). Hyderabad: Andhra Pradesh Sahitya Akademi.

Rama Sharma, M. H.

1978. *The History of the Vijayanagara Empire, Beginnings and Expansion (1308–1569).* Edited by M. H. Gopal. Bombay: Popular Prakashan.

Ramaswami, A.

1972. *Tamil Nadu District Gazetteers: Ramanathapuram.* Gazetteer of India. Madras: Government of Tamil Nadu.

Ramayyapantulu, Jayanti.

1914. "Rāyavācakamu." *Āndhra Sāhitya Parisat Patrikā* 3:11–40, 49–64, 125–136, 175–182, 207–210.

1933. *Rāyavācakamu.* Āndhra Sāhitya Pariṣat Pracuraṇa, no. 33. Kākināḍa, A.P.

Reynolds, Holly Baker.

1987. "Madurai: *Kōyil Nakar.*" In *The City as a Sacred Center: Essays on Six Asian Contexts*, ed. Bardwell Smith and Holly Baker Reynolds, pp. 12–44. International Studies in Sociology and Social Anthropology, ed. K. Ishwaran. Leiden: E. J. Brill.

Rice, Edward P.
1934. *The Mahābhārata: Analysis and Index*. London: Humphrey Milford, Oxford University Press.
Roghair, Gene H.
1982. *The Epic of Palnāḍu: A Study and Translation of Palnāṭi Vīrula Katha, a Telugu Oral Tradition from Andhra Pradesh, India*. London: Oxford University Press.
Rosenfield, John M.
1967. *The Dynastic Arts of the Kushans*. Berkeley: University of California Press.
Sarasvati, A. Rangasvami.
1926. "Political Maxims of the Emperor-Poet, Krishnadeva Raya." *Journal of Indian History* 4 (3): 61–88.
Sathianathaier, R.
1956. *Tamilaham in the Seventeenth Century*. Madras.
Sathyanatha Aiyar, R.
1924. *History of the Nayaks of Madura*. Madras.
Scholes, Robert, and Robert Kellogg.
1966. *The Nature of Narrative*. New York: Oxford University Press.
Sewell, Robert.
1962. *A Forgotten Empire (Vijayanagara): A Contribution to the History of India*. 1900. Reprint. Delhi: Government of India.
Shapiro, Alan.
n.d. "The Kalyāṇotsava of Pampādevī and Pampāpati." Unpublished manuscript.
Shastri, Hari Prasad, trans.
1957–1959. *The Ramayana of Valmiki*. 3 vols. London: Shanti Sadan.
Shulman, David D.
1980. *Tamil Temple Myths: Sacrifice and Divine Marriage in the South Indian Śaiva Tradition*. Princeton, N.J.: Princeton University Press.
1985. *The King and the Clown in South Indian Myth and Poetry*. Princeton, N.J.: Princeton University Press.
Sircar, D. C.
1965. *Indian Epigraphy*. Delhi: Motilal Banarsidass.
1966. *Indian Epigraphical Glossary*. Delhi: Motilal Banarsidass.
Sitapati, P.
1981–1982. *Srisailam Temple Kaifiyat, Andhra Pradesh*. 2 vols. Hyderabad: Government of Andhra Pradesh.
Sridhara Babu, D.
1975. *Kingship: State and Religion in South India According to South Indian Historical Biographies of Kings (Madhuravijaya, Acyutarayabhyudaya, and Vemabhupalacarita)*. Inaugural dissertation, Georg August University, Göttingen.

Stein, Burton.

1978. "All the King's *Mana:* Perspectives on Kingship in Medieval South India." In *Kingship and Authority in South Asia,* ed. John F. Richards, pp. 115–167. Madison: University of Wisconsin, Department of South Asian Studies.

1980. *Peasant, State and Society in Medieval South India.* Delhi: Oxford University Press.

1989. *Vijayanagara.* New Cambridge History of India, vol. 1, pt. 2. Cambridge: Cambridge University Press.

Sturtevant, William C.

1966. "Anthropology, History, and Ethnohistory." *Ethnohistory* 13:1–51.

Sundaram, K.

1984. *The Simhachalam Temple.* 1969. Reprint. Simhachalam: Simhachalam Devasthanam.

Swaminathan, K. D.

1957. *The Nayakas of Ikkeri.* Madras.

Swearer, Donald K.

1987. "The Northern Thai City as a Sacred Center." In *The City as a Sacred Center,* ed. Bardwell Smith and Holly Baker Reynolds, pp. 103–113. Leiden: E. J. Brill.

Taylor, Rev. William.

1835. *Oriental Historical Manuscripts in the Tamil Language.* Madras.

Thapar, Romila.

1976. *A History of India.* Vol. 1. Harmondsworth: Penguin Books.

Thapar, Romila, Harbans Mukhia, and Bipan Chandra.

1969. *Communalism and the Writing of Indian History.* Delhi: People's Publishing House.

van Buitenen, J. A. B., trans.

1973. *The Mahābhārata.* Bk. 1, *The Book of the Beginning.* Chicago: University of Chicago Press.

1975. *The Mahābhārata.* Bk. 2, *The Book of the Assembly Hall.* Bk. 3, *The Book of the Forest.* Chicago: University of Chicago Press.

1978. *The Mahābhārata.* Bk. 4, *The Book of Virāṭa.* Bk. 5, *The Book of the Effort.* Chicago: University of Chicago Press.

Vansina, Jan.

1985. *Oral Tradition as History.* Madison: University of Wisconsin Press.

Venkataramanayya, Nelaturi.

1935. *Studies in the Third Dynasty of Vijayanagara.* Madras University Historical Series, no. 11. Madras: Madras University.

1939. *Velugōṭivārivaṃśāvaḷi* (in Telugu with an English introduction). Edited with introduction by N. Venkataramanayya. Bulletin of the Department of Indian History and Archaeology, no. 6. Madras: University of Madras.

1954. "Madhura Taṃjāvūru Nāyaka Rājula Nāṭi Āṃdhra Vāṅmayamu" (in Telugu). *Bhārati* 31 (February): 143ff.

1972. *Kṛṣṇadēvarāyalu* (in Telugu). Andhra Pradesh Government Archaeological Series, no. 33. Hyderabad: Government of Andhra Pradesh.

1974. *Inscriptions of Andhra Pradesh: Warangal District.* Andhra Pradesh State Department of Archaeology and Museums, Epigraphical Series, no. 6. Hyderabad: Government of Andhra Pradesh.

Venkata Rao, Nidudavolu.

1960. *Dakṣiṇadēśīyāndhra Vāṅmayamu* (The southern school in Telugu literature) (in Telugu). Madras University Telugu Series, no. 16. Madras: Madras University.

Venkataraya Sastry, Vedamu.

1964. *Āmuktamālyada, nāmāntaramu Viṣṇucittīyamu, Śrīkṛṣṇadēvarāyamahārāyapraṇītamu; Sanjīvanīvyākhyā Vēdamu Venkaṭarāya Śāstripraṇītamu* (in Telugu). 1927. Reprint. Madras: Vedamu Venkataraya Sastri & Bros.

Vriddhagirisan, V.

1942. *The Nayaks of Tanjore.* Annamalainagar.

Wagoner, Phillip B.

1991. "Architecture and Mythic Space at the Hemakuta Hill: A Preliminary Report." In *Vijayanagara: Progress of Research, 1985–87,* pp. 142–148. Mysore: Directorate of Archaeology and Museums.

in press "From 'Pampā's Crossing' to 'The Place of Lord Virūpākṣa': Architecture, Cult, and Patronage at Hampi before the Founding of Vijayanagara." In *Vijayanagara: Progress of Research, 1988–91.* Mysore: Directorate of Archaeology and Museums.

n.d. "From 'The Place of Lord Virūpākṣa' to 'The City of Victory': Architecture, Cult, and Patronage in the Genesis of the Vijayanagara Capital." Unpublished manuscript.

Welch, Stuart Carey.

1985. *India: Art and Culture, 1300–1900.* New York: Metropolitan Museum of Art and Holt, Rinehart & Winston.

Yazdani, Ghulam, ed.

1982. *The Early History of the Deccan.* 2 vols. New Delhi: Oriental Books Reprint Corp.

Zimmer, Heinrich.

1951. *Philosophies of India,* ed. Joseph Campbell. Bollingen Series, no. 26. Princeton, N.J.: Princeton University Press.

I·N·D·E·X

Names and technical terms are listed in the standardized spellings employed in the translation, with actual Telugu spellings and variant forms found in the text following in parentheses. General identifying or defining notes follow, with information not supplied in the text given in parentheses. Page numbers are preceded by a brief indication of events associated with the figure, place, etc., in the passage in question. Small caps are used to identify names of persons, places, and localized divinities whose historical existence is verifiable on the basis of other sources.

chief present at Krishnadevaraya's coronation, 87
Ayyalayya *(Ayyalayya-gāru),* subordinate of Krishnadevaraya in charge of the captured fort at Nagarjunakonda, 144
AYYAMARASU (*Ayyamarasu,* probably identified with Ayyapparasu, son of Kondamarasu, who according to Nuniz succeeded Saluva Timmarasu as chief adviser to Krishnadevaraya), minister of Krishnadevaraya: present at Krishnadevaraya's coronation, 87; instructs Krishnadevaraya in ruling the kingdom, 89–96; Krishnadevaraya asks him to suggest further reforms, 101; praises Appaji's extraordinary qualities, 107–108; listens to the spies' reports from Bijapur, 109–112; decries the Turks' addiction to wine and opium, points out that their advisers have little power, and argues that Krishnadevaraya would not need a large force to overcome the Turks, 113–114; praises the spies Arava Ramudu and Fakir Gopaji for their courage with the barbarian Turks, 119; explains to Krishnadevaraya the reasons for the Turks' battle preparations, 120–121; joins other ministers in advising Krishnadevaraya to subdue the forts of the Turks and the Gajapati, 142; joins other ministers in sowing dissension in the Gajapati's camp, 152–153
Ayyappa Nayadu *(Ayyappa Nāyaḍu),* one of the military commanders *(daḷanāyakulu)* of Krishnadevaraya summoned to report on the strength of his forces, 121
Ayyapparaju *(Ayyapparāju), sthānāpati* of the Lord of Ahmadnagar at the court of the Gajapati, 127

Baboji Pantulu *(Bābōjī Paṃttulu), sthānāpati* of the ruler of Bāgānagaram at the court of the Gajapati, 127
Bacharasu *(Bācarasu),* minister of Krishnadevaraya: at Krishnadevaraya's coronation, 87; joins Appaji in instructing Krishnadevaraya in ruling the kingdom, 89–96; joins Appaji in advising Krishnadevaraya to subdue the forts of the Turks and Gajapati, 142
Baddena's Hundred Verses (Padya Śatakamu), a work on royal conduct: a verse recited by Padyaniti Chandrayya's son inspires Krishnadevaraya to implement military reforms, 99, 104
Baddena's Nīti (Padya Nīti, apparently identical with *Padya Śatakamu),* a work on royal conduct recited in the morning at the Vijayanagara court of Viranrisimharaya, 77. See *Baddena's Hundred Verses*
BAGANAGARAM (*Bāgānagaraṃ,* present-day Hyderabad), city in Golconda territory: its ruler is represented by a *sthānāpati* at the court of the Gajapati, 127
BAHUBALENDRA. *See* GAJAPATI
Bakula (*Vakuḷa,* the tree *Mimusops elengi,* known for its fragrant flowers), Krishnadevaraya circumambulates the Bakula grove at the pilgrimage site of Gokarna while returning from his battle campaigns, 159
Balabhadra Patra *(Balabhadra Pātruḍu),* one of the Sixteen Patras or "Worthies" in the service of the Gajapati, 147
Balavankam family *(Balavaṃkkaṃ),* a family of Amaranayakas summoned by Krishnadevaraya in preparation for launching his campaign against the Turks, 136
BANARAS. *See* KASHI
BARID OF BIDAR (*Beḍadakōṭa Barudu,* Qasim Barid [d.1504], minister and de facto ruler of the Bahmani kingdom of the Deccan during much of the reign of Mahmud Shah [1482–1518]; later considered the eponymous founder of the Barid Shahi kingdom of Bidar): founders of kingdoms of Ahmadnagar, Bijapur, and Golconda started their careers as servants in his court, 123
barijis (a type of weapon, precise sense uncertain), 146
Basuva Reddi *(Basuvā Reḍḍi),* a Reddi prince in the service of Krishnadevaraya summoned to report on the strength of his forces, 121
Bekoji Pantulu *(Bēkōji Paṃttulu), sthānāpati* of the Lord of Bidar at the court of the Gajapati, 127
BELLAMKONDA *(Bellaṃkoṃḍḍa, Bellaṃkoṃḍa),* Gajapati fort in coastal Andhra: Krishnadevaraya sends spies to, 97; Gajapati orders to secure the fort against Vijayanagara's impending

A·B·O·U·T T·H·E A·U·T·H·O·R

Phillip B. Wagoner is curator at the Mansfield Freeman Center for East Asian Studies and adjunct assistant professor of art history at Wesleyan University in Connecticut. He was trained in Telugu literature and South Asian art and history at the University of Wisconsin, where he received his Ph.D. in 1986. Since then, his research has focused primarily on the architecture and urban history of Vijayanagara and medieval Telugu historiography, two strands which intersect in *Tidings of the King*.

Production Notes

Composition and paging were done on the Quadex Composing System and typesetting on the Compugraphic 8400 by the design and production staff of University of Hawaii Press.

The text and display typeface is Galliard.

Offset presswork and binding were done by The Maple-Vail Book Manufacturing Group. Text paper is Glatfelter Offset Vellum, basis 50.